Self-Care

for the

Mental Health PRACTITIONER

The Theory, Research, and Practice
of Preventing and Addressing the
Occupational Hazards of the Profession

Alfred J. Malinowski

Jessica Kingsley *Publishers*
London and Philadelphia

First published in 2014
by Jessica Kingsley Publishers
73 Collier Street
London N1 9BE, UK
and
400 Market Street, Suite 400
Philadelphia, PA 19106, USA

www.jkp.com

Library of Congress Cataloging-in-Publication Data
Malinowski, Alfred J., author.
Self-care for the mental health practitioner : the theory, research and practice
of preventing and addressing the occupational hazards of the profession /
Alfred J. Malinowski.
    p. ; cm.
Includes bibliographical references and index.
ISBN 978-1-84905-992-3 (alk. paper)
I. Title. [DNLM: 1. Psychotherapy. 2. Burnout, Professional--prevention &
control. 3. Professional Role--psychology. 4. Professional-Patient Relations.
5. Self Care--psychology.
WM 62]   RC480   616.89'14--dc23   2014015339

British Library Cataloguing in Publication Data
A CIP catalogue record for this book is available from the British Library

ISBN 978 1 84905 992 3
eISBN 978 0 85700 931 9

Printed and bound in Great Britain by Bell and Bain Ltd, Glasgow

Contents

Preface

Someone once said, "You don't know what you can do until you try." This has been my experience throughout my life. However, without the encouragement of other people and challenging myself to meet those goals in my life, I would not have accomplished the completion of this book.

Writing this book has not only been a journey, but a learning experience. The more I researched and gathered materials and information on topics pertaining to its content, the more questions came to mind as to what hazards I am open to in my practice of psychotherapy, and what self-care strategies I should be practicing to ensure my own psychological well-being.

This book was written for a variety of reasons. One of the main reasons was that one of my mentors encouraged me to write it. He noticed how much material I had researched and gathered in completion of my dissertation and strongly advised me to consider writing a book. He not only suggested to me that I write this book, but he was also instrumental in my entering a PhD program. Another main reason for writing this book was to give back to my profession and colleagues all that I have been given. My professors, instructors, mentors, and society have done so much for me that it is my pleasure and, I feel, my responsibility to improve my field in some form. Some other reasons for writing this book are actually seeing experienced colleagues leaving the counseling profession in pursuit of other careers because of disturbances mentioned in this book, hearing from peers about their own difficulties regarding the performance of psychotherapy, and reading various research articles about the lack of training for student mental health practitioners regarding the hazards and self-care strategies of performing psychotherapy.

Finally, I want to thank all my fellow colleagues, friends, and clients where I practice, who have been inspirational in the creation of this book. It is because of them that I have learned through experience about my strengths, limitations, and need for self-care in my daily life.

PART 1

Introduction to a Demanding Profession

CHAPTER 1

Why Self-Care?

During the past decades, there have been a number of reports into the degradation of psychotherapists' psychological well-being. In a national study involving 800 psychologists, 61% acknowledged being depressed, 29% mentioned feeling suicidal, and 4% reported having made a suicidal attempt (Pope and Tabachnick 1994). Another study conducted by Mahoney (1997) discovered 51 out of 155 therapists suffered from various symptoms related to depression and/or anxiety. Similarly, Gilroy, Carroll, and Murra (2002) found that out of 1000 counseling psychologists 62% were depressed and 42% experienced thoughts related to suicidal ideation. In addition, the American Psychological Association (APA) discovered in the 2009 APA Colleague Assistance survey that 40–60% of practicing psychologists had symptoms related to depression, anxiety, and/or burnout with 18% suffering with thoughts of suicidal ideation (APA 2010).

Gibson, McGrath, and Reid's (1989) study of 176 social workers found that 89% of the participants had some type of symptoms related to job burnout, ranging from moderate to high intensity. Bohnert and O'Connell (2006) also reported that psychiatrists have faced high rates of suicide, divorce, and substance abuse. Finally, other studies have shown that psychotherapists have continued to suffer from such things as psychological distress, Compassion Fatigue (CF), and job burnout (Figley 2002; Hannigan, Edwards, and Burnard 2004; Maslach 1982). Of course, not every clinician suffers from such issues; the problem lies in not placing enough emphasis on self-care (Skovholt 2001).

So, self-care must be an imperative if the psychotherapist is not only to perform his/her duties at peak performance but also to maintain his/her psychological well-being. This attention needs to start with learning about self-care very early in a therapist's educational process and throughout his/her career (Hill 2004; Myers and Sweeney 2005; Roach 2005; Skovholt 2001). In addition, Jones (2007) noted that learning and continually practicing self-care techniques early in the educational process helps the therapist maintain a focus on caring for his/her needs.

Throughout this book, terms such as psychotherapist, therapist, and counselor will be used interchangeably as they pertain to individuals who perform psychotherapy, unless otherwise indicated. The purpose of this chapter is to define self-care, ethical concerns related to self-care, and vulnerabilities as these pertain to the psychotherapist.

Self-care defined

So how can self-care be defined as it pertains to the mental health practitioner and his/her psychological well-being? This is a very important question that will affect the therapist throughout his/her career. According to Baker (2003b), self-care is the process a psychotherapist takes in understanding how to maintain his/her psychological well-being and applying this knowledge through many different means. Wise, Hersh, and Gibson (2012) describe self-care as not only being knowledgeable and applying this knowledge to ensure the therapist's psychological well-being, but most importantly, it means being self-aware and cognizant of one's weaknesses and limitations so the practitioner can effectively treat his/her clients. Likewise, Meyer and Ponton (2006) emphasize that the counselor must be knowledgeable, self-aware, and constantly applying these self-care principles to maintain a state of well-being.

Throughout this book, self-care will be seen as consisting of three parts. The first part involves knowledge and awareness of the hazards and self-care principles of the mental health practitioner. This knowledge and awareness should be learned very early in one's training program and practiced throughout one's career. The second part comprises the acceptance that the hazards and vulnerabilities of the clinician's profession should be taken seriously. Therapists with this type of attitude know their weaknesses and limitations and are honest with themselves. These professionals know what to do and how to seek help when they have problems. The third part stresses the need to continually incorporate and practice self-care principles. This means that self-care should be always be at the forefront of a therapist's mind.

So, self-care is the key and well-being is the goal. If the therapist does not take an active part in self-care, then he/she will not achieve a healthy psychological well-being (Linley and Joseph 2007). Being active may consist of participating in such activities as personal therapy and seeking supervision (Linley and Joseph 2007), mindfulness-based stress reduction (Shapiro, Brown, and Biegel 2007), being more self-aware (Baker 2007), the practice of meditation (Boellinghaus, Jones, and Hutton 2013), and/or participating in leisure activities (Dubrow 2011). Continually practicing activities such as these can buffer a counselor against stressors during the performance of his/her duties and help maintain a healthy well-being.

Coster and Schwebel (1997) describe well-being or well functioning as "...the enduring quality in one's professional functioning over time and in the face of professional and personal stressors" (p.5). On the other hand, Carruthers and Hood (2004) report that well-being is a state that is characterized by the principles governed by positive relationships, personal growth, self-determination, a sense of purpose in one's life, and self-acceptance. By contrast, Myers, Sweeney, and Witmer (2000, p.252) define wellness as:

a way of life oriented towards optimal health and well-being in which body, mind, and spirit are integrated by the individual to live life more fully within the human and natural community. Ideally, it is the optimum state of health and well-being that each individual is capable of achieving. (p.252)

One thing that is implied in maintaining a healthy psychological well-being through self-care is the ability to use coping strategies when the therapist is under stress (Stevanovic and Rupert 2004). Brucato and Neimeyer (2009) indicate that there is a difference between self-care and coping. While self-care emphasizes preventative measures a clinician takes before stress is felt, coping strategies modify the individual's response once stress is encountered. So, according to this definition, self-care is the on-going activities the therapist performs to stay emotionally and psychology healthy, whereas a coping strategy is an activity or activities a clinician performs to stay calm during an emotional situation. An example of this is the therapist taking a deep breath and remembering to relax his/her body when interacting with a client threatening to commit suicide (Granello 2010).

There are a variety of strategies that the therapist can use in stressful situations. Parkinson (1997) reports that strategies such as humor, expressing feelings and emotions, and avoiding disturbing thoughts help in one's daily life when the therapist's caseload is focused on treating traumatized clients. Case and McMinn (2001) noted that prayer and meditation gave clinicians peace of mind when dealing with difficult clients. McAdams III and Foster (2002) showed that talking to family friends, peers, and supervisors relieved distress after a client's suicide. Using positive talk in difficult situations was also shown as another way of keeping therapists calm (Stevanovic and Rupert 2004). However, not all counselors use positive strategies. Jordaan *et al.* (2007) have shown that some psychotherapists employ self-blame, self-distraction, and substance abuse to deal with the stress of their job. It follows, if a therapist does not constantly practice self-care, this can affect not only his/her psychological well-being but that of the client.

An ethical concern

How does the therapist's practice of self-care affect clients and how is this an ethical concern? At first, self-care might not seem to be related to ethics, but indirectly it does relate (Wise *et al.* 2012). Many professional ethical codes stress the need for counselors and therapists to take certain actions if their psychological well-being degrades to a point that it is having a negative affect on their clients. The APA's *Ethical Principles of Psychologists and Code of Conduct, General Principle A: Beneficence and Nonmaleficence* states: "Psychologists strive to benefit those with whom they work and take care to do no harm" (APA 2002, p.1063). In addition, Ethical Standard 2.06, "Personal Problems and Conflicts" dictates that psychologists are to refrain from treating clients when they become aware that personal problems are affecting their work-related activities (APA 2002). Counselors working with the American Counseling Association (ACA) and/or the American Mental Health Counselor Association (AMHCA) also have ethical codes mandating that their members terminate treatment and make referrals with clients when their mental health and psychological well-being are in question (ACA 2005; AMHCA 2010).

As professional practitioners involved in helping those who are suffering, psychotherapists have the responsibility to do no harm to their clients. This goes along with the Hippocratic oath to "do no harm." Wise *et al.* (2012) note that a clinician who does not care for his/her psychological needs will eventually become impaired and this impairment will over time degrade the counselor–client's relationship and produce a poor treatment outcome. Symptoms related to depression, substance abuse, anxiety, and/or job burnout can degrade the cognitive and psychological functioning of the practitioner where he/she can be uncaring and insensitive and may possibly even injure the client by his/her actions or by not acting (Gilroy *et al.* 2002; Mahoney 1997; Maslach 1982; Williams *et al.* 2010; Wurst *et al.* 2011). In this state of impairment, the therapist will not only be in distress, but be in danger of causing the client's symptoms to worsen (Williams *et al.* 2010).

So how does one define impairment? Wise *et al.* (2012) define impairment as "...an objective change in the psychologist's professional functioning that may result in ineffective services or cause harm to those with whom we work" (p.488). Swearingen (1990) defines an impaired psychiatrist as a professional who has a significant amount of difficultly in treating clients and performing duties in an objective and competent manner. Furthermore, the APA describes psychologists who are impaired as those who display poor professional functioning that is shown in their quality of work (Schwebel, Skorina, and Schoener 1996). Gilroy *et al.* (2002) write that impairment is a condition that may be shown by a therapist's isolation from his/her colleagues and a diminished capacity to communicate effectively with clients. These definitions highlight that the psychotherapist is not only in distress, but that this distress has affected his/her psychological functioning in a way that clients could be harmed. In this context, distress is different than impairment. Munsey (2006) describes distress as the intense stress response a therapist experiences that affects his/her mood, thinking, and/or physical health in a way that may degrade professional functioning, whereas impairment is the condition that may impede psychological functioning to the point of bringing harm to a client. In fact, Kleespies *et al.* (2011) emphasize that if psychotherapists do not use self-care strategies during times of intense emotional distress, they may not only become impaired, but some therapists may become vulnerable to suicide ideation. Additionally, Sherman and Thelen (1998) discovered that there is a high positive correlation between distress and impairment. The question to ask is, at what point is the clinician impaired enough to bring harm to the client?

Many therapists may have been wondering "At what point is one impaired enough to justify reducing or terminating one's caseload?" This may sound like a philosophical question with a variety of answers, but it is an important question with implications both for the therapist and for clients. Williams *et al.* (2010) developed a rating scale for therapists based on five levels of impairment on being depressed, where symptoms at Level 1 were mild and infrequent, and symptoms at Level 5 were intense and were felt frequently. A rating of 3.5 was described as being too impaired to practice. At this level, symptoms and intensities were described as being sad all day, at least once a week; crying at least once a week; feeling lethargic one day a week; and experiencing trouble sleeping at least once a week. Williams *et al.* (2010) indicated that the consequences of therapists experiencing these symptoms result in problems in concentrating and maintaining interest in clients, and also frequently being late, missing, and/or canceling sessions.

In the area of competence, psychotherapists of any profession should be knowledgeable and competent enough to know what their ethical responsibilities are in the area of impairment and self-care. In fact, the APA's Ethical Standard 2.03, "Maintaining Competence" mandates psychologists to maintain and develop the knowledge of their duties and responsibilities of their profession (APA 2002). Goncher *et al.* (2013) emphasize that when self-care is taught early in one's educational training and new techniques are learned and practiced later in one's career, the quality of life can be much improved. Richards, Campenni, and Muse-Burke (2010) noted that when experienced mental health professionals learn new self-care techniques such as self-awareness and mindfulness their well-being is greatly enhanced and as a result they are able to treat clients more effectively. Therefore, competence is an ethical imperative in the area of self-care in order to prevent impairment.

A critical question that needs to be asked is, why do some therapists not seek help when they are impaired? Because mental health practitioners are in the profession of helping people in distress, some may be in denial that they could be impaired or that their condition could harm the client (O'Connor 2001). In another case (Barnett and Hillard 2001), a clinician might feel that if he/she sought help for some type of psychological distress, then family members, colleagues, friends, and/or clients might be critical of him/her. According to Bearse *et al.* (2013), several other reasons why some mental health practitioners might not get help when they are experiencing distress and impairment include difficulties finding an acceptable therapist, lack of time, financial reasons, or difficulty admitting distress.

Vulnerabilities

Self-care is not only an ethical concern, but it demands a psychotherapist to be aware and take care of his/her vulnerabilities. In this context, a clinician's vulnerabilities can be within himself/herself. One type of vulnerability could be due to a therapist's past history. Barnett (2007) discusses how a therapist with narcissistic traits in the form of "narcissistic injury" could negatively affect the therapeutic relationship between the counselor and client. Narcissistic injury is an event in an individual's past where one's "true" self was not responded to or validated and subsequently developed a "false" self (Winnicott 1960). In this case, Barnett states that a therapist who is unaware of this past injury could develop a false image of himself/herself to protect others from seeing his/her limitations and inadequacies. The danger here is that the clinician may not be himself/herself and therefore not meet the needs of the client because of fear of failure in the counseling process (Barnett 2007).

Another vulnerability a therapist must be aware of because of his/her developmental history is known as parentification. Parentification is a term used to describe the process of the child taking over the responsibilities of the parents, and in effect, parenting the parent (DiCaccavo 2006). In this case, the child cares for the parent(s) because of a disability or the parent just being irresponsible and relinquishing all parental duties to the child. The child then internalizes this process and may care for the needs of others more than his/her own, even at later points in his/her life (Nuttall, Valentino, and Borkowski 2012). A therapist affected by parentification early in his/her development might find the counseling profession satisfying, but ignoring one's needs and totally focusing on others can bring a host of disturbances and disorders that can eventually lead the therapist to be ineffective (Barnett 2007; Hooper *et al.* 2011). Moreover, counselors who experience the effects of parentification might feel totally responsible for a client's successful treatment outcome and might feel guilty if this does not occur within a specific amount of time (DiCaccavo 2002).

Many therapists who have entered the counseling field with past histories of psychopathologies may be vulnerable to previous symptoms that may affect their psychological well-being in the present (Cain 2000; Wheeler 2007). One example is a clinician who mentioned her personal experiences with dealing with the effects of major depression earlier in life and her need to be consciously aware of stress to prevent present and future occurrences (Sawyer 2011). This heightened awareness was due to the fact of her vulnerability to similar reoccurrences when encountering present-day stressors. In addition, Cain spoke of the stress caused by countertransference experienced by clinicians due to past psychiatric hospitalizations. This consisted of cases associated with one psychiatrist, two psychologists, and seven social workers. Each case discussed steps individuals took in controlling the anxiety of their past while treating their clients in the present. In several studies, psychologists were found to have a higher number of occurrences concerning childhood trauma than found in the general public (Elliott and Guy 1993; Nikcevic, Kramolisova-Advani, and Spada 2007; Pope and Feldman-Summers 1992). These occurrences can make the therapist more empathic to their clients who have experienced similar incidents, but at the same time can place the therapeutic relationship at risk if the psychotherapist is not aware of the effects this can have on their present condition. Therefore, many mental health practitioners have found that personal psychotherapy helps maintain their psychological well-being in spite of their chronic conditions, past histories, and vulnerabilities (Bike, Norcross, and Schatz 2009).

Clinicians also may be vulnerable to distress due to their personality. As Armon, Shirom, and Melamed (2012) remarked, if a practitioner has personality traits associated with neuroticism, then he/she will be more open to distresses and job burnout. Likewise, Lent and Schwartz (2012) found that there was a high correlation between neuroticism and burnout. In fact, Lent and Schwartz noted that individuals who displayed characteristics of neuroticism had higher levels of emotional exhaustion and depersonalization, with lower levels of feelings of personal accomplishment, than those individuals who were not neurotic.

Costa and McCrae (1994) described neuroticism as being related to such disturbances as depression, impulsiveness, self-consciousness, anxiety, and hostility. Furthermore, Costa and McCrae (1987) add the following to the definition of neuroticism:

> By Neuroticism we mean a broad dimension of individual differences in the tendency to experience negative, distressing emotions and to possess associated behavioral and cognitive traits. Among the traits that define this dimension are fearfulness, irritability, low self-esteem, social anxiety, poor inhibition of impulses, and helplessness. (p.301)

Brooks, Holttum, and Lavender (2002) emphasize that how one's personality develops and becomes stable will determine how an individual will cope with stress and apply self-care techniques. Because neuroticism becomes a stable personality dimension in adulthood (Terracciano, Costa, and McCrae 2006), the therapist needs to have self-awareness and self-knowledge of his/her weakness and strengths to be able to use coping mechanisms when he/she experiences stress in the daily performance of duties.

Another personality type that can make the clinician vulnerable to high levels of distress is the Type-A personality. What makes therapists with a Type-A personality vulnerable to distress is that these individuals are highly driven, highly competitive, and success oriented (Sharma 2003) and have tendencies towards workaholism (Erden, Toplu, and Yashoglu 2013). Heilbrun and Friedberg (1988) noted that, since these individuals have such a highly driven nature, they impose demands on their performance that results in feelings of stress and anxiety.

Some other negative elements of therapists with a Type-A personality is that they are highly critical of their thoughts and actions (Friedman and Ulmer 1984) and they become impatient when progress is not seen during treatment in clients (McCarthy and Frieze 1999). Resistant clients also may pose a significant problem for mental health practitioners who display a Type-A personality (Kraus 2005). Erden *et al.* (2013) say this is due to the fact that one of the main characteristics of individuals with Type-A personality is their sense of urgency in completing tasks in the shortest amount of time. Additionally, McKenzie Deighton, Gurris, and Traue (2007) discovered that psychotherapists who are rigid and overly involved with their clients could develop distress because of their desire to control situations in their work environment.

The temptation of having sexual relationships with clients can also be a vulnerability for some psychotherapists. In one national research study consisting of 323 mental health practitioners, Jackson and Nuttall (2001) found that 15 participants had sexual contact with clients. In another study, Pope and Bouhoutsos (1986) discovered that male clinicians were involved in sexual contact with their clients approximately 10% of the time, whereas female clinicians were involved in sexual relationships with clients about 2% of the time.

Of course, these percentages might seem small, but there can be severe consequences for the client and the counselor who have such an encounter. Consequences for clients may involve symptoms including the inability to trust, depression, guilt, rage, flashbacks, nightmares, risk of suicide (Pope 1988), and those symptoms associated with incest victims (Sonne and Pope 1991). Feldman-Summers and Jones (1984) reported that female clients who had a sexual encounter with their therapist developed a mistrust and anger towards most men, accompanied by psychological and psychosomatic symptoms. The consequences for psychotherapists may also be painful. Therapists may be involved in civil lawsuits, removal of their license by their state board, and losing present career and future job opportunities at institutions, clinics, and hospitals (Hotelling 1988). Moreover, Layman and McNamara (1997) stress that sexual contact impairs the counselor's ability to interact objectively with the client and produces a poor treatment outcome.

There are various reasons why therapists develop sexual relationships with clients. The first of these reasons is physical attraction. Pope, Keith-Spiegel and Tabachnick (2006) found that in one study 87% of 575 psychotherapists had been sexually attracted to a client on at least one occasion. Likewise, Rodolfa *et al*. (1994) noted that out of 908 APA psychologists, 88% of the participants were sexually attracted to a client at least once in their practice. It must be noted that in both studies only a minority had any sexual contact with clients, but sexual misconduct is increasingly becoming a problem to the profession these days (Pope *et al*. 2006).

It does seem that sexual attraction to some clients is a normal response of the human experience (Hoffman 1995), although Pope, Keith-Spiegel, and Tabachnick (1986) discovered that most therapists in their study felt anxious, guilty, or confused about this type of attraction. So, the issue is not the attraction that the clinician has towards the client, but how the therapist manages his/her feelings of being sexually attracted and, most importantly, not acting on these feelings (Martin *et al*. 2011; Rodolfa *et al*. 1994).

Hoffman discusses measures that a therapist can take in dealing with his/her feelings. First, the therapist should acknowledge, not deny or ignore, such feelings. Second, the clinician needs to differentiate between being aware of these feelings and acting on them. This means that such feelings are part of the human experience. However, the counselor must not act on them in the form of sexual contact. Finally, the psychotherapist should discuss such feelings with supervisors and colleagues to get a proper perspective of how this is affecting his/her psychological well-being and therapeutic relationships with clients (Rodgers 2011).

There is another reason why mental health practitioners have sexual relationships with their clients. Jackson and Nuttall (2001) record clinicians who are most vulnerable to sexual misconduct are those who have a history of childhood abuse. This may be due to the fact that the therapist may have not properly dealt with the trauma of abuse in his/her childhood (Schwartz 1992). Green (1993) reported that some practitioners who were involved in sexual misconduct may be acting out their countertransference, whereas others may be sexually compulsive because of a history of childhood sexual abuse (Schwartz 1992).

There is a need to incorporate more teaching of the topic of sexual misconduct into ethical courses associated with training psychotherapists (Pope 1988). Hoffman (1995) stresses the need for counselors to have more awareness about the dangers of sexual misconduct and to implement steps to prevent this from happening in their practice. Additionally, clinicians should establish measures within themselves and in their environment to prevent any type of violation against the client (Wylie and Oakley 2005). It does need to be mentioned that not every therapist who has had a history of sexual abuse will have sexual contact with their clients, and not every clinician who has sexually exploited his/her client(s) will have a history of being sexually abused (Jackson and Nuttall 2001). So far, several internal characteristics that would make the psychotherapist vulnerable to distress have been discussed. The following chapters will examine the external factors in the clinician's environment that make him/her vulnerable to distress.

The work of a counselor treating individuals with mental health issues can take a toll on his/her psychological well-being. The emotional stress of interacting with clients day after day can lead to burnout if adequate steps are not in place (Everall and Paulson 2004). Psychotherapists who treat clients who suffer from severe symptoms (Vredenburgh, Carlozzi, and Stein 1999) and are resistant to therapeutic change (Kraus 2005) can experience frustration and distress. Eventually, this frustration and distress can lead a clinician to develop symptoms associated with job burnout. Maslach, Schaufeli, and Leiter (2001) state that the symptoms related to job burnout are emotional exhaustion, depersonalization, and a lack of a sense of personal accomplishment. This condition can over time cause a therapist to lose his/her effectiveness and begin questioning his/her desire to stay in the helping profession (Maslach *et al.* 2001).

It should also be noted that working specifically with traumatized clients can cause clinicians to develop what is known as Secondary Traumatic Stress (STS) (Stamm 1995). Figley (1995) states that the cause and symptoms related to STS are similar to those of Post Traumatic Stress Disorder (PTSD), except the therapist is not directly exposed to a life-threatening event but instead hears of it from clients.

Furthermore, the practitioner may be vulnerable to distress due to the work environment. This includes having little or no control over the work environment (Rupert and Morgan 2005), rigid schedules (Vredenburgh *et al.* 1999), excessive work loads (Hannigan *et al.* 2004), and conflicts between work and family life (Rupert, Stevanovic, and Hunley 2009). Topics such as job burnout, STS, and so on have only been briefly discussed and will be expounded in more detail later in this book.

Summary

This chapter has reviewed the many definitions and importance of self-care in the profession of a psychotherapist. Mainly, self-care has been shown as consisting of three parts: knowledge and self-awareness of the therapist's weaknesses and strengths, acceptance of one's shortcomings, and the ability to consistently apply self-care principles to maintain the clinician's psychological well-being. It has also examined the importance of self-care in relationship to ethics, impairment, and properly treating clients. Finally, this chapter has explored the various types of vulnerabilities that the psychotherapist may face in his/her profession, including those related to his/her inner world and external work environment. The next chapter will look at the therapist's profession in regards to why individuals become psychotherapists, issues concerning transference and countertransference, and a brief description of how stressors outside the work environment can affect one's professional responsibilities.

CHAPTER 2

The Therapist's Profession

The profession of the psychotherapist can be very intense, yet satisfying for many individuals. This intensity can vary depending on many personal elements. These elements will determine the therapist's effectiveness in treating clients and his/her ability to maintain a healthy psychological well-being (Wise *et al.* 2012). Some of these elements include one's personal traits and life experiences (Saarnio 2010; Taber, Leibert, and Agaskar 2011; Wogan 1970), education, training, counseling skills, practicums, and internships (Boellinghaus *et al.* 2013; Pillay and Johnston 2011).

To be successful performing psychotherapy, a therapist must care both for himself/herself and for those who come for relief of their symptoms (Collins 1995). Many therapists may not be aware how one's past experience, limitations, and weaknesses can affect one's psychological well-being and performance during the counseling session, but this knowledge is imperative to performing one's duties at an optimum level (Hatcher *et al.* 2012; McConnaughy 1987).

This chapter was written to examine and emphasize the many variables that can affect the psychological well-being of the psychotherapist during his/her profession. It will focus on why individuals become therapists, issues associated with transference and countertransference, and briefly examine how stressors outside of work can affect one's ability to perform one's duties and responsibilities.

Reasons for becoming a therapist

What motivates an individual to become a psychotherapist, and what reasons lead a person to their decision to enter the mental health field? Even though there may be many reasons why an individual chooses to become a clinician, Barnett (2007) writes that a person's history and life experiences associated with emotional distress, in many cases, has been associated with his/her decision to enter the counseling field. Even the renowned Albert Ellis stated that he entered the field of psychotherapy to learn how to become a less anxious and happier individual (Ellis 2005).

But why does one's past experiences have such an influence in one's seeking to become a psychotherapist? Probably one of the main reasons a person's past experiences have such an influence in entering the mental health field is that some of these people may have experienced some type of psychological disturbance early in life. Because of these experiences, an individual may feel he/she can experientially understand what clients are feeling and how best to treat them, based on his/her knowledge, training, and experience (Cain 2000; Ellis 2005). In this case, one can say that the psychotherapist has already been in the clients' shoes.

Research shows that one's past life events and experiences have an effect on a person's choice to become a counselor/therapist (Barnett 2007; DiCaccavo 2002; Leiper and Casares 2000). In this context, this would refer to what some would call "wounded healers." Wheeler (2007) describes wounded healers as therapists who had bouts of their own unique psychopathology, and these experiences have driven them to help others with similar disturbances. In this way, the clinician has an inner emotional knowledge of the client's world through personal experience. Research conducted by Orlinsky and Ronnestad (2005) showed a relationship between individuals' past emotional experiences and their desire to become psychotherapists. In this study, 48% of the 3577 participants indicated that their career choice was associated with the resolving and coping of past emotional disturbances. Elliott and Guy (1993) showed that women who experienced a dysfunctional family of origin were highly motivated in choosing a career in mental health. These clinicians reported having childhood traumas related to the death of a sibling or parent, parental alcoholism, sexual molestation, or hospitalization of a parent due to mental illness. Elliott and Guy described how most of these women therapists used imaginative and creative ways of coping to decrease their feelings of depression, anxiousness, and sleep problems, compared with women in other professions. Other studies have shown that issues associated with past attachment (Leiper and Casares 2000), early-life psychiatric hospitalization (Cain 2000), parentification (DiCaccavo 2002), and problems with grief and narcissistic needs (Barnett 2007) have had a major impact on many mental health practitioners' decision to enter the mental health field.

Personal therapy is another experience that has been shown to motivate people's interest in entering the mental health field. A study conducted by Geller, Norcross and Orlinsky (2005) discovered that approximately three-quarters of participants who were treated with psychotherapy in their past acknowledged that this experience had a large part to play in their decision to become therapists. Most likely these individuals saw great value and relief in dealing with their problems and felt comfortable that they might be able to help people in similar ways. In fact, Farber *et al.* (2005) wrote that many therapists chose their career because they saw becoming a clinician as the next sequence in their life in terms of helping people, which started with themselves experiencing distress, seeking out and participating in therapy, gaining relief, and using this experience to help others. Again, the point here is that overcoming experiences associated with emotional distress motivated these individuals to want to help others with similar problems.

Certainly not all individuals who become therapists have had a past associated with mental health issues, and not all people who have had emotional disturbances become clinicians. In fact, there are those who become mental health practitioners who have no psychological issues at all. Instead, they may have an overwhelming curiosity about people and why they feel, think, and behave as they do (Henry, Sims, and Spray 1973). They seek to know what type of variables contribute to the development of an individual's personality. Farber *et al.* (2005) noted that there are many people who enter the field of mental health because of the desire to understand themselves and others. From early childhood they are constantly looking for the "whys" behind behavior. They seek to understand how each person is similar but different in the way he/she thinks, feels, and acts.

Furthermore, Henry *et al.* (1973) discovered that many of these individuals frequently read books dealing with human nature, often analyze their thoughts and feelings, and are primarily introspective. They are constantly observing the way they feel and think about various topics, and become sensitive towards the emotions of people in their environment. They seek to understand themselves by questioning their feelings, thoughts, and behaviors. Farber *et al.* (2005) state that these people are stimulated intellectually and try to discover the causes behind many individuals' thoughts and actions. Additionally, they read articles, view shows, attend seminars, and take courses to get a better understanding of what makes people unique in their thoughts and behaviors (Henry *et al.* 1973).

So, what are the other reasons individuals would choose to enter the mental health field? One of the answers to this question has to do with the influence of another person, and how this individual becomes a model for choosing a future career (Karel and Stead 2011; Kniveton 2004). Modeling has been shown to be a powerful influencer because it requires little effort on the part of the individual who is being influenced to emulate the behaviors of the model (Leitner 1973; Reeves 2009). A role model could come from one's immediate family. Edmundson (2007) notes that Anna Freud, the daughter of the famous Sigmund Freud, was inspired by her father to pursue the same type of career as a psychoanalyst. Melanie Klein, developer of the object relations theory, became a physician because of the inspiration of her father's desire to help others in distress (Feist and Feist 1998).

Exposure to people and events early in an individual's life can also have an influence on the selection of the work one will perform in his/her career. This exposure could even come from theological events and teachers (Nesbitt 1995). Feist and

Feist (1998) found that famous theorists and therapists such as Edward Thorndike, Carl Rogers, Erich Fromm, and George Kelly were influenced by religious leaders and theology, which in turn enhanced the development of their concern for people who were in distress.

Another group of individuals who may have an impact on one's selection of a career are teachers and professors. How many readers can relate to taking a course in psychology that stimulated their interest so much that it motivated a desire to pursue a career in mental health? Henry, Sims, and Spray (1971) mention that professors and teachers have been known to play a major role in a person's choice of career. Similarly, Farber *et al.* (2005) agree that teachers play a significant part in stimulating curiosity in one's field of interest. Even though many people in one's past had a powerful effect on the direction one will go in life, the individual person still has the responsibility of choice in this matter.

While influential people often have an impact on the direction of one's career, mentors especially have been found to be major influences on an individual even after he/she has chosen his/her profession. According to Johnson (2002), mentoring is a one-on-one relationship that has its basis in teaching, challenging, support, counseling, and friendship. This relationship is not formal, but personal, and is directed towards the growth of the mentee (Levinson *et al.* 1978). Dannenfelser (2007) emphasizes that mentoring assists in showing what a mentee may expect in his/her future career, which may not be taught in a university curriculum. So, what does it mean to be a mentor? Green and Hawley (2009) note:

> Being a mentor means having a genuine human relationship and making a commitment to an individual to help shape his or her professional and personal growth. With this responsibility also comes the challenge of being aware of diversity issues, serving as a steward of psychology and preserving its history, and being consistent in one's own life with what one expects from the mentee. (p.211)

Being a mentor means displaying certain characteristics towards the mentee. Two of the most important characteristics a mentor can display are confidence and encouragement (Kummer 2006). By the time an individual's training is completed, the mentee has learned and attained what will be needed to perform his/her job effectively. But will the person be confident enough to use this knowledge in difficult and stressful situations as a psychotherapist?

One of the main objectives of mentors is to prepare the future clinician to deal with stressful and intense situations in a work environment (Lazarus 2012). Casto, Caldwell, and Salazar (2005) discuss how a mentor can expose the individual to situations that challenge the mentee's ability to stay calm and handle intense situations. This might mean allowing the mentee to treat a depressed and suicidal client under the mentor's guidance, while giving helpful and encouraging advice.

Albert Ellis is one mentor that Johnson, Digiuseppe, and Ulven (1999) describe as having a powerful influence on his mentees because of his personal characteristics and interactions. Johnson *et al.* (1999) portray Ellis as having the characteristics of being unconditionally accepting, supportive, warm, and encouraging towards his mentees. Albert Ellis was also described as a supervisor who displayed transparency about himself and his thoughts about his profession. One of the most noticeable and impressive qualities that Ellis exhibited was his personal commitment to each of his mentees, in which he tried to be involved in their personal lives, giving emotional support when needed. Some examples that Johnson *et al.* give are consoling when one of his mentees lost a loved one, giving letters of recommendation for employment, listening to the mentees' worries and anxieties, and giving them unconditional emotional support.

The final and most important characteristic that a mentor can display to their mentees is ethical behavior. Demonstrating ethical behaviors can have an influential and instructional effect on future psychologists and is a requirement of the Ethical Principles of Psychologists (APA 2002). These principles help to direct psychologists' behavior towards their mentees, colleagues, and clients so they can have a positive effect without harming them. Many studies have shown that mentors have had a substantial influence over their mentees just by their behaviors and by being role models (Kitchener 1992; Pettifor *et al.* 2011; Ronnestad and Skovholt 2003; Sugimoto 2012). According to Kitchener, many unethical behaviors exhibited by psychologists could have been corrected in their early training and internships if mentors had been critical in a supportive way. Behaviors such as talking about one's client in public, breaching confidentiality, and writing accurate progress notes have to be brought to the attention of future clinicians to ensure they understand the serious impact of their actions.

In addition, unethical behavior by mentors can have negative effects on mentees. Kitchener (1992) describes incidents of mentors misusing their power and authority, for example, by having mentees perform the mentor's research responsibilities to meet deadlines, taking frustrations out on mentees, and having sexual contact with learners. In fact, several surveys conducted on female psychologists indicated that between 14 and 18% had sexual contact with a mentor (Glaser and Thorpe 1986; Robinson and Reid 1985). The consequences to the mentee for this type of behavior led to a drop in their self-esteem for years afterwards. The reason the novice therapist might be vulnerable to allowing unethical behaviors by their mentors to go unnoticed or unreported are in order to receive a high grade or a letter of recommendation (Kitchener 1992).

Furthermore, Sugimoto (2012) stresses that the main goal of mentoring is to guide the mentee towards making good decisions, whether decisions are practical and/or ethically based. Mentoring also means correcting unethical behavior when it is noticed in the mentee, and supporting him/her in times of stress and discouragement.

To summarize this section, various reasons have been shown to affect an individual's choice to enter the mental health profession. These include dealing with some type of psychological disturbance earlier in life, attending personal therapy, curiosity about the psychological make-up of individuals, the influence of family or religious leaders, and the encouragement and guidance of mentors. Of course, a therapist's past experiences and training associated with these reasons will have an important impact on his/her performance in treating clients, including issues pertaining to transference and countertransference.

Dealing with transference

One of the main factors that the clinician will have to deal with effectively in treating clients is transference. Transference is a term, first developed by the well-known psychoanalyst Sigmund Freud, which refers to the unconscious re-enactment of the client's unresolved conflicts with such individuals as parents and/or siblings that resulted in some emotional crisis (Tara 2007). This unconscious re-enactment is displayed by the client towards the therapist during treatment sessions (Freud 1958). Gammelgaard (2003) explains that the unconscious re-enactment may be some type of heightened emotional display brought out by the client. The client's emotions are a force that the counselor has to outwardly control. What is meant by outward control is that the therapist is responsible for ensuring that the client's emotional behavior does not get out of control during the counseling session (Wolstein 1996). One example is that a client could become verbally loud during the session and may even threaten the therapist because of some memory that has surfaced in the client's mind. Another example is the psychotherapist's ability to control behaviors of clients diagnosed with Borderline Personality Disorder who react to memories associated with their transference. Hart *et al.* (2013) emphasize that these individuals have trouble with emotional regulation. The symptoms these clients display are centered around problems with self-identity, fear of abandonment, distrust, marks of impulsivity, and difficulty controlling anger (APA 2000). Symptoms characterized by Borderline Personality Disorder have been shown to develop during the early childhood and adolescent period and are projected onto clients' everyday relationships (Joyce *et al.* 2003; Van Den Bosch *et al.* 2003).

Johnson (1997) informs that one of the main responsibilities of the clinician is to observe and try to help clients reduce the intensity of their symptoms. These symptoms may be related to impulsivity, anger, threats, explosive and irrational behaviors, evasiveness, and dependent attitudes that may have developed early in childhood or because of some biological, and/or environmental reason. The important point is that the therapist must stay calm, assess the situation continually, be ready for any situation that may arise, and control the behavior of the client as much as possible (Rambo, Heath, and Chenail 1993).

Since the client's response in session will depend on a variety of factors, the clinician must remain calm and be prepared for any situation. One of these factors is how a client reacts according to his/her temperament. Temperament can also be defined as an individual's emotional responses to different circumstances in his/her environment that become stable over time (Cloninger *et al.* 1994). Hutchinson, Stuart, and Pretorius (2010) state that temperament can be seen as biology based and an internal part of the personality developed early in life. Another factor involved in how a client will respond to a therapist is the early environment and caregivers that the client had early in his/her life. Additionally, during the client's early years, there could have been some kind of trauma, such as emotional, physical, and/or sexual abuse (Becker-Weidman 2006). There may even have been some type of neglect (Widom, Marmorstein, and White 2006).

The main concern is that the counselor's psychological well-being can be weakened to the point of emotional and physical exhaustion (Maslach, Jackson and Leiter 1996) by being continually exposed to this type of environment day after day. A therapist is not only responsible for dealing with the behavior of the client while in session, but is also responsible for being aware of his/her reactions towards the client.

Dealing with countertransference

Transference is not the only element the therapist must be aware of while treating clients. The clinician must also be aware of his/her countertransference. Again, Freud (1959) was the first to coin this term, which he referred to as the psychotherapist's remembrance of past relationships that contain the unconscious, unresolved, and neurotic conflicts which surface during his/her interaction with clients in session. In addition, Rosenberger and Hayes (2002) state that during the counseling session the client may say or do something that triggers the therapist to remember some type of conflict that occurred earlier in a clinician's life. However, in opposition to Freud's past theory of countertransference, the modern view of countertransference contains both the unconscious and conscious remembrance of unresolved conflicts from the therapist's childhood (Fauth and Hayes 2006).

How a therapist reacts to these memories will determine how the counselor thinks and feels, and how he/she might project this onto the client (Holmqvist 2001). Cain (2000) discusses how counselors can be overwhelmed by feelings of anxiety, anger, discomfort, and stigmatized while identifying with the client if the therapist had symptoms in his/her past similar to the client's. In like fashion, Sarasohn (2005) writes that, in some cases, identifying with the client's past may produce feelings of dread and shame within the counselor.

Occurrences of countertransference may not only affect the well-being of the therapist, it also may affect how the counselor relates to the client. In one study, the therapist's unresolved feelings of bereavement were found to be inversely proportional to how many clients perceived the therapist as being empathic (Hayes, Yeh, and Eisenberg 2007). Hayes *et al.* found that if counselors do not examine their past feelings of loss and work towards resolution in an appropriate way, then these feelings could eventually hinder the effectiveness of the therapist in treating his/her clients. According to Richards (2000), a therapist who is not aware of his/her countertransference could act on these thoughts and feelings and possibly bring harm to the therapeutic relationship by saying or doing something to upset the client. In another study, Fauth and Hayes (2006) noted that identifying with the client, as far as countertransference is concerned, may cause some therapists to feel threatened and challenged, and to emotionally distance themselves from the client. In a similar study, Rosenberger and Hayes (2002) showed that the therapist's countertransference could produce a defensive attitude, distorted recall of the client's conversations, and an avoidance of material that is disturbing to the client.

Countertransference does not always necessarily have a negative effect on the counselor and the counselor–client relationship. According to Holmqvist (2001), the identification of the therapist with the client's past disturbances can be viewed as positive in that the therapist can obtain useful information and relay it back to the client, but this will depend upon the therapist being aware of his/her countertransference. Bernard (2005) writes, "...self-aware therapists have the opportunity to scrutinize their experience in the treatment situation to achieve greater understanding of the people with whom they are working. What therapists do with this understanding then becomes a matter of therapeutic technique" (p.154). Likewise, Rober (2005) comments that the therapeutic process can be enriched by the counselor reflecting and being aware of his thoughts and memories during the therapy session and using this information to understand the client in a deeper way. For example, many times the therapist will treat a client who has had a similar experience as themselves. This experience might be some type of child abuse or a depression episode. A therapist, being aware of remembering these events and knowing that these memories and feelings are part of the countertransference experience, can be more empathic towards the client and strengthen the counselor–client bond (Beck and Buchele 2005). In some studies, being aware of one's countertransference can make a difference as to whether a therapist will make a positive or negative evaluation of his/her client (Fauth and Hayes 2006), and/or be in control of a traumatized group of individuals during session (Bernard 2005). The critical piece in the therapist's reaction is being aware of the internal processes and able to cope with them in such a way that the therapeutic process is not affected. Not only does a therapist need to engage the client in session and be aware of his/her own past experiences, but a therapist also needs awareness of his/her present stressors outside of work.

Dealing with outside stressors

As with most people, the stressors that a counselor encounters outside the work environment may affect the performance of his/her duties while treating clients. These stressors can and do affect the therapist's well-being and can cause an additional strain on the counselor–client relationship (Lawson 2007). Rupert, Stevanovic, and Hunley (2009) found that outside forces such as one's financial, household, and family care could become a distraction even to long-time, experienced therapists. A therapist not taking care, or being overwhelmed with matters in other areas of his/her life, can find his/her mind wandering and focusing on things happening at home or other places rather than his/her full attention being focused on the client. At the beginning of each workday, the therapist should perform an assessment on himself/herself to discover if he/she is focused and free from any type of distress. If the counselor is bothered with outside stressors which result in not giving undivided attention to the client, then the therapist should consider taking time away from his/her duties to resolve the matter (APA 2002).

The intent of this section was not to have an in-depth discussion of the forces outside of the therapist's work environment, but to make the clinician aware that worries at home can affect the treatment of clients. The mental health practitioner must ensure he/she is free from all distractions and is focused completely on the treatment of the client.

Summary

In this chapter, various elements were examined as to how a mental health practitioner develops into his/her profession. This examination showed how individuals are influenced and motivated to select a career as a mental health practitioner. This motivation could have been due to the influence of a family member, teachers, religious leaders, and/or mentors. The past experiences of the clinician have also been shown to play a major factor in how he/she functions as a therapist and how this can affect him/her in both positive and negative ways during the therapy session. In addition, this chapter has explored how the therapist must be continually in control of different aspects of the counseling session, including the client's display of emotional behaviors and the therapist's own countertransference. A brief discussion of stressors outside of the work environment were also reviewed and it was shown how these may affect the therapist's psychological well-being and interaction with the client. Finally, the main emphasis of this chapter was to make the mental health practitioner aware of how his/her past experiences, limitations, and weaknesses can affect his/her psychological well-being and interaction with clients. The next chapter of this book will explore various duties and responsibilities that clinicians perform, with the emphasis placed on how the more comfortable with being a mental health practitioner one is, and the more one is prepared, the less stress will be encountered.

CHAPTER 3

The Therapist's Duties and Roles

A therapist's duties and roles are more complex than the average person may perceive. A mental health practitioner not only talks to people about their problems, but also must be well versed in the legal, ethical, and administrative responsibilities of the profession. Some of these responsibilities may pertain to such things as client confidentiality (Kampf *et al.* 2008), duty to warn (Costa and Altekruse 1994), and how to treat various clients according to their cultural and ethnic differences (Mogudi-Carter 2001), as well as when to make referrals. A clinician must also be an accurate record keeper and maintain current notes and assessments of all clients being treated. Scaife and Pomerantz (1999) emphasize that a psychotherapist should have a system and know where all clients' notes are and how to keep these records confidential from people who are not authorized to read them.

The mental health practitioner will encounter many stressors and dilemmas that will test his/her psychological well-being to perform his/her duties under pressure. This chapter was written to help the clinician perform his/her duties more efficiently whether the individual is an intern or a seasoned professional. The purpose of this chapter is to focus primarily on four specific roles of the mental health practitioner:

1. a social influencer
2. an effective organizer

3. a goal planner

4. a psychological helper.

Being a social influencer

What does being a social influencer mean in reference to a counselor/therapist? The answer means much in regard to how successful the clinician will be in treating clients. This is not to say it is the only role, or that it is the most important role, but without being a social influencer the therapist cannot have a strong therapeutic alliance with his/her clients (Thomas, Werner-Wilson, and Murphy 2005).

One can view being a social influencer as corresponding to one's professionalism in being a mental health practitioner. According to Rashotte (2006), "Social influence is defined as change in an individual's thoughts, feelings, attitudes, or behaviors that results from interaction with another individual or a group" (p.4426). In therapy, isn't the goal of treatment to change the thoughts, emotions, and behaviors of the client searching our help? Similarly, Dorn (1984) also acknowledges that counseling is basically a process where the counselor uses verbal and non-verbal behavior to influence the client to change his/her emotions, thoughts, and behaviors for the betterment of his/her psychological well-being.

Whether one is conscious of it or not, we do influence each other by the way we act and present ourselves, especially in front of new clients who have never seen a therapist before. According to Dorn (1984), the social influence theory suggests that therapy is an interpersonal influence process in which the counselor can influence the client's participation by such things as his/her education, training, reputation, and even attire and personality. Thomas *et al.* (2005) emphasize that social influence is an important part of the therapeutic process in which the client sees the therapist as being credible, reliable, and knowledgeable. This type of influence happens even before the therapist meets the client and is the first part of the counseling process. One might call this stage of being a social influencer as the preparation because it prepares the therapist physically, emotionally, and cognitively to influence the client towards a desire to change. First impressions, especially in the initial session, set the stage for the client wanting to change and to willingly follow the advice and the direction of the counselor (Laungani 2002).

During this time of preparation, the therapist should wear the appropriate attire, should have rehearsed a pleasant and warm welcome, and should have a clean and orderly office, so the client will feel comfortable enough to disclose personal distresses as soon as possible (Senour 1982). A professional appearance (how the counselor dresses and being groomed) and communication style are imperative if the therapist wants to influence the client and change the client's way of thinking about his/her mental health (Strong 1968). The appearance of the therapist's office is also an important part of this first stage. Nasar and Devlin (2011) emphasize that this is an important element in how influential the therapist will be. If the physical environment of one's office is orderly, personalized with certificates and diplomas, and looks comfortable and attractive, then clients will be more willing to disclose personal information and participate in therapy.

The second stage of being a social influencer is also important because it is the time when the therapist meets the new client and presents himself/herself. Gass (1984) has found that during the initial interview clients will form impressions based on the counselor's attire, presentation, and office environment that will determine if the client will return for a second session. Similarly, Harris and Busby (1998) noticed that many clients on the initial visit will judge the therapist rather quickly, based on personal characteristics such as physical appearance, attractiveness, openness, and friendliness. Other types of non-verbal communication that play an important part in the initial session are body posture and facial expressions. Tang (1990) calls this type of interaction during the initial session "interpersonal competence." In relationship to therapy, interpersonal competence could be defined as the counselor's effective use of both verbal and non-verbal forms of communication to create a feeling of friendliness and safety among new clients (Tang 1990). When one thinks about how the therapist acts as a social influencer, one can understand that this is the outward demonstration of one's professionalism.

The following is a list of questions that a clinician can address before meeting with new or long-term clients to increase his/her influence. The list of questions is as follows:

- When a therapist meets a client for the first time, how is the clinician dressed?

- Is the clinician wearing fairly new and color-coordinated clothing?

- What about grooming? Is the hair clean and combed so it looks presentable and attractive?

- Does the therapist meet the client with a smile and a handshake?

- Does the clinician display a warm and relaxed appearance that makes the client feel safe?

- Does the therapist acknowledge the family and friends that came with the client by introducing himself/herself to them?

This all has to do with influencing the client to the counselor's way of thinking or social influencing. However, the clinician's main concern is not only with being a social influencer, but also with being an effective and efficient organizer.

Being an efficient organizer

Another important role a clinician has to perform is that of an organizer. Most, if not all, therapists will be involved in organizing their caseload of clients to some extent. This includes performing initial assessments, reviewing clients' charts to assign a diagnosis, assigning follow-up sessions (Seligman 2004), and deciding how to deal with calls from clients outside of the therapist's work hours.

Some therapists who work for corporations, hospitals, or clinics may have their clients assigned to them, whereas those in private practice or who are contractors will have to fill their open time slots and negotiate times with the people they treat (Cohn and Hastings 2013). Whether the clinician is employed by a corporation or not, the counselor will have to organize and negotiate times with clients to meet their needs. Beck (1994) states that there is a further consideration to take into account if the clinician works part time and if his/her availability conflicts with that of his/her clients.

One possible way that may make it easy for the client and therapist to remember when to meet for sessions is to meet on the same day and same time each week. This makes it easy for the client and therapist to remember when their session is and makes the client more accountable for attending or calling to cancel a session. This may not always be possible, especially with clients who the clinician sees multiple times throughout the week or a few times during the month (Seligman 2004). The point here is to make the scheduled times between the therapist and client as simple and consistent as possible so they are easy to remember. Using this principle will make things more reliable for the counselor with regard to clients attending their sessions on time and will also help the clients remember when their scheduled times are for therapy. In addition, having a calendar with a listing of all clients who are scheduled for at least two months from the present date is a good way to be aware of what one's caseload looks like each week and to make the necessary changes when emergencies occur. Another recommendation is to review one's schedule of clients for the next day, and personally telephone them as a reminder.

Next, the counselor should have a policy about clients who are "no shows" or "cancel," and those who drop out of therapy prematurely; that is, how to fill their time slots, and actions to be taken as far as payments and terminations are concerned (Owen et al. 2012). The idea here is to develop a plan so all time slots will be filled. One must remember that the therapist earns money by seeing and treating clients. Research shows that clients experience a reduction of the severity in their symptoms when they come consistently to therapy and participate in their treatment compared to clients who come less frequently (Hitch 2012; Messari and Hallam 2003; Nock and Photos 2006).

The second important part of being an organizer is record keeping. This is one of the more important activities that a therapist will perform. It includes keeping notes, billings, assessments, and treatment plans and storing these in a secure location where they cannot be accessed by any outside parties (Drogin *et al.* 2010). As any clinician knows, keeping organized documents related to clients' treatment is critical to justifying payments from third parties and a means of remembering, assessing the progress, and documenting the types of treatments used on clients (Scaife and Pomerantz 1999). Bemister and Dobson (2012) noted that record keeping is important from an ethical and legal consideration. During the course of treatment the counselor might discover times when a client has been abused and/or neglected, threatened to commit suicide, or threatened to hurt someone. In these cases keeping accurate notes is critical to relaying this information to the proper authorities if and when it is needed (Grossman and Koocher 2010).

Another consideration for recording information about the client is if the clinician will be taking psychotherapy notes. Just what are psychotherapy notes, and is there a difference between these notes and the client's medical record? In one study conducted by DeLettre and Sobell (2010) of 464 doctoral level psychologists, 29% of participants reported having no knowledge of the difference between a client's medical record and a client's psychotherapy notes. Scaife and Pomerantz (1999) explain that, while the client's medical records contain things such as diagnoses, symptoms, assessments, progress notes, payment information, medical prescriptions, and treatment received, the client's psychotherapy notes are different in that they are mainly the clinician's subjective impressions about clients that can be used as a means of remembering and can be analyzed at later times. Most importantly, psychotherapy notes do not have to be released to third-party payers such as insurance companies if these notes are kept totally separate from the client's medical record (DeLettre and Sobell 2010). In this case, Grossman and

Koocher (2010) acknowledge that the only way that these notes could be released would be if dictated by state law or a signed consent to release this information by the client.

Having a system where one can readily find information is imperative to a clinician's line of work (Scaife and Pomerantz 1999). Since most practitioners schedule one client after another, psychotherapists do not have a lot of time to look for clients' files or write notes. A clinician would be wise to have all files of clients that he/she will be seeing on hand and review them at the beginning of the day. Additionally, forms such as consent, release of information, progress notes, treatment plans, diagnostic questionnaires, and policies of the practitioner or the institution should be on hand and arranged in such a way that the clinician can find them at a moment's notice (Seligman 2004). Zuckerman (2008) notes that whether the mental health practitioner is in private practice or works for a corporation, he/she only has a limited amount of time in which to accomplish tasks and so being more organized will help him/her to become more efficient and reduce stress.

Furthermore, Bemister and Dobson (2012) stress the need for confidentiality in most situations concerning one's client, especially in regard to those conversations that are written in the individual's file. In cases where clients' documentation is handwritten, these records should be in locked cabinets and kept away from anyone's line of sight except those who are authorized to open these records in performance of their duties (Mir 2011). Drogin *et al.* (2010) emphasize that in most cases confidentially is essential in protecting the client's privacy.

Speaking on the topic of keeping records confidential, assigning numbers to clients' names and their files is a good way of preventing any unauthorized people from knowing what information is associated with specific clients. Many times, when the clinician is busy, he/she may leave a client's file on his/her desk. If the client's file has a number on it, another client would not know whose name is on the specific file. A list that correlates each number to a client can be kept in a locked filing cabinet or locked desk drawer until it is needed.

In the advent of computers and electronic recording, many facilities are using electronic medical records programs to keep the client's information (Mir 2011). Smolyansky *et al.* (2013) state that additional requirements are needed in the case where most of the clients' information is recorded in a computer's data base to ensure that confidentiality is kept since some of this information may be used to collaborate with other organizations, institutions, and/or physicians using these electronic data bases. Items such as assessments, evaluations, diagnoses, treatment plans, progress notes, and medical information pertinent to the client may be included (Maheu *et al.* 2012). Having certain safeguards including passwords with encryption can prevent breaching confidential information. Now that the importance of a therapist being a social influencer and organizer has been discussed, the next item that will be examined will be the importance of the practitioner being a goal planner.

Being a goal planner

One of the more important duties that a therapist will perform is working with clients to establish goals. Egan (1998) notes that developing and working towards goals gives clients motivation, purpose, and direction. The motivation comes because of the encouragement of the clinician with the development of goals, the continual review, and positive reinforcement until completion (Andresen, Oades, and Caputi 2003; Mackrill 2011). Pound and Duchac (2009) found that hope is one key element which enables clients to work on the goals through to successful attainment. Furthermore, the attainment of these goals can give clients a sense of accomplishment and at the same time can help to relieve distress that they are experiencing (Clarke *et al.* 2009).Goals help clients focus their thoughts and energies towards a specific endpoint where they can feel and notice the severity of their symptoms being reduced or eliminated. Like a roadmap, goals give a starting point and a point of completion. Without goals, therapy could go anywhere and may last for years without the knowledge of how much progress was achieved (Egan 1998).

Goals also help individuals attain a specific objective. An objective for someone suffering from major depression could be feeling happy in his/her life. One can have multiple goals towards reaching a specific objective. An example of a goal is taking a walk for 15 minutes three times a week. Another example is journaling four times a week. Meeting these two goals could provide the motivation and direction for accomplishing an objective of feeling happier.

In addition, the establishment of goals is essential to the development of any effective treatment plan (Hutchinson, Bland, and Kleiber 2008). During the initial assessment, the clinician will usually ask specific and general questions to discover the client's symptoms and their level of severity (Seligman 2004). The therapist may also ask how the client would like to feel after the course of treatment. This type of logic has the present condition of the client in mind, and also the desired future state, free of distress. It gives the clinician and client a starting and end point for therapy. The client in this scenario can think and try to imagine what his/her life would be like if free of symptoms of mental illness. An example of this could be someone who has been depressed and sad for weeks and sees no hope in his/her condition getting better. In this case, the client might want to see his/her future condition as being happy, and traveling around to different parts of the country, which was the way the individual felt and acted before the onset of depression.

Goals may differ from one therapist to the next, depending on the clinician's theoretical orientation, past education, and experience (Alloy, Jacobson, and Acocella 1999; Dirmaier *et al.* 2006; Philips 2009). According to Alloy *et al.* (1999), a clinician who practices a psychodynamic approach would focus on uncovering unconscious developmental conflicts associated with the client's past, especially in the person's family relationships, whereas a counselor who practices a cognitive approach would be interested in changing the present distorted thinking patterns of the client. Other theoretical orientations, such as behavioral or family approaches, would lean towards developing goals consistent with their specialty. There are clinicians who are also eclectic in their development of the client's treatment plans, so the goals will vary according to different methods (Dirmaier *et al.* 2006).

For any type of treatment to be effective, goals should be specific, measurable, and developed by both the client and therapist (Egan 1998). Likewise, Dyer and Vriend (1977) found that for goals to be successful they should contain the following components:

- be specific enough to eliminate problematic behaviors
- be measurable and quantifiable
- be achievable and success-oriented
- be developed and agreed upon by both the client and therapist.

It is noteworthy that Elliot and Church (2002) also wrote that development of goals first start with hearing the client's story. Goals are then formulated by using specific and measurable criteria to determine if the goal will be met within a specific time period. Goals are then written down and tracked from session to session to note the progress towards the client's objective. This process happens with the continual input and mutual agreement of both the counselor and client and is not the endpoint of the client's treatment plan. After several weeks of therapy, Seligman (2004) states that the treatment plan should be reviewed and re-evaluated to determine if the goals were achieved and have been effective. If the goals were not effective they can be readjusted, or new goals can be made. A goal planner is but one role and duty a clinician has to perform aside from other roles such as a social influencer and organizer. The next and final role is probably the most crucial of all to successfully treating the client. It is the role of being a helper.

Being a psychological helper

The role of helper is probably the most important of the clinician's four roles and should be the main reason for being a mental health practitioner. There are various techniques that can help the helper be more effective (Okun and Kantrowitz 2008). In this context, Egan (2013) states that a therapist helps clients overcome distress and the severity of one's symptoms through the verbal interaction that takes place during the therapy session. This verbal interaction has been termed either, "psychotherapy" or "counseling." Egan (1998) says that there are similarities and differences between these two terminologies, but for the purposes of this book the terms "psychotherapy" and "counseling" will be defined as follows: "The essence of counseling is to consistently summon the energy to engage with another human's emotions while at the same time balancing our own personal experiences and challenges outside the job" (Cummins, Massey, and Jones 2007, p.35). In this definition, the therapist acts as a helper, focusing his/her energies to help to relieve clients of their distress while ensuring his/her personal past memories do not interfere with treatment.

Being a helper is at the heart of a therapist's main function (Egan 2013). Gary R. Collins (1995) in his book *How to be a People Helper* discusses how being a helper begins with a desire in one's heart to help someone through some difficulty in his/her life. This desire should be authentic because most clients will sense this caring or lack of caring, and this may determine whether there will be a strong therapeutic alliance or premature termination on the part of some clients (Egan 1998). This desire to help people, especially those suffering from mental disorders, does not stop with desire but is the motivational piece for the therapist to use his/her basic therapeutic techniques to provide a safe and trusting environment for the client to interact with the counselor.

These therapeutic techniques are fundamental to most mental health practitioners and are associated with the teachings and theory of Carl Rogers (Rogers 1980). The main emphasis of Rogers' theory is on establishing a safe and trusting environment where the client can openly address issues that are causing him/her distress (McLeod 2008). The reason for discussing Carl Rogers' theory is that, during two surveys, taken in 1982 and 2006, Carl Rogers was rated as the number one most influential psychotherapist of approximately 3,000 members of the American Psychological Association (APA) (Samstag 2007).

The first therapeutic technique that will be discussed is unconditional positive regard. Wilkins (2000) describes unconditional positive regard as the acceptance of the client's feelings, no matter how good or bad, positive or negative these feelings may be. Similarly, Rogers (2007) defines unconditional positive regard in these terms:

> It involves as much feeling of acceptance for the client's expression of negative, "bad," painful, fearful, defensive, abnormal feelings as for his expression of "good," positive, mature, confident, social feelings, as much acceptance of ways in which he is inconsistent as of ways in which he is consistent. (p.243)

Many people who come to therapy are overwhelmed by some type of emotional distress and need some place to come to talk about their hurts without the fear of being criticized (Sanyal 2011). Providing a safe, accepting, and therapeutic environment is a good way for the client to feel that someone cares and keeps their interests at heart. In this respect, the client can come into therapy and tell the clinician their deepest secrets and greatest distresses. When a client feels this relaxed, it is an excellent way for the counselor to establish where and what the problems are.

The second technique that will be discussed is empathy. Rogers (1980) says that empathy could be defined as the way a therapist perceives and creates the feelings of the client in himself/herself. Creating these feelings should not detract the therapist in to feeling sorry for the client, but instead should be used in an objective matter to help and understand the client's specific situation. According to Sanyal (2011), empathy gives the practitioner accurate knowledge of the client's emotions and thoughts, which helps the therapist develop an inner picture of the client. A therapist at this point not only knows what the client is emotionally experiencing but can feel specific emotions such as fear, joy, frustration, or disgust. Empathy begins with listening to the client's story as he/she opens up the world of hurts, distresses, and disappointments to the therapist (Feller and Cottone 2003).

Listening is the third technique used in counseling. Listening may not seem so much like a technique, but it is how an individual listens that makes this unique. Listening, in the context of therapy, is the most important duty a clinician will perform, and it is the foundation of all therapies (Egan 1998; Hibel and Polanco 2010; Ivey 2000; McGlasson 2012; Rogers 2007). A study conducted by Littauer, Sexton, and Wynn (2005) found that listening was an essential quality in performing effective therapy. In another study, clients viewed their successful treatment outcomes as linked to the personal qualities of their therapists, especially the clinician's ability to listen to their stories and to engage them in the specific details of their discussions (Howe 1993). Listening in this way demands that the counselor focuses his/her full attention on the client continuously. This is what is known as attentive listening, and it not only focuses on the words of the client but also on the bodily and facial expressions of the client (Egan 1998). According to Myers (2000), this type of listening combined with the empathy on the part of the clinician produces a feeling of being heard and understood in the client. Seikkula and Trimble (2005) noted that when these types of ingredients are active in the dialogue between a counselor and client, then positive changes can be displayed in the form of the reduction of the severity of symptoms in clients.

Summary

In summary, this chapter has covered many different types of roles that a mental health practitioner performs on the job. One of these roles is that of being a social influencer. A social influencer in this context has to do with how the clinician presents himself/herself to the client. This presentation should motivate the client to want to listen and change his/her thoughts and behaviors to that recommended by the therapist. Another role of the counselor is that of an organizer. Being an organizer means not only having one's inner thoughts organized but also having one's external materials organized as well. This has to do with the clinician's case files, office, progress notes, and caseload of clients. A third role performed by a therapist is that of a goal planner. During the performance of this role, the clinician guides and works with the client to develop measurable and quantifiable goals with the main objective being to improve some part of the client's psychological well-being. The final and most important role of the mental health practitioner is that of a helper. This is the most important role of a clinician because it deals with the treatment of the client and the reduction and elimination of symptoms.

This section has explored the question of why the mental health practitioner needs self-care strategies to maintain his/her psychological well-being. In addition, it has examined the counselor's profession including his/her duties and responsibilities with reference to the stressors and difficulties that the practitioner will encounter. The next section will discuss various stressors and disturbances a counselor is vulnerable to, such as job burnout and Secondary Traumatic Stress Syndrome.

PART 2

Hazards of the Profession

CHAPTER 4

General Stressors Associated with the Profession

There is little doubt that the counseling profession is one of the most demanding and stressful careers an individual can pursue (Horowitz 2008; Jordaan *et al.* 2007; Kim 2007). Several stressors in the counseling profession include role conflict, role ambiguity, large caseloads (Kirk-Brown and Wallace 2004), and treating severely disturbed clients (Vredenburgh *et al.* 1999). Over time these stressors may cause the clinician to suffer from such impairments as anxiety, depression, and alcohol or drug abuse (Emerson and Markos 1996; Lawson 2007; Saakvitne 2002). Additionally, Rupert and Morgan (2005) emphasize that any impairment suffered by a therapist may eventually cause potential harm to clients.

The purpose of this chapter is to examine stressors that the mental health practitioner will encounter in his/her career. These stressors include various types of issues involving clients, ethics, and employment status.

Issues involving clients

Some of the most stressful duties psychotherapists perform involve watching over the health and safety of their clients and those in the clients' environment. The point here is that the therapist is responsible and accountable for performing multiple types of duties involving monitoring, not only for the health and safety of the client, but also for the safety of people in the client's environment (Walfish *et al.* 2010).

Any therapist or counselor who has been in the field for any amount of time will come across those clients who are especially hard to treat. These clients might have problems with anger, communication, psychotic or irrational behavior, depression, or unresponsiveness to treatment. Whether a client has these symptoms or not, many mental health practitioners would agree that treating clients who have threatened, attempted, or eventually completed suicide can be one of the most stressful and devastating experiences one can have in one's professional life (Darden 2011; Wurst *et al.* 2011). In one study, Hendin *et al.* (2004) concluded that "most clinicians are not prepared for the intense emotional responses that accompany a patient's suicide or for the reactions of the patient's family and institutions in which the therapists work" (p.1446). According to the Centers for Disease Control and Prevention (CDC), nearly 38,500 people in the year 2010 committed suicide in the United States (CDC 2010). Many people do seek professional help before committing suicide (Gulfi *et al.* 2010) and this places the responsibility for the health and welfare of the client in the hands of the mental health practitioner.

It seems that some types of psychotherapists will encounter a higher percentage of clients who commit suicide than others (Chemtob *et al.* 1989; Koosowa 2009; Lesage 2005; McAdams III and Foster 2000; Singer and Slovak 2011). One type of psychotherapist who encounters a larger amount of suicidal clients is the psychiatrist. According to Gulfi *et al.* (2010) 51–82% of psychiatrists have lost at least one patient to suicide during their professional career. The reasons noted for this is that many psychiatrists work in a hospital setting and treat many patients who usually suffer from severe affective, psychotic, and substance abuse disorders (Chemtob *et al.* 1989). Chemtob *et al.* also noted that the severity and the classifications of these mental disorders make the risk factor for suicide high. Additionally, Gulfi *et al.* (2010) found that 22–39% of psychologists had at least one client commit suicide in their career, whereas 33% of social workers had at least one client who had committed suicide. According to these studies, the mental health practitioner has a high probability of losing at least one client to suicide during his/her career.

It is known that psychotherapists experience a broad range of emotions when one of their clients decides to take his/her own life. Many psychiatrists who experienced the death of a client expressed feelings of depression, guilt, sadness, and hopelessness (Thomyangkoon and Leenaars 2008). Several experienced psychiatrists in one study (Gitlin 2007) expressed feelings of shock, disbelief, and denial upon initially hearing about a client's suicide, and at a later time mentioned reactions of grief, shame, guilt, anger, and fear of blame.

While many experienced psychiatrists expressed psychological distress from a client's suicide, a larger percentage of the early career psychiatrists acknowledged having a greater severity of symptoms (Fang *et al.* 2007; Hendin *et al.* 2004; Ruskin *et al.* 2004). One study conducted by Ruskin *et al.* (2004) discovered that many psychiatrist trainees who experienced a client's suicide reported symptoms similar to those of Post Traumatic Stress Disorder (PTSD), whereas another study (Gitlin 1999) found a psychiatrist who had recently finished residency displaying feelings of self-doubt, shame, and embarrassment upon the death of one of his clients. In fact, Fang *et al.* (2007) informed that without some type of intervention from supervision, an intern could experience severe reactions, which in some cases may last for years.

Counselors and other psychotherapists face similar distresses to that of psychiatrists. According to Richards (2000), counselors and psychotherapists who have had clients commit suicide displayed feelings of helplessness, hopelessness, and a sense of failure. In one study, counselors reported having higher levels of avoidant and intrusive thoughts than either psychologists or psychiatrists (McAdams III and Foster 2000). Private practitioners also have noted feelings of guilt, shame, and inadequacy, accompanied by thoughts of incompetence for the failure of not spotting the signs of an impending suicide, which resulted in the therapist isolating himself/herself from peers (Fox and Cooper 1998). In response to some clients' suicide, Christianson and Everall (2009) discovered how many school counselors faced the fear of litigation, questioning of their competence, a strong reaction of grief and loss, and/or the suppression of emotional grief.

Distress experienced by therapists due to a client's suicide can last a very short time or persist for years (Wurst *et al.* 2011). In one study conducted by Sanders, Jacobson, and Ting (2005), clinicians mentioned having negative psychological reactions such as depression, trauma, and feelings of personal failure for as many as 15 years after a client's death. Similarly, Brown and Kulik (1977) reported that social workers who counseled clients who eventually committed suicide could recall specific details and emotions that were felt many years after the death of the client. Because of individual characteristics and experiences, not all therapists will have the same reactions, severity, and/or intensity due to a client's suicide (Ting, Jacobson, and Sanders 2011; Wurst *et al.* 2011).

The distress a therapist could experience following a client's suicide may depend on a variety of factors. These factors include a clinician's age, years of experience, personal characteristics, caseload, type of clients, and/or place of employment (Chemtob *et al.* 1988; Chemtob *et al.* 1989; Hendin *et al.* 2004; Horn 1994; McAdams III and Foster 2000; Wurst *et al.* 2011). However, it seems like a psychotherapist's schema has a significant part to play in his/her level of distress (Horn 1994). Markus (1977) describes a schema as a cognitive structure of information that determines how an individual processes and uses new information about himself/herself. According to Horn (1994), the emotional impact and amount of distress that a therapist will experience depends upon the clinician's schema (core beliefs) and life experiences (personal and professional). This reaction also involves the therapist's expectations about himself/herself and feelings of responsibility for another person's behavior. For example, if the counselor believes that the lack of improvement in a client's cognitive, emotional, and behavioral processes is the clinician's sole responsibility, then this will affect the intensity of emotion the therapist experiences. However, if the counselor knows he/she has done all in his/her power to treat the individual and that the therapist is not responsible for the client's actions, then the intensity of the negative emotions will probably be mild (Veilleux 2011; Wurst *et al.* 2011). Additionally, Horn (1994) found that psychotherapists who have more training (a PhD), additional course work in ethics, practical limitations, and experience treating clients with suicidal ideation, have a more realistic view into how to view their clients' behavior and actions. However, no matter how much training and experience a clinician has had, he/she must always be on guard for clients who are experiencing suicidal ideation or want to harm themselves.

It has also been shown that mental health practitioners who treat clients with severe symptoms of mental illness are under constant tension to assess and evaluate the risk for suicide in clients (Wagner, Wong, and Jobes 2002). Fujimura, Weis, and Cochran (1985) inform that suicidal threats and behaviors are an individual's cry for help to relieve the unbearable emotional distress that he/she is experiencing. These cries may be direct or indirect, verbal or non-verbal. Assessing for the risk of suicide may be as easy as asking clients if they are thinking of hurting or killing themselves, observing the way a person talks about death, noticing the individual giving valued possessions away, or observing changes in the client's mood or affect (Fujimura *et al.* 1985). In addition, mental health practitioners should not think that because they treat children who are very young or treat those who are very old, they are exempt from encountering such situations. There have been reports of children as young as six years of age, and adults over 80 years old, who have committed suicide (Erlangsen, Bille-Brahe, and Jeune 2003; Hannan 2010). In their experience, many psychotherapists who have treated clients who eventually committed suicide may have also taken care of clients who have threatened self-harm.

While some clients may be intent on taking their own life, counselors may encounter those individuals who contemplate deliberate self-harm without a desire to die (Miller *et al.* 2013; Tuisku *et al.* 2006). Hawton and Harriss (2008) define deliberate self-harm as a non-fatal act that inflicts some type of bodily damage to cause an individual pain. Inflicting damage to one's person may include such things as slashing one's wrist, cutting or bruising parts of the body, inflicting blows, and/or swallowing objects. This action against one's body can be summed up as a deliberate act to inflict pain without the intention of causing death (Austin and Kortum 2004). Dycian, Fishman, and Bleich (1994) mention that at times a client may perform an act of self-harm such as slashing an artery or taking an overdose without any intention of killing himself/herself, but nevertheless the action leads to death. The reasons for self-harm/ non-suicide behaviors may vary. Hawton and James (2005) name some primary reasons such as to relieve tension, escape a stressful situation, manipulate the behavior of others, escape unbearable emotional distress, make other people feel guilty, and a cry for help. Whatever the reason for self-harm, the therapist must stay calm, assess the situation, and determine the next course of action to take. Suicide, the threat of suicide, and/or the act of a client performing deliberate self-harm can tax a therapist's psychological well-being to a point where he/ she becomes ineffective treating other clients under his/her care (Hendin *et al.* 2006; Sharry, Darmody, and Madden 2002).

The psychotherapist not only has to face situations that involve harm to the client or to others, but at times, the therapist may be involved in circumstances where his/her physical well-being may be in jeopardy. In one research study, Gentile *et al.* (2002) found that some clients, especially those who suffer from mood and personality disorders, have threatened or stalked their therapist. In a national survey of therapists, Pope and Tabachnick (1993) reported that more than 18% of participating mental health professionals were physically attacked by at least one client. Purcell, Powell, and Mullen (2005) discovered that stalking and physical attacks have led many psychotherapists to leave their field of specialization and transition into other types of non-clinical work. But what can a clinician do about a threat of an attack? Does he/she continue treating a client and risk personal harm, or risk liability charges from the client for abandonment? Fortunately, the "Ethical Principles of Psychologists and Code of Conduct" was revised to allow psychologists to refer or abruptly terminate a client when the psychologist feels his/her safety is in danger (APA 2002).

Another group of individuals who may be difficult for the counselor to treat are diverse cultural groups. These groups may be difficult to treat because their beliefs, lifestyle, and attitudes may be different from those of the therapist. Counselors who are not well versed on culture, ethnicity, language, lifestyle, or racial differences should make a referral to a knowledgeable counselor or receive the proper training and experience to treat a specific population (APA 2002). Sue and Sue make note that, "each cultural/racial group may have its own distinct interpretation of reality and offer a different perspective on the nature of people, the origins of disorders, standards of judging normality and abnormality, and therapeutic approaches" (Sue and Sue 2003, p.15). In fact, a therapist who is ignorant of a client's culture, race, or lifestyle could unknowingly harm the client (Sue and Sue 2003). In a research study conducted by Wang and Kim (2010), clients indicated that the quality of the counseling effectiveness was higher for therapists who were knowledgeable about multicultural characteristics versus therapists who were not. Even knowledge concerning religious beliefs of specific populations may make a difference between a client's successful treatment outcome or the client dropping out of therapy prematurely (Raiya and Pargament 2010).

Issues involving ethics

A counselor not only has the responsibility to ensure that the client does not harm himself/herself, but is accountable for the safety of the public (Goodman 1985). What this means is that if the client indicates harm against a specific individual, then the therapist must decide to breach confidentiality and warn the intended victim and police. Kell (1999) explains that confidentiality pertains to keeping the information, whether verbal or written, private between the counselor and client unless the client gives written/verbal consent to release it. Breaching confidentiality is never an easy decision because the consequences could cost the therapist his/her professional license and possibly lead to legal action. On the other hand, if the client fulfills the threat of harming a specific individual, and the therapist has not warned the intended victim, then the therapist could face liability charges (Younggren and Harris 2008).

One famous court case, which stressed the counselor's responsibility to warn an intended victim, is known as "Tarasoff v Regents of the University of California" (Gostin 2002). In this case, the client told his therapist of his intent to kill Tatiana Tarasoff, thought by the client to be his girlfriend. The therapist called the campus police to detain the individual, but later was informed by his supervisor to release the client and not to take any further action against him. At this point no one warned Miss Tarasoff or her family of this threat. After a few months the client did, in fact, kill Tatiana Tarasoff. It would seem like this is a case involving several issues including confidentiality. However, the parents filed a lawsuit against the therapist and supervisors for negligence. The Supreme Court of California ruled that when the life of an intended victim is in jeopardy, then the counselor has a responsibility to breach confidentiality and warn the intended victim. Since the ruling of a duty to warn, most states have adopted California's stance, but a few states still consider this release of information as a breach of confidentiality (DiMarco and Zoline 2004). Clinicians need to consult the state law concerning confidentiality in whichever states they practice.

As with most ethical questions, especially those involving the duty to warn and confidentiality, dilemmas are created in the mind of the therapist. A dilemma is "a situation necessitating a choice between two equally desirable or undesirable alternatives" (VandenBos 2007, p.282). In other words, asking oneself what should be done, even though it may seem to be a no-win situation. This kind of conversation with oneself can develop into worry and anxiety as the situation becomes more critical. Ethical dilemmas can create a great amount of indecision, especially when it involves the therapist's professional conduct concerning a client's well-being (Scaturo 2002).

One situation that can cause the clinician a great amount of distress is working with parents or caregivers who may be physically, sexually, and/or emotionally abusing their children. During their career, therapists may often come across stressful situations in which the client's parents have abused or neglected their children in one form or another (Ainsworth 2002). Since therapists are mandated reporters, any type of emotional, physical, and/or sexual abuse or neglect that is suspected must be reported to the proper authorities. The important word here is "suspected." But just what does it mean to "suspect?"

Individual states have instituted laws requiring and mandating professionals who work with children to report suspicions of abuse and neglect to the proper state authorities. It may be of interest that the word "suspicion" is interpreted differently by a variety of professionals (Crowell and Levi 2012), which adds to ambiguity and anxiety for many psychotherapists. According to Levi and Portwood (2011), the wording in most state laws in regard to mandated reporting for child abuse include terms such as belief, suspicion, and reasonable suspicion among others. Unfortunately, in the context of mandated reporting, the professional "MAY NOT" or "DOES NOT" have to be "ABSOLUTELY SURE" (Levi and Portwood 2011). This dilemma of reporting a suspected case of abuse or neglect on the part of a clinician has been written about in many research articles because of the serious consequences it poses for the parents, the well-being of the child, and also the counselor (Iwaniec, Larkin, and McSherry 2007; Miller and Weinstock 1987; Risin and McNamara 1989; Walters 1995).

The important thing to remember is that the safety of the child is paramount and false positives are acceptable if this means protecting the life of even one child. In this case, the practitioner is exempt from legal action if he/she is incorrect, and it is the state's responsibility to prove the allegations (Crenshaw and Lichtenberg 1993). However, Saulsburg and Campbell (1985) note that if the suspicions are correct and the clinician fails to report them, then he/she may face charges and/or prosecution by the state authorities.

There are other concerns about breaching confidentiality that may be on practitioners' minds in terms of state-mandated reporting laws. This pertains to how it will affect the family, caregiver(s), and suspected victim if the allegations of abuse and/or neglect are unfounded. When state protective services investigate allegations of suspected child abuse, they put aside the family's right of privacy in order to interview relatives, friends, neighbors, and other acquaintances (Newman, Dannenfelser, and Pendleton 2005). Even if the investigation does not turn up anything against the alleged perpetrator, the family's reputation can be questioned by people (Besharov and Laumann 1996). Besharov and Laumann also report each year that approximately 700,000 families go through investigations in which the allegations are unsubstantiated.

Another concern of the clinician may be the caregiver's right to remove the child from therapy whether the allegations of abuse or neglect are true or false (Walters 1995). This is a realistic concern, especially when the child has been diagnosed with some type of severe mental disorder. The therapist may want to help and protect the child, but when the caregiver is the legal guardian there is nothing that can be done. At this point, it is up to the child protective services and the state authorities to decide the fate of the client.

Another stressor that many counselors have had to work with is the managed care system. Lawless, Ginter, and Kelly (1999) define managed care as that combination of organizations and businesses that control the delivery and financing of mental health services. Managed care was developed in response to the Health Maintenance Act of 1973 to provide quality of care and to eliminate unnecessary treatments while controlling and/or reducing cost (Karon 1995).

Because of managed care restrictions to control costs, organizations usually impose certain limitations that can create ethical dilemmas for the healthcare provider (Glosoff *et al*. 1999). Dyckman (1997) reports that insurance companies may set a certain amount of therapy sessions that may be given in a set amount of time. An example may be that an insurance company may state that a client may only receive five therapy sessions in a month, but the client might actually need eight sessions in that month. This leaves the counselor with the dilemma of not properly treating the client or providing the proper treatment without being paid (Alleman 2001). Insurance companies will pay for only a limited amount of therapy sessions in any given period, and may also require specific documentation to verify the quality of care performed by the clinician.

Before most insurance carriers will reimburse the counselor for treatment, these organizations require personal information about clients, such as diagnoses, assessments, evaluations, treatments plans, and progress notes (Austad and Hoyt 1992). One of the ethical dilemmas that many businesses confront therapists with is the release of confidential information about the client. Austad and Hoyt emphasize that confidentiality is for the protection of the client from any unauthorized release of information that may harm the client.

During the initial session, the clinician will have the client sign a "release of information" form. The client's signature authorizes the clinician to release information to the managed care company for purposes of payment for treatment. Even though the therapist receives the client's permission to send their information to third-party payers, many practitioners may still be concerned that this may affect their patient in some way (Alleman 2001).

Again, Glosoff *et al.* (1999) emphasize that in most cases counselors must give a substantial amount of information about their clients to receive payment from these managed care institutions. According to Alleman (2001), the requirement of releasing private information to outside sources goes against the concept of confidentiality established by most professional organizations and through agreement between the counselor and client. Fortunately, and similar to other situations mentioned in this chapter, most ethical codes allow for such kinds of releases, if clients are told about them and sign the appropriate paperwork (Davidson and Davidson 1996). Still, the counselor must use discretion and keep any disclosures to a minimum.

Issues involving employment status

Depending on his/her work status, a psychotherapist will encounter different stressors. The three working statuses that will be discussed in this section are being an intern, being a full-time employee within some institution, and working in private practice. One of the most stressful times that a clinician will experience in his/her career will be during an internship.

Gibson, Dollarhide, and Moss (2010) note that this is because the counselor is in the process of learning and beginning to practice his/her profession. Interns face unique stressors because of their unfamiliarity with a therapist's professional duties and responsibilities (Kleespies 1993; Nelson and Jackson 2003). An internship is a transitional period where the counselor in training is starting to develop his/her professional identity, to incorporate attitudes and skills, and discover how he/she fits into the professional community (Gibson et al. 2010). Since this is a developmental period, there will be times when the intern questions and doubts himself/herself, and it can be a time of great worry and anxiety (El-Ghoroury et al. 2012). Similarly, Rodolfa, Kraft, and Reilley (1988) acknowledged that interns usually suffer from greater stress and anxiety than established full-time clinicians and those in private practice. These stressors may involve the perception of an inability to help clients feel better, receiving criticism from a supervisor, observing the lack of a client's progress, and giving painful feedback to a client. In addition, the effect of these stressors can produce feelings of incompetence and inadequacy in how to perform one's job effectively (Kaslow and Rice 1985). That is why it is imperative for interns to seek out supervisors, mentors, and peers who can instruct them in the practice of being a conscientious practitioner and how to cope properly with early career stressors.

Gelso and Hayes (2001) also discuss the importance of developing an awareness of one's feelings of countertransference during internships. As mentioned by Burwell-Pender and Halinski (2008), countertransference pertains to the internal thoughts and memories of the mental health practitioner that may cause distress and anxiety during a session. If anxiety management within the clinician is not achieved, then it may lead to hostile responses to the client's negative emotions (Van Wagoner et al. 1991). However, Rodolfa et al. (1988) emphasized that many early career therapists usually learn to manage their internal world as they develop and mature in their profession.

Another stressor that most interns will face is the financial debt caused by his/her education and training. The debt that graduate and PhD students accumulate during their training and internships is substantially high (Eby *et al.* 2011; Fagan *et al.* 2007). In fact, King and Bannon (2002) reported that 39% of the psychology students in their research study were graduating with unmanageable student loan debts, and Robiner *et al.* (2002) discovered that most pre-doctoral psychology interns expected that their starting salary would be $2,000 less a year than they needed to meet their basic living expenses. Additionally, many interns receive little or no compensation in the form of money and/or benefits, so many interns continue to pay tuition without receiving any income. Indeed, the mounting expenditure increases associated with graduate school and internships place an enormous amount of stress on the future clinician to think of ways to keep up with expenses.

It will take a period of time after becoming licensed before the clinician becomes relaxed with his/her duties and responsibilities. Both maturity and gaining experience from performing psychotherapy will help the professional in this area (Bradley, Drapeau, and DeStefano 2012). Lim *et al.* (2010) indicate that the reason for this adjustment period may have to do with a lack of maturity in life and professional experiences. The longer the practitioner treats clients, especially in an institution or agency, the quicker he/she will become more competent, but there may still be times when the practitioner questions himself/herself (Theriault and Gazzola 2005).

Many stressors encountered by the full-time experienced clinician will be different than those encountered by an intern. In one study, Vredenburgh *et al.* (1999) reported that mental health practitioners in hospital settings reported higher levels of stress than those in private practice or interns due to larger caseloads, lack of autonomy, long working hours, and demanding work schedules. Similarly, Maslach and Leiter (1997) noted that working in organizations such as hospitals and outpatient agencies can create anxiety over time that can affect the clinician's work–life balance, especially for those therapists working full time.

An unstable work–life balance has been known to take an enormous toll on many well-established, experienced practitioners (Rupert and Morgan 2005). The pressure to continually complete one's administrative duties, meet scheduled deadlines for special projects, and/or complete clients' notes can influence one to spend more time in the office or take work home (Rupert *et al.* 2009). In fact, Rupert and Morgan (2005) found that stress levels for agency workers were exceptionally high because of long working hours, less control of their work environment, and attending too much to administrative duties rather than treating clients. Many other studies noted how agencies increase stress levels on their therapists by such things as selecting the amount and type of clients the clinician will treat, role ambiguity, role conflict, a lack of reward, long workdays, large caseloads, and excessive demands (Kramen-Kahn and Hansen 1998; Lim *et al.* 2010; Maslach and Leiter 2008; Rupert *et al.* 2012). When institutions place this type of pressure and stress constantly on their workforce, then feelings of stress and anxiety develop and the effectiveness in treating clients diminishes (Maslach and Leiter 2008). The stressors encountered in institutions and agencies can lead to disturbances such as job burnout and Secondary Traumatic Stress, which may place the clinician at risk of harming clients (Everall and Paulson 2004).

Not all clinicians will choose to work for a full-time employer, and some may want to go into private practice. Private practice might have the appeal of being one's own boss and running one's own business. It brings with it the advantages that are not seen in being employed by agencies or institutions, such as the flexibility of choosing work hours, clients, and the policies that will be followed. However, private practice does have its own unique set of stressors. Beck (1994) writes that counselors in private practice don't have the convenience of a stable salary. In fact, clinicians receive no paid vacation days, sick leave, disability pay, pension plans, and/or continuing education reimbursements, which are included in full-time employment at most institutions or agencies.

Psychotherapists in private or independent practice have a more personal stake in their financial and working conditions (Appelbaum 1992). In this context, the therapist is responsible to publicize his/her practice and attract clients. There may be difficult times in the beginning of one's practice, especially with the establishment of a residence to treat clients. Even when the clinician's residence is established, he/she still has to deal with the stressor of isolation from colleagues and supervision.

To help fill the therapist's caseload, many mental health practitioners in private practice may choose to be involved with one or more managed care organizations. Broskowski (1991) reports that managed care uses health insurance plans that contract with medical facilities and healthcare providers to offer services to its members. Being involved in managed care brings with it the advantage of receiving clients and payment from the contracted organization(s) (Alleman 2001), but problems may exist for many therapists under managed care.

There are a few disadvantages to being involved with a managed care organization. One of the disadvantages is how it affects clients. In one study consisting of 718 therapists from the American Psychological Association (APA), Tucker and Lubin (1994) discovered that 90% of the participants indicated that managed care interfered with their clients' treatment, while 49% emphasized that their clients suffered because of managed care denying or delaying authorization for clients' treatment, and 72% said that the quality of care was negatively affected. Likewise, in another study consisting of 108 licensed mental health counselors, 60% of participants stated that managed care impacted their delivery of mental health services in negative ways (Danzinger and Welfel 2001). Furthermore, Phelps, Eisman, and Kohut (1998) observed that four out of five participants (15, 918 licensed psychologists participated) experienced concerns about managed care; for example, excessive pre-certification, receiving a limited amount of clients, and only allowing specific types of treatments to be performed.

In addition, the clinician must also conform to the benefit structure of the payer (Austad and Hoyt 1992). Again, limitations are usually placed on the number of sessions a client can receive in a year, co-payment, and length and frequency of sessions. This means that managed care organizations dictate the amount of payments the therapist will receive and also the number of clients. Because the main purpose for managed care is to control costs, many psychotherapists may find it difficult to meet their business expenses and enjoy a comfortable living (Rupert and Baird 2004).

Summary

In summary, the practice of psychotherapy is a stressful and demanding profession that tests the psychological well-being of the counselor in clinical settings. First, the therapist must always be aware of any psychological disturbances that may cause the client to harm themselves, other people, or the counselor. Second, the interaction with other populations, such as multicultural groups and managed care organizations, also brings its own unique stressors. Third, the clinician employment status can determine what types of stressors and levels of intensities he/she may encounter. Finally, this chapter has reviewed only a portion of the general stressors a mental health practitioner will face during his/her career. The next chapter will review a specific disturbance that the therapist may encounter, known as job burnout.

CHAPTER 5

Job Burnout

In the previous chapter some of the general stressors encountered by psychotherapists were explored. One stressor pertained to clients who threatened and/or committed suicide, inflicted self-harm upon themselves, and/or threatened harm to others or the therapist. Another stressor had to do with ethical issues involving dilemmas with making decisions on breaching confidentiality, reporting child abuse/neglect, duty to warn for threatening of an individual(s), and releasing clients' information to managed care organizations. The final stressor had to do with being an intern, being a full-time employee with an institution or agency, or having a private practice.

In this chapter, the disturbance known as job burnout will be examined as it pertains to psychotherapists. Members of many professional organizations experience the symptoms related to job burnout, but mental health practitioners have been shown to be especially vulnerable because of the particular work they perform (Maslach *et al.* 1996). Clinicians affected by job burnout may suffer from symptoms such as emotional distress, inflexibility, sleep disturbances, and impairments in their cognitive functioning (Dam *et al.* 2012; Emery, Wade, and McLean 2009; Peterson *et al.* 2008). Having a knowledge and awareness of the debilitating effects of burnout can help maintain the clinician's psychological well-being and effectiveness in treating clients. The main focus of this chapter is to discuss the theories, causes, and self-care strategies pertaining to the disturbance known as job burnout.

Theories associated with job burnout

The initial research on job burnout was started during the mid-1970s. As noted by Maslach *et al.* (2001), these studies focused on individuals who worked in the healthcare and human service fields, treating people suffering from severe emotional disturbances. The outcome of this early research resulted in the discovery of impairments associated with interpersonal and emotional stressors (Freudenberger 1975; Maslach and Jackson 1981).

Herbert Freudenberger, a German-born American psychologist, was one of the first researchers to study and describe the phenomenon known as job burnout (Freudenberger 1974). He defined job burnout as the state of physical and emotional exhaustion brought about by being overly committed and dedicated to one's occupation (Freudenberger 1977).

According to Freudenberger (1975), people who experience job burnout display signs of rigidity, irritability, and cynicism. It was noticed that these people worked harder and longer than other co-workers, even to the point of bringing their work home. Freudenberger also noted that since this condition is chronic and gradually develops over time, the individual may not be aware of its effects (Freudenberger 1974).

Around the same time, Christina Maslach, a researcher and psychologist, also discovered that mental health practitioners developed emotional exhaustion and other debilitating symptoms associated with job burnout (Maslach and Jackson 1981). Furthermore, she noticed that clinicians who suffer from emotional exhaustion experience fatigue, loss of energy, feelings of being drained, and the inability to recuperate after sufficient rest (Maslach 1993). In her research, she found that there was a significant relationship between the development of these symptoms and the intense interaction of helping people with psychological distress (Maslach 1982). At this point the therapist may have difficulty meeting the needs of clients at a psychological level (Maslach and Leiter 1997).

In later years, Maslach theorized that job burnout consisted not only of emotional exhaustion, but was also associated with symptoms of depersonalization and a sense of a lack of personal accomplishment (Maslach *et al.* 1996). Depersonalization can best be described as the degradation of the therapeutic relationship between the counselor and client. At this stage, the therapist develops a cynical attitude towards the client, which erodes the counselor–client relationship into one that is superficial. Maslach *et al.* (1996) mentioned that when psychotherapists develop a cynical attitude, they start viewing their clients as impersonal objects, become callous, and develop an unsympathetic attitude toward the clients' situations. In essence, the counselor loses the ability to empathize with the client and becomes hardened to the client's misfortunes.

According to Maslach *et al.* (2001), the final stage of job burnout is described as the therapist developing a sense of a lack of personal accomplishment. After some time of having experienced emotional exhaustion and depersonalization, psychotherapists may come to the realization that they are unable to meet the psychological needs of the client. Therapists, at this point, begin to evaluate their lack of effectiveness and may even begin to doubt if they should continue in the counseling field. Maslach *et al.* (1996) state that psychotherapists may ask questions of themselves such as: "Am I having a positive influence on people?" "Do I feel like I am making accomplishments in my job?" "Is my job worthwhile?"

During the past few decades, Maslach's theory has been used by researchers to examine the amount of burnout levels that exist in the clinical community. Maslach's theory of job burnout was unique unlike other theories and surveys, because, it not only focused on the mental health professional's psychological well-being, but also observed the breakdown of the therapeutic relationship between the client and therapist and the negative evaluation that the therapist made of himself/herself (Maslach 1993). Another significant element that Maslach's theory brought to the understanding of job burnout was how some therapists, at times, might make a negative self-evaluation that may lead to a belief that they may be incompetent (Angerer 2003). This belief over time may cause the clinician to reconsider his/her choice of career and leave the counseling profession.

Maslach and her colleagues developed what came to be known as the "Maslach Burnout Inventory-Human Services Survey" (MBI-HSS) to quantify the amount of distress that human services professionals, especially mental health practitioners, were exhibiting due to their job responsibilities (Maslach *et al.* 1996). The MBI-HSS has three categories, which have already been discussed:

1. emotional exhaustion

2. depersonalization

3. a sense of a lack of personal accomplishment.

In using the MBI-HSS, Maslach *et al.* (2001) found that counselors who had high scores of emotional exhaustion and depersonalization, combined with low scores for feelings of personal accomplishment, displayed high levels of job burnout; however, those who recorded low scores of emotional exhaustion and depersonalization, combined with high scores for feelings of personal accomplishment, had low levels of job burnout.

More recently, a new theory and survey were developed, which examined job burnout as it specifically pertains to counselors. This survey was named the "Counselor Burnout Inventory" (CBI) (Lee *et al.* 2007). The survey contains five dimensions:

1. exhaustion

2. devaluing the client

3. negative work environment

4. deterioration of one's personal life

5. incompetence.

According to Lee *et al.* (2007), exhaustion can be defined as the emotional and physical exhaustion that the therapist experiences in performing his/her duties. Devaluing clients, on the hand, is the cold and callous attitude taken by the counselor towards clients. The negative work environment dimension can best be described as how the counselor feels emotionally about the place where he/she performs therapy, whereas deterioration of his/her personal life develops due to the stressors imposed by the counselor's professional duties. Finally, the incompetence dimension reflects the counselor's evaluation of himself/herself concerning the effectiveness of clients' treatment.

According to Lee *et al.* (2010), the CBI is different from any other burnout inventory because it not only explores the internal stressors related to therapists, but also examines how the work environment promotes burnout. The CBI is both similar to and different from the MBI-HSS, in that three of the CBI's dimensions correlate highly with the MBI-HSS, whereas the other two dimensions of the CBI explore additional stressors that a counselor may encounter. The CBI's exhaustion dimension has been shown to have a positive correlation with the MBI-HSS's emotional exhaustion scale, and the CBI's devaluing client scale has a positive correlation with the MBI-HSS's depersonalization scale. The fourth dimension of the CBI, the deterioration of one's personal life, has a negative correlation to the MBI-HSS's sense of personal accomplishment. The other two dimensions of the CBI—the negative work environment and incompetence—are additional categories not specifically explored in the MBI-HSS; they pertain to counselor burnout and more fully explain the stressors involved with being a psychotherapist.

Causes associated with job burnout

Over the last few decades, various factors have been linked to job burnout among mental health practitioners. One of these factors is known as over-involvement as it relates to empathy (Koeske and Kelly 1995). Rogers (1980) described empathy as "...temporarily living in the other's life, moving about it delicately without making judgments" (p.142). Empathy allows the therapist to feel as the client feels, and think as the client thinks, except in an objective manner. In this way, the counselor has an idea of the distress the client is experiencing and is able to help the client move towards a point of relief. Likewise, Osborn (2004) has noted that empathy is a one-way process where the counselor tries to feel and think as the client. Every therapist has learned early in his/her training the necessity and importance for empathy in the counselor–client relationship. The therapist in session probes the client for signs of distress by asking questions, and imagines how he/she would feel in the client's shoes. This empathy, taken to an extreme, can cause the therapist great stress in some cases. An example is that the psychotherapist could become so obsessed thinking about the client's situation that he/she starts developing symptoms of emotional exhaustion in trying to solve the problems of the client. Maslach calls this type of empathy "emotional empathy" because the emotions of the counselor bring distress and difficulty, and an inability to think clearly to help the client because of being over-involved in the client's problems (Maslach 1982). In this situation, the therapeutic process is headed for a poor outcome.

Another factor contributing to job burnout is the therapist's perception of a lack of therapeutic effectiveness in the psychotherapist's practice. McCarthy and Frieze (1999) pointed out that many counselors who are young and new to the profession have higher rates of job burnout due to the discouragement of not seeing positive changes in clients in a short amount of time. According to Emery *et al.* (2009), many inexperienced therapists may have rigid ideas that they should always work at peak efficiency. As an example, a counselor may think he/she should always be in control of all situations and always have a competent answer for all questions that a client may ask. Additionally, many early career therapists may have rigid, inflexible, and dogmatic ideas about using one specific type of therapy on most of their clients. Having this type of attitude towards treatment may only lead to frustration and resentment on the part of the client and lack of therapeutic success (Baird and Jenkins 2003). In fact, in one research study, Baldwin, Wampold, and Imel (2007) reported that it was the clinician's flexibility, not the client's ability to make changes, which was responsible for strong therapeutic alliances and successful treatment outcomes. Moreover, several attributes of therapists found to support the development of strong alliances with clients were trustworthiness, and being experienced, confident, friendly, warm, and open (Ackerman and Hilsenroth 2003). Similarly, Zuroff *et al.* (2010) noted that successful treatment outcomes of depressed clients were determined by the personal characteristics of the therapist in the use of the Rogerian principles and not using specific therapies such as Cognitive Behavioral Therapy (CBT) and Interpersonal Therapy (IPT).

Moreover, Wilkerson (2009) discusses the importance of older counselors teaching younger therapists to be flexible with their approach to treating people to prevent frustration and burnout. In addition, Schaufeli, Maslach, and Marek (1993) found some young and inexperienced therapists expected some "pay off" for the efforts put towards counseling. When this "pay off" (in the form of clients' symptoms being relieved) does not happen, or if results are not seen quickly, the counselor may get frustrated and be easily discouraged. Furthermore, in another study, Ross, Altmaier, and Russell (1989) discovered a significant number of early career postdoctoral therapists who suffered from symptoms related to job burnout, compared to therapists who had been in the counseling field for many years. As has been shown in many of these studies, when reality does not match expectations over time, frustration and discouragement could set in, which can lead to job burnout.

Being inexperienced does not mean that a counselor will develop job burnout as there are other causes associated with this disturbance. The results of one study showed that some therapists who treated clients with trauma histories developed symptoms of burnout (McKenzie Deighton, Gurris, and Traue 2007). McKenzie Deighton *et al.* informed that these symptoms developed because of counselors' fears of confronting the client with the reality of the traumatic events. This, in turn, may lead to fear avoidance and stress reactions on the part of the therapist, which could lead to emotional exhaustion. In one study, Perseius *et al.* (2007) found that the combination of learning Dialectical Behavioral Therapy (DBT) and using it to treat self-harming clients could produce harmful effects of job burnout in therapists. These effects may be produced, in many cases, because DBT is normally a very stressful type of therapy to learn, and also DBT is used to treat many clients threatening self-harm (Perseius *et al.* 2007). The combination of unfamiliarity with DBT and clients who have the potential for self-harm has caused many stressful reactions within psychotherapists.

Mental health practitioners were also found to be vulnerable to job burnout while working in a more stressful environment. Vredenburgh *et al.* (1999) demonstrated that counseling psychologists, treating patients in a hospital environment who suffered from severe psychological problems, displayed a higher level of job burnout than psychologists in private practice. This is because clients who need to be hospitalized usually suffer from severe symptoms such as suicidal ideation, some type of psychosis, and/or extreme impulsive tendencies. Treating these individuals has been shown to place a strain on one's patience, frustration level, and ability to stay calm (Vredenburgh *et al.* 1999). Furthermore, clients who are resistant to therapy (Kraus 2005; Perseius *et al.* 2007), have trauma histories (McKenzie Deighton *et al.* 2007), and have symptoms related to Borderline Personality Disorder (BPD) (Perseius *et al.* 2007) can produce feelings of frustration and emotional exhaustion within the clinician.

The work environment is yet another cause of job burnout. In this context, the work environment consists of the counselor's caseload and institutional stressors (Maslach and Leiter 1997). According to Hannigan *et al.* (2004), excessive caseloads can affect therapists in such a way as to decrease job satisfaction and increase symptoms associated with job burnout. Additionally, excessive caseloads can also lead the counselor to develop feelings of being emotionally drained and physically fatigued, with an inability to rejuvenate after a lengthy night's sleep (Maslach 1982). Therapists who treat clients for many hours without a break may experience feeling stressed and anxious. The reason for this distress is that the counselor not only has the residual of the clients' emotions on their minds, but also has to keep up with writing progress notes on each client during session. While many therapists prefer to write notes during the therapy session, there are some who focus all their attention on the client, leaving writing of the progress notes to the final ten minutes. It takes much discipline and energy to remember and complete progress notes for each client, so ten minutes is not much time for writing them up and preparing to meet the next client. Lloyd, McKennan, and King (2005) noticed similar results related to stress when the therapist's caseloads became excessive.

Moreover, the increased workload has been shown not only to affect the therapist at a physical level (Ilies, Dimotakis, and DePater 2010), but also to affect the therapist's family life (Ilies *et al.* 2007). However, a study conducted by Hauck, Synder, and Cox-Fuenzalida (2008) found no increase in stress reaction when the workload became excessive, but there was a noticeable reduction in job performance over a period of time.

Personal factors have also been shown to have a significant relationship to job burnout (Schaufeli *et al.* 1993). Maslach *et al.* (2001) researched the relationship between various personal factors pertaining to counselors and the degree of increase in job burnout rates. Three personal factors that stand out as high indicators for job burnout are:

1. age

2. work experience

3. personality type.

In a meta-analysis involving 3,613 mental health professionals from 15 studies, Lim *et al.* (2010) noted that age was the most significant predictor of all three dimensions of job burnout (emotional exhaustion, depersonalization, lack of a sense of personal accomplishment). Lim *et al.* presume that novice and physically young therapists who come into the field are inexperienced both in their profession and life and this can make them more vulnerable to job burnout. Since age and work experience are highly correlated, past research has shown that symptoms of job burnout in counselors may develop due to either or both of these factors (Ackerley *et al.* 1988; Maslach *et al.* 2001; Schaufeli *et al.* 1993). Nevertheless, Maslach *et al.* (2001) discovered that a complex interaction of age, years of work experience, and personality factors could produce high levels of burnout.

Associated with age and work experience, personality characteristics have a part in the development of burnout. In a study, conducted by Lent and Schwartz (2012), consisting of 340 professional counselors who work in a community mental outpatient clinic, neuroticism was found to be the strongest predictor of job burnout. This was especially so in burnout that produced high scores in emotional exhaustion and depersonalization, and low scores in a sense of self-accomplishment. Thomas (2009) defines neuroticism as "an individual's propensity to respond to life challenges with negative emotionality that goes beyond the reasonable amount of negativity that any person might exhibit when stressed and provoked" (p.727). In addition, Lahey (2009) describes neuroticism as traits associated with anger, vulnerability, self-consciousness, and anxiety. Lent and Schwartz (2012) indicate counselors should have an understanding and self-awareness of their own personal characteristics that may interfere with the therapeutic process.

Another personal characteristic related to job burnout is a Type-A personality. Maslach *et al.* (2001) stress that therapists who exhibit a Type-A personality (time-pressured, highly competitive, excessive need for control) and/or are categorized as being a "feeling type" rather than a "thinking type" on the Myers-Briggs Type Indicator (Jungian analysis), are highly prone to job burnout. Moreover, other characteristics that have shown to be related to job burnout are individuals who have a high need for affection and approval, have problems controlling certain emotions such as hostility, fear, and impatience, and those who feel overwhelmed when dealing with the problems of others (Maslach 1982).

As noted, job burnout can have devastating effects on a counselor's ability to maintain his/her psychological mental health and his/her capacity to treat clients successfully. Effective strategies need to be developed in areas that pertain to the therapist and his/her work environment to prevent and reduce burnout.

Self-care strategies

There are a number of strategies that can be used to prevent and/or reduce the effects of job burnout. One strategy to this problem is to take a personal approach. This involves the therapist being more in control of himself/herself and the environment (Maslach 1982). Many inexperienced therapists, especially within the first five years of graduation, expect success to come quickly in the form of clients' symptoms being relieved in a short amount of time (Maslach 2003; Maslach *et al.* 1996). Emery *et al.* (2009) state that novice therapists think if they work harder and get more involved with helping clients, success will come more quickly. In most cases, this is furthest from the truth. In fact, over time, emotional exhaustion and discouragement can develop (Maslach *et al.* 2001; McKenzie Deighton *et al.* 2007). To help prevent this type of discouragement, the therapist can develop awareness through peer supervision. Gibson, Grey, and Hastings (2009) reported that novice therapists who seek out supervision from experienced counselors have a more realistic approach to success in therapy than other novice therapists who do not. Even experienced psychotherapists need supervision and consultation to ensure they are remaining objective in critical cases (Melamed, Szor, and Bernstein 2001; Reid *et al.* 1999). Clinicians who are more experienced need to be role models and mentors to younger therapists to help them avoid the pitfalls and difficulties associated with early career development.

Another strategy mental health practitioners can use to prevent or reduce job burnout is developing an attitude of flexibility. Clients with mental health issues can be very unpredictable and the therapist many times will have to make adjustments in his/her treatment approach to the client's behavior. Emery *et al.* (2009) found therapists who are flexible and less controlling with their clients have a more positive attitude to their work. Of course, this has to do with allowing clients to express their emotionality and not applying specific therapies when clients resist. Many therapists are trained to go into session with a treatment plan, such as performing a specific therapy or treatment for an individual suffering from major depression. The client, in this narrative, might just want to talk and not listen to the therapist regarding changing his/her cognitive approach to life. The more the therapist might try to get the client to participate in his/her specific therapy, then the more frustration and anger might be generated by both parties. It is wise at this time to allow the client to dictate the flow of the session until the client feels more at ease with the situation.

Learning not to be so self-critical helps to ease the stress of the therapist's job and improve job satisfaction (Linley and Joseph 2007; Skovholt and Ronnestad 2003). Again, this is especially true of inexperienced and novice therapists but applies to experienced therapists as well. When one expects clients to continue coming to therapy, it can be disheartening when some leave prematurely. Some therapists, at this point, may blame themselves for clients leaving, thinking it is because of something they said or did. In some cases, the clients might not have been ready for the commitment and work that therapy brings. Learning to put situations in context and realizing that the counselor cannot help every client is an important step towards being less self-critical. Skovholt and Ronnestad (2003) talk about the importance of therapists developing a positive and less critical attitude about themselves, which is an important step to building self-confidence and the ability to treat individuals more effectively. Learning to put situations in context and realizing that the counselor cannot help every client is an important step to being less self-critical.

There are other strategies that a mental health practitioner can use to combat job burnout. Zur (2008) mentions these strategies include being involved in non-work related activities such as participating in community events, developing diverse friendships, and, most importantly, taking time off from work and going on vacations. Self-care will be discussed in greater detail in Part 3 of this book, but a short discussion of these topics will follow. First, in the area of non-work-related activities, getting involved in different hobbies and activities is a great way to rejuvenate the mind and develop a peaceful perspective towards life. Activities such as hiking, boating, baseball, basketball, reading an interesting book, and/or taking a long walk are good distractions from continually thinking of work when at home. Second, being involved in the community can mean involvement in coaching children in activities such as baseball, football, and/or baseball, or even volunteering on the local school board or a community council position. Third, the clinician can develop and foster diverse friendships away from work, where his/her main goal is to relax and enjoy the company of others. Lastly, enough cannot be said about leisure activities, especially taking time off for vacations. Leisure activities, especially in the form of vacations, have been shown to rejuvenate the professional and improve the individual's psychological health (Maslach 1982).

The final strategy that will be discussed to prevent and/or to reduce the severity of symptoms associated with job burnout is to decrease one's caseload, especially if one feels overwhelmed. Since many cases of job burnout have been reported from the direct interaction with clients, the reduction of the therapist's caseload has been shown to reduce the symptoms of therapists suffering from the effects of client overload (Lawson and Myers 2011; Walsh and Walsh 2002). Ballenger-Browning *et al.* (2011) noted that the size of a clinician's caseload and in particular the severity of clients' symptoms had a significant positive relationship to job burnout. Emery *et al.* (2009) also found that the amount and quality of care delivered to clients could have a draining and emotional effect on a therapist's psychological well-being. Even diversifying by treating clients who suffer from different disorders can help. An example could be if a therapist's caseload consists strictly of clients suffering from psychotic or anxiety disorders; then the clinician might start to phase in clients with depressive or personality disorders (Hellman and Morrison 1987). These recommendations also pertain to the clients' ages and genders. The main point here is diversity and cutting back on the number of clients seen if the conditions warrant it. In addition, taking breaks of 5–10 minutes between sessions to socialize with co-workers can also help distract the therapist from the stress of his/her job and help to refocus his/her thoughts for upcoming clients (Maslach 1982).

Summary

In summary, the development and research associated with the concept of job burnout was examined as it pertains to the mental health practitioner. This concept of job burnout was first researched and theorized to be one-dimensional. Upon further research, theories were developed to explain that job burnout was not one-dimensional, but multi-dimensional. In addition, several causes of job burnout were discussed. One cause was that clinicians may, in some cases, become over-involved and over-empathize with their clients. Another cause could be the counselor's misperception of his/her therapeutic effectiveness due to his/her age and/or inexperience. A third cause that was explored was the rigid organizational rules and expectations of the therapist's work environment, and the fourth cause discussed was the individual personality characteristics of the practitioner. Finally, a variety of strategies that a mental health practitioner could use were also briefly examined. Since this chapter has dealt with various causes and self-care techniques to prevent and/or decrease the severity of the symptoms associated with job burnout, the next chapter will examine another disturbance that counselors are often exposed to, known as Secondary Traumatic Stress Syndrome.

CHAPTER 6

Secondary Traumatic Stress Syndrome

In the previous chapter, various factors that make a mental health practitioner vulnerable to the specific disturbance known as job burnout were discussed. Research has indicated that job burnout is not the only disturbance that can affect a clinician's psychological well-being. Another disturbance that may take a greater toll on a psychotherapist's mental health is known as Secondary Traumatic Stress (STS) (Cieslak *et al.* 2013; Craig and Sprang 2010; Kraus 2005; Sprang, Clark, and Whitt-Woosley 2007). Figley (1999) describes STS as "...the natural, consequent behaviors and emotions resulting from *knowledge about* a traumatizing event experience by a significant other. STS is the stress resulting from *helping* or *wanting to help* a traumatized or suffering person" (p.10). In this context, the therapist is known as a significant other, and performing psychotherapy is the means to help the traumatized person.

There are a variety of studies indicating that STS is a significant problem among psychotherapists. In fact, Pearlman and Saakvitne (1995) stated that psychotherapists who specialize in treating traumatized clients would eventually experience symptoms related to STS to some extent during some point in their career. During one study, 198 social workers out of 282 who worked with traumatized clients reported at least one STS symptom and more than half exhibited symptoms related to avoidance, intrusion, and arousal (Bride 2007). In another study,

Ting *et al.* (2005) reported that more than half (53%) of the 515 mental health practitioners who worked with traumatized clients acknowledged having difficulties in their professional and personal lives. Furthermore, in a meta-analysis consisting of 41 studies and a total of 8,256 professionals who work with trauma survivors, a high correlation was found between STS and their performance of their duties with clients (Cieslak *et al.* 2013). Additionally, Cieslak also indicated that this shows that working with clients who have been traumatized can lead not only to STS, but also to burnout. During this chapter, many terms, such as Secondary Traumatic Stress (STS), Compassion Fatigue (CF), and Vicarious Traumatization (VT), will be used to describe the experiences and symptoms that the therapist may encounter while treating traumatized clients. In this chapter, Secondary Traumatic Stress Syndrome (STSS) will be used as the general term that combines STS, CF, and VT. The purpose of this chapter is to describe the theory development, mechanisms involved, and strategies to prevent STSS.

Theory development of STSS

Various researchers have been involved in coining of the term known as STS (Figley 1995; McCann and Pearlman 1990; McCann and Saakvitne 1995). STS has been described as a clinician's non-pathological response to treating traumatized clients, resembling that of Post Traumatic Stress Disorder (PTSD). The term "Secondary Traumatization" is used to define the effect on the therapist being indirectly traumatized due to hearing horrifying stories from clients (Regan *et al.* 2006).

Various terminologies have been used to describe the symptoms a therapist may suffer while treating traumatized clients. Although STS, CF, and VT may be thought to be interchangeable with one other, each has their own separate meaning (Jenkins and Baird 2002; Newell and MacNeil 2010; Stamm 1995). Whatever terminology is used or whatever symptoms are involved, all researchers would agree that the consequences involved in these disturbances arise from the responses of the therapists on hearing terrifying and traumatizing stories from clients they are treating (Jenkins and Baird 2002; McKenzie Deighton *et al.* 2007; Stamm 1995).

Research concerning the development of STSS began in the early 1990s. Charles Figley (1995), one of the first researchers to study this phenomenon, described STS as a clinician's disturbance whose symptoms are similar to that of PTSD. According to the *Diagnostic and Statistical Manual of Mental Disorders, Fourth Edition, Text Revision (DSM-IV-TR)*, individuals who are diagnosed with PTSD exhibit symptoms of intense fear or helplessness, distressing and intrusive thoughts of a traumatic event(s), the inability to recall specific parts of the traumatic event(s), irritability, difficulty concentrating and hypervigilance (APA 2000). Figley also noticed that psychotherapists who treated traumatized clients showed signs and symptoms of anxiety, irritability, isolating types of behaviors, and detached and intrusive memories (Figley 1995). Additionally, Chrestman (1999) observed clinicians displaying symptoms of guilt, grief, sleeping problems, dread, and feelings of horror while treating traumatized individuals.

Devilly, Wright, and Varker (2009) noted that the symptoms associated with PTSD and STS are very similar. The major difference between a person suffering from PTSD and a clinician suffering from STS is that a person suffering from PTSD has been exposed, witnessed, and/or has been directly confronted with a serious injury or life-threatening event, whereas a psychotherapist who suffers from STS has only been subjected to hearing traumatic stories from the client, and starts exhibiting the signs and symptoms similar to that of the traumatized client. Moreover, Jenkins and Baird (2002) also defined STS as the thoughts, memories, and recollections of counselors, who in their treatment of traumatized clients, start exhibiting symptoms of trauma themselves. Stamm (2010) noted that symptoms related to STS usually have a quick onset with symptoms involving sleep problems, anxiousness, and avoidance of conversations associated with clients' trauma. Additionally, Figley discovered that the effects of trauma counseling could become so serious in a therapist's life that it could lead some to leave their chosen field of psychotherapy (Figley 1999).

CF is another term developed during the 1990s from research involving indirect traumatization of therapists. Charles Figley was directly responsible for coining the term "Compassion Fatigue" (Figley 1995). Figley found that there were mental health practitioners who not only experienced symptoms related to PTSD, but who also displayed symptoms of helplessness, confusion, and isolation, which caused clinicians to feel physically and emotionally exhausted. In fact, at times, Figley (1999) used the terms STS and CF interchangeably. It is worth noting that Regan *et al.* (2006) wrote that CF was different from STS in that psychotherapists who suffer from CF not only display symptoms related to PTSD, such as avoidance, intrusive thoughts, and hypervigilance, but also suffer from physical and emotional exhaustion. Furthermore, Stamm (2010) noted that CF included elements of both STS and burnout and was characterized by the therapist feeling overwhelmed by his/her work.

Most notably, White (2006) commented on the differences between the constructs known as CF and STS. White noted that the differences lie in the names. Since the definition of compassion incorporates sympathy and compassion for another individual's suffering, White concluded that CF develops within psychotherapists due to empathizing with a client who has been traumatized. On the other hand, White (2006) stressed that a clinician could develop STS just by hearing and having knowledge of the traumatic event, without having empathy. Whatever the distinction between STS and CF, the main point here is that the symptoms associated with both STS and CF can degrade the psychological well-being of the psychotherapist and affect the therapeutic relationship in such a way as to make it ineffective (Meadors *et al.* 2009).

The third construct related to STSS is VT. McCann and Pearlman were responsible for developing this concept in the 1990s. According to McCann and Pearlman (1990), VT involves the harmful but normal change in the way a clinician views himself/herself, others, and the world, as a result of hearing and empathizing with traumatized clients. As in CF, the main component responsible for moderating the effects of VT is the therapist's use of empathy (Brockhouse *et al.* 2011; Newell and MacNeil 2010). Brockhouse *et al.* also mentioned that other factors responsible for the development of VT are the type of traumatic event and time involved in hearing it from the client, the therapist's caseload of traumatized clients, and the personality traits of the clinician. Newell and MacNeil emphasize that the main difference between VT and CF is that VT is not related to symptoms of PTSD, but rather to changes in the psychotherapist's cognitive schema. These changes are in the areas of trust, esteem, safety, control, and intimacy (Baird and Kracen 2006). In addition, McCann and Pearlman (1990) state that these changes in the therapist's schema are cumulative, pervasive, and permanent. An example is that at one point in the therapist's life, he/she may have believed the world was a safe place in which to live; then, as a result of treating traumatized clients and developing VT, this belief changed to one of being fearful and unsafe about his/her environment. Furthermore, symptoms related to STS and CF can develop over a short time, whereas symptoms related to VT are cumulative and develop over a long period of treating traumatized clients. Finally, concerning the differences between all the terms associated with STSS (STS, CF, and VT), Craig and Sprang (2010) remarked that there is no definitive data that would suggest that there is a difference between these terminologies (STS, CF, and VT), but awareness and taking action against the symptoms by the therapist are the most important elements in helping to prevent and/or eliminate their effects.

In speaking of the effects of STSS, whether it is STS, CF, or VT, Canfield (2005) emphasizes that symptoms associated with STSS not only affect the therapist, but also affect the therapeutic relationship between the client and therapist. Because of this, the counselor may start to distance himself/herself from the client to avoid dealing with his/her internal feelings of trauma. In addition, the counselor's views of people and the world might also be changed, where the world might be viewed in a more negative and cynical way (Herman 1992). According to Canfield (2005), constantly hearing stories of horror and human cruelty not only causes the counselor to become traumatized but also changes the practitioner's belief system about trusting others in the world.

During the past two decades, various studies have contributed to the development and insight of STSS. Steed and Downing (1998) reported that counselors' psychological well-being was affected by treating individuals who were survivors of sexual abuse. In this study, clinicians' view of the world changed from one of being trusting and feeling safe to one of being distrusting and suspicious. Additionally, the psychological well-being of these therapists was also affected in such a way that they displayed sleeping problems, anger outbursts, sadness, feelings of numbness, flashbacks, intrusive thoughts, and fatigue. In another study conducted by McKenzie Deighton *et al.* (2007), psychotherapists who treated torture survivors acknowledged displaying symptoms related to a combination of CF, distress, and burnout. Other types of studies in which mental health practitioners have been affected are related to clients suffering from sexual assault and domestic violence (Jenkins and Baird 2002), sexually abused children (Pistorius *et al.* 2008), victims of the 9/11 attack in New York City (Pulido 2007), and criminal victimization (Salston and Figley 2003).

Not all studies that researched the development of STSS in clinicians and its relationship to the treatment of traumatized clients indicated significant results. In one study, consisting of 221 mental health professionals who treated clients suffering from sexual violence, cancer, and/or mental disorders, Kadambi and Truscott (2004) reported not finding any correlation between the treatment of traumatized clients and its effect on therapists. Similarly, the results of a study consisting of 152 mental health psychotherapists showed that exposure to a client's traumatic history did not degrade clinicians' psychological well-being to a point of becoming ineffective in performing their professional duties (Devilly *et al.* 2009). However, a study consisting of 1,121 clinicians found that a significant number of participants suffered from symptoms related to CF while treating traumatized clients (Sprang *et al.* 2007). The point here is that there may be more variables to consider in the development of STSS than just listening to the stories of traumatized clients.

In a recent meta-synthesis study of 20 published articles that examined the impact on psychotherapists who treated traumatized clients, Cohen and Collens (2012) found that there were both negative and positive changes to clinicians' cognitive schemas, which were related to VT theory. However, the results of the negative changes were similar to those of other studies in which the therapists' view of the world changed from feeling safe to feeling unsafe, untrusting, and suspicious; the positive change observed was that therapists viewed humanity as resilient, based on seeing the client's growth and overcoming symptoms relating to PTSD. It must be noted that the positive change in the clinicians' cognitive schema did not come about unless they noticed growth in their client.

During the past two decades, various questionnaires and surveys have been developed to assess if the psychotherapist is suffering from STSS and the intensity level of symptoms related to it. Questionnaires such as the Secondary Traumatic Stress Scale (Bride *et al.* 2004), Secondary Trauma Questionnaire (Motta *et al.* 1999) and Compassion Fatigue Self-Test for Psychotherapists (Figley 1995) have been developed to evaluate the mental health practitioner's level of distress.

One of the more widely used instruments to measure the symptoms related to STSS is the Professional Quality of Life Scale (PROQOL) (Stamm 2010). The PROQOL is a 30-item questionnaire that measures three constructs including CF, compassion satisfaction and burnout. Each construct has its own scale and measures items on a 5-point Likert scale ranging from 1 (never) to 5 (very often). Stamm (2009) indicates several questions that are asked including, "I jump or am startled by unexpected sounds," "I feel as though I am experiencing the trauma of someone I have treated," "I feel happy," and "I feel worn out because of my work as a therapist." This instrument is primarily concerned with both the positive and negative aspects of caring.

This PROQOL instrument's psychometric properties are quite satisfactory. Alpha reliability coefficients for the scales of

CF, burnout, and compassion satisfaction are .77, .71, and .86, respectively (Craig and Sprang 2010), with all three scales having an average score of 50 and a standard deviation of 10 (Stamm 2010). Stamm (2010) states that in all three scales 25% of participants usually score below 43, and 25% of participants score above 57. The PROQOL has been used for the last 15 years and has proven to be valid in measuring symptoms related to STSS and compassion satisfaction.

If a therapist develops STSS through hearing the traumatic stories of clients, then what are the mechanisms responsible for creating this disturbance within the psyche of the psychotherapist?

Mechanisms responsible for STSS

There are a number of mechanisms responsible for the development of STSS. One of these mechanisms is known as empathy. As discussed previously, empathy is a technique that counselors use to treat clients effectively (Koeske and Kelly 1995). Good and Beitman (2006) state that empathy is the therapist's way of feeling the emotions of the individual being treated, and without that empathic experience by the therapist, proper treatment of the client would most likely be ineffective. In studying the effects of STSS on counselors, Sexton (1999) discovered that empathy was not only a major strength of a successful counselor, but also a major weakness. Sexton found this to be true because empathy made therapists vulnerable to experiencing the emotional trauma that their clients suffered. For example, as a psychotherapist thinks and imagines what it would be like being physically abused or tortured in a similar way to how the client was treated, the therapist may start to feel the terror, fear, pain, and horror of the traumatic experience of the client. These thoughts and feelings may stay with the counselor long after the client has departed. In this way, the major component known as empathy, which is the strength to treat clients effectively, can eventually over time become a liability to therapists who exclusively treat traumatized clients (Figley 1999).

A second mechanism responsible for developing STSS is countertransference. Countertransference is a term first coined by Sigmund Freud (Freud 1959) and is largely referred to in the practice of psychodynamic therapy. Freud explains countertransference as the therapist's reaction to the client's transference, due to the psychotherapist's unconscious and unresolved issues of his/her childhood. This could include the unresolved unconscious conflicts that the therapist has had in past relationships with his/her primary caregivers. These unconscious past conflicts could interfere with the present-day therapeutic relationships between the therapist and client. In this view, a counselor who was abused in some way earlier in his/her life could possibly be affected by unconscious memories of past trauma, which could lead to treatment of clients being ineffective and in some cases harmful (Chassman, Kotter, and Madison 2010; Freud 1959).

Moreover, if the counselor has a history of trauma, then the symptoms of STSS could be more severe (Beck and Buchele 2005; Chassman *et al.* 2010). One interesting study conducted by Nikcevic *et al.* (2007) found that aspiring clinicians had more histories of sexual abuse and neglect than psychology students who were not interested in therapeutic work and preferred to pursue a career in other fields. Chassman *et al.* (2010) noted the reason for this is that counselors who had histories of abuse had more empathy and understanding of the feelings of their clients' past. Similar studies showed a relationship between symptoms related to STSS and a psychotherapist's past trauma (Cunningham 2003; Kassam-Adams 1999; Meyers and Cornille 2002; Pinto 2003), whereas other studies determined that there was no relationship (Follette, Polusny, and Milbeck 1994; Schauben and Frazier 1995).

A more contemporary view of countertransference includes not only all the unconscious memories and unresolved intrapsychic conflicts of the therapist's past, but also incorporates the conscious present-day unresolved conflicts of the counselor's psyche (Johansen 1993). From this modern view, both the unconscious and conscious conflicts of the therapist are emphasized.

Good and Beitman (2006) mentioned that, while transference may mean the transferring of the client's past interpersonal experiences onto the therapist, countertransference refers to the internal working of the counselor's interpersonal experience that may be transferred unto the client. This experience of the counselor may be unconscious or conscious. What this means is that the mental health practitioner should always be aware of his/her past history, emotional states, and feelings in session, especially if the therapist has a history of abuse (Chassman *et al.* 2010). According to Canfield (2005), STS can develop just as a product of hearing of the traumatic stories expressed by clients. It must be emphasized that both empathy and countertransference are natural processes that happen within the context of the therapy session and can be used to successfully treat clients who have experienced traumatic events.

There are other contributors that are responsible for the development of STSS in mental health practitioners. One of these contributors is a clinician supporting or advocating a client to "work through" his/her traumatic experience, while the therapist is not willing to work through the traumatic event with the client (McKenzie Deighton *et al.* 2007). Gendlin (1996) referred to "working through" as the process a psychotherapist uses in the treatment of traumatized clients, with methods such as exposure, imaginative techniques, psychodrama re-enactment, narrative methods, flooding, and Eye Movement Desensitization and Reprocessing (EMDR). McKenzie Deighton *et al.* (2007) found psychotherapists who advocated, but did not work through traumatic events with their clients, displayed high levels of symptomology related to CF when compared to those who worked through the trauma with their clients.

The clinician's caseload was also shown to contribute to the formation of STSS. In a recent study, Voss Horrell *et al.* (2011) discovered that there was a correlation between the percentage of traumatized clients in a therapist's caseload and the display of symptoms related to STSS. Research conducted by Schauben and Frazier (1995) discovered that clinicians who treated a greater percentage of victims of sexual violence acknowledged having greater changes in their cognitive schemas about themselves and the world. Similarly, several studies have shown that psychotherapists who had especially heavy caseloads were highly vulnerable to symptoms related to VT (Chrestman 1999; Lind 2000), whereas other studies did not find any such correlation (Cunningham 2003; Landry 1999).

Another contributor to the development of STSS is a therapist's level of exposure to traumatic material, including frequency, severity, and type of exposure (Cornille and Meyers 1999; Dutton and Rubinstein 1995). Dutton and Rubinstein stressed that symptoms related to STSS did not develop in therapists just by hearing clients' traumatic stories, but by being exposed to the client's fear, panic, pain, rage, and hopelessness. So, the development of STSS is related to hearing the factual and emotional response of the horror that happened to the client in an empathic way. In addition, Baird and Kracen (2006) determined that such factors as a psychotherapist's trauma history, coping styles, lack of peer support, and supervision oversight had an impact on the development and severity of STSS. However, Craig and Sprang (2010) discovered that the development and severity of STSS was related to the number of traumatized clients who the therapist was treating.

It does seem that there are different variables at work with a clinician's development of symptoms related to STSS, but the common contributor in each case was hearing and empathizing with clients' horrifying stories. If STSS has such a debilitating effect on many mental health practitioners who treat traumatized clients, then what strategies can clinicians perform to maintain or improve their psychological well-being?

Strategies to prevent STSS

There are a number of recommended strategies to help combat the effects of STSS for psychotherapists. Trippany *et al.* (2004) noted several methods that could be used to prevent or reduce the severity of symptoms associated with STSS. These strategies include peer supervision and self-awareness of the hazards involved in treating traumatized clients. In the area of peer supervision, Trippany *et al.* (2004) stress the need for counselors to talk about cases of traumatization with peers even though the

practitioner is not experiencing any type of distress. This will give the counselor insight into his/her feelings towards the client (countertransference) and whether the client's treatment is being effective in relieving distress. Talking with peers about cases involving traumatized clients is an excellent way to increase self-awareness of distress in oneself (Saakvitne 2002; Sexton 1999). Similarly, Williams and Sommer (1999) recommend clinicians regularly meet and discuss cases with other practitioners who treat traumatized individuals to help maintain their psychological well-being and objectivity, and to discover if they may be developing symptoms associated with STSS.

Another method of preventing STSS is developing a well-balanced lifestyle between work, leisure, and rest. Trippany *et al.* (2004) emphasize that balancing the clinician's lifestyle is an excellent way to provide enough distraction from his/her duties, and relaxation to counteract against the stress of his/her job. Likewise, Inbar and Ganor (2003) agree that the balancing of work, leisure, and rest is critical to prevent or reduce the effects of STSS in the life of a mental health practitioner. During Figley's (2002) research of STSS, he found that several ways to reduce its effects was for the therapist to properly process any history of trauma, increase social support both at work and at home, and to educate himself/herself on the hazards of treating clients with histories of trauma. Furthermore, Sommer (2008) discovered that a lack of training in the educational and internship programs was responsible for the development of symptoms related to STSS. Similarly, Everall and Paulson (2004) commented that many graduate courses do not include much information about the harmful effects of STSS on practicing clinicians, and this is one factor why many therapists may be confused when they start experiencing symptoms of PTSD themselves.

Several studies have indicated positive results in protecting the psychological well-being of the clinician against the effects of STSS, yet there is other research that has indicated that there is no such correlation (Bober and Regeher 2005; Carmel and Friedlander 2009; Creamer and Liddle 2005). Bober and Regeher (2005) discovered that many of the well-known strategies mentioned do not work. In their study consisting of 259 therapists who performed therapy for traumatized individuals, Bober and Regeher found that there was no association between activities associated with self-care and leisure with a reduction or prevention of STSS symptoms. However, other studies have found that reducing counselors' caseloads of traumatized clients could have a significant effect in preventing or reducing symptoms associated with STSS (Carmel and Friedlander 2009; Creamer and Liddle 2005).

Summary

In summary, this chapter examined how the concept and terminologies of STSS developed. This included a discussion into the associations and differences between terminologies such as Secondary Traumatic Stress, Compassion Fatigue, and Vicarious Traumatization. The review of STSS not only included symptoms similar to those of PTSD, but also a change in the therapist's perception of the world from that of being safe to unsafe. In addition, a major component in the development of STSS in therapists was shown to be that of hearing and empathizing with clients who have been traumatized.

An explanation of the two mechanisms, empathy and countertransference, were also reviewed to discover how these brought about the symptoms associated with STSS in the practitioner. Finally, some self-care techniques responsible for preventing and reducing symptoms of STSS were also discussed. These include peer supervision, increasing one's self-awareness of the hazards of treating traumatized clients, receiving additional training in the hazards and self-care when treating clients with histories of trauma, and balancing the therapist's lifestyle of work, leisure, and rest. The next section of this book will examine some of the self-care techniques to help prevent or reduce distress within the life of the psychotherapist according to psychological, spiritual, physical, and social dimensions.

PART 3

Self-Care Dimensions

CHAPTER 7

The Psychological Dimension

The previous section of this book examined the occupational hazards that may cause the mental health practitioner's psychological well-being to degrade to the point of becoming ineffective in treating clients. These hazards may also be responsible for the development of disturbances associated with psychological disorders, job burnout, or Secondary Traumatic Stress Syndrome (STSS). In this section of the book, self-care strategies will be explored in four different dimensions: the psychological, spiritual, physical, and social.

The psychological dimension is one area in which the mental health practitioner has invested many years of education, training, expense, and practice in learning to treat individuals with psychological issues. During this training period, the therapist should have developed a certain level of confidence in assessing clients' psychological problems and treating them effectively. For some unknown reason(s) whether it is denial, ignorance, or unawareness, the therapist may develop symptoms similar to those of his/her clients, which can affect the therapeutic relationship in a negative way (Barnett *et al*. 2007; Schoener 2007). These symptoms may be associated with anxiety, depression, emotional exhaustion, or trauma. Symptoms related to these disturbances can bring about distress within the practitioner during the performance of his/her duties (Figley 2002; Hannigan *et al*. 2004; Mahoney 1997; Maslach 1982).

One of the most important duties for the clinician to keep in the forefront of his/her mind is the responsibility to take care of his/her own psychological well-being before attending to others (APA 2002). A few ways that a practitioner can reduce and/or prevent distress in his/her work environment is through awareness, attending personal therapy, developing a positive attitude towards life, and use of humor.

Awareness

Awareness in therapy plays an important part in the success of any therapist (Richards, Campenni and Muse-Burke 2010). The two types of awareness related to the counseling process are the therapist being self-aware of his/her thought processes and the awareness of the hazards of the counseling profession. Many researchers in recent years have viewed self-awareness as one of the most important characteristics a counselor can develop during a long and stressful career (Lacewing 2005; Miller 2008; Richards, Campenni and Muse-Burke 2010). In fact, in one research study, Schwebel and Coster (1998) found that 339 licensed psychologists and 107 heads of professional psychology programs rated self-awareness as one of the highest ranked items that a psychologist could perform for maintaining his/her psychological well-being.

Self-awareness has been defined in various ways. Brown and Ryan (2003) emphasized that self-awareness is an internal process that leads a person to become more fully aware of his/her cognitions and emotions, making the individual more sensitive to the association of his/her negative cognitions and emotions with distress. Cook (1999), on the other hand, described self-awareness as a state that helps a mental health practitioner become cognizant of his/her prejudices, values, assumptions, countertransferences, feelings, and limitations. Additionally, Abu Baker (1999) mentions self-awareness as a way in which mental health practitioners can learn more about themselves at any given moment in time and why they react in specific ways. Freshwater (2002) uses the terms self-awareness and the therapeutic self interchangeably to define a process whereby an individual evaluates his/her interactions with those in the environment to gain insight and understanding into his/her emotional and cognitive processes. However, Williams (2003) noted that therapists who were extremely self-aware became overly anxious, which reduced their effectiveness in treating their clients. So, there does seem to be a moderate level of self-awareness that a therapist should possess, but it should not be taken to an extreme. As has been discussed, having a personal knowledge of himself/herself and an awareness of his/her personal characteristics can help a therapist distinguish if he/she is becoming anxious, frustrated, or depressed, and take the corrective action(s) necessary to relieve this distress so it does not interfere with the treatment of the client.

Another term similar to self-awareness is self-monitoring. Self-monitoring is similar to self-awareness in that both self-awareness and self-monitoring refer to a therapist being conscious of his/her thoughts, cognitive processes, and emotions. Self-monitoring is different from self-awareness in that self-monitoring involves the regulation of one's behavior to fit the demands of specific situations (Synder 1987). One can say that self-monitoring is a feedback system that may help an individual reduce the amount of distress being experienced and move towards a state of tranquility. This type of feedback can help the counselor realize when he/she is becoming uncomfortable and anxious in a session, thereby allowing the therapist to take the appropriate actions to relieve the distress. In this situation, the counselor can take a deep breath and think about what to say and/or do next in the therapy session.

Under the process of self-care, developing and sustaining a healthy psychological well-being can be seen as consisting of three parts: awareness, acceptance, and action (Hansen 2009; Hutchinson and Skinner 2007; Williams *et al.* 2003). Being aware of the hazards is the first step in this process. Whether the clinician is an intern, novice, or experienced, the American Psychological Association Practice Organization (APAPO 2013) emphasizes that being aware of the hazards and self-care through learning is an imperative for all psychotherapists. Training concerning principles of self-care must start at the university level when individuals are learning to become therapists. Skovholt (2001) makes note that graduate courses need to incorporate material into training courses to make students aware of the hazards of their profession.

If more awareness into the need for self-care is taught at this level, Jones (2007) stresses, therapists would be less likely to experience psychological distress. Unfortunately, even though some programs teach self-care, this information is being taught at a limited level (Busacca, Beebe, and Toman 2010). Those counselors who are informed about the principles of self-care learn from other experienced therapists or by experiencing symptoms of distress for themselves and seeking help (APAPO 2013). Myers and Sweeney (2005) recommend that experienced clinicians who have had courses on the hazards and self-care of the profession should take refresher courses. Awareness concerning the knowledge of the distresses produced within the counselor's profession is but the first step towards self-care. The second step is acceptance.

While awareness involves consciousness, acceptance is concerned with consciousness and decision-making (Cook 1999; Zaborowski and Slaski 2004). When a therapist knows about the hazards of the counseling profession, he/she has the responsibility to decide whether to take preventative measures or not. This decision might not come so easy. Some counselors may be in denial because they may feel that they are the expert in dealing with psychological well-being and therefore immune from psychological distress themselves. Then, there are other practitioners who think they should not show or talk about any of their weaknesses with co-workers or even supervisors. Yet another group of therapists may think that they do not have time to take off from work to care for themselves (Shallcross 2011).

Baker (2007) writes that if a mental health practitioner does not want to admit weakness, come to terms with his/her own condition, or consciously refuses to care for his/her own psychological well-being, the therapist is in violation of one of the most sacred duties in the counseling profession. This duty is to do no harm. The counselor may think that he/she is not harming anyone. But in fact, the therapist is harming his/her own mental health. Whether the psychotherapist is practicing under the American Psychological Association's Ethical Code (APA 2002) or the American Counseling Association Code of Ethics (ACA 2005), the therapist has a sworn obligation to take care of himself/herself. Meek (2005) notes that when practitioners refuse to care for themselves, it can lead to a degradation of their psychological well-being and a negative impact on the therapeutic relationship with clients. Therapists should understand that no one is immune from high levels of occupational stress. Seeking personal therapy during times of distress or just talking over personal issues with a trusted colleague is the responsible way of handling life's issues and a preventative measure towards self-care.

Finally, not only does the therapist have the responsibility to be aware of the hazards of his/her profession, the therapist must be aware of how these hazards can affect his/her psychological well-being and what steps need to be taken to prevent and reduce psychological, emotional, and physical distress. Another self-care technique related to awareness is mindfulness-based stress reduction (MBSR).

MBSR is a meditation-type practice that is an integration of contemporary clinical and psychological techniques combined with Buddhist mindfulness meditation (Kabat-Zinn 2003). Carmody and Baer (2008) mention that the major component of MBSR is mindfulness, and it is performed by using body scans, yoga, and various types of meditation. Although MBSR has many similarities to awareness, there are differences. Richards *et al.* (2010) writes that "self-awareness is considered to be knowledge of one's thoughts, emotions, and behaviors; mindfulness is maintaining awareness of and attention to oneself and one's surroundings" (p.258). Thus, this definition states, mindfulness is the process involving maintaining awareness of oneself (internal) and one's environment (external).

Mindfulness has been shown to produce many benefits in the area of cognitive functioning. In one study, mindfulness was shown to reduce trait anxiety and ruminative thinking, and increase self-compassion and empathy in healthy individuals (Chiesa and Serretti 2009). In another study conducted by Van den Hurk *et al.* (2010), mindfulness improved attention processing that led to a reduction of errors during stressful situations. Wilkinson-Tough *et al.* (2010) determined that mindfulness could reduce obsessive and intrusive thoughts and at the same time promote positive effects in one's emotional well-being. In addition, several studies (Beddoe and Murphy 2004; Galantino *et al.* 2005) involving health care professionals showed that using mindfulness reduced stress levels and increased their coping ability. Mindfulness, not only reduced stress levels in mental health practitioners, but was also found to prevent job burnout, Compassion Fatigue (CF), and Vicarious Traumatization (VT) (Christopher and Maris 2010). As reported earlier in this book, these disturbances are major contributors that could cause crippling distress in a psychotherapist's life.

Mindfulness was shown not only to help improve the psychological well-being of individuals, but also the physical well-being. Zeidan *et al.* (2010) demonstrated that practicing mindfulness for one hour in a three-day period could improve cardiovascular functioning related to such things as heart rate and blood pressure. Similarly, Carmody and Baer (2008) provided evidence that mindfulness meditation can lead to benefits associated with a reduction of chronic pain.

As mentioned earlier, the main focus of MBSR is on being consciously aware of one's body, thoughts, and emotions in a non-judgmental manner. In one example, focusing on one's breathing can help an individual reduce anxiety (Zeidan *et al.* 2013). This may be accomplished by noticing when one's breathing is becoming shallow during a stressful event and taking several deep breaths until one becomes relaxed. Another example of the use of MBSR is observing something distressful going through one's mind and not reacting to it (Christopher and Maris 2010). The individual notices the thought going through his/her mind and replaces that thought with other thoughts. Thus, MBSR teaches that thoughts are transitory and can be replaced with more pleasant thoughts. In this instance, an individual does not overreact or become overly anxious because of what he/she is thinking (Praissman 2008). To illustrate this, a therapist may anticipate how badly a session may go because of a highly resistive client, even before the session starts. Then, after the session is over, the clinician notices that the session did not go as badly as the therapist first thought. In this example, the importance of being aware that thoughts come and go into one's mind helps the therapist see that thoughts are temporary and can be changed to produce a better outcome.

Finally, one of the most important areas concerning awareness for the therapist is known as countertransference. As discussed earlier in this book, countertransference is the remembrance of an unconscious and/or conscious unresolved conflict(s) from the therapist's childhood that could hinder the therapeutic relationship if the counselor reacts to these memories (Fauth and Hayes 2006; Rosenberger and Hayes 2002). A therapist being aware of his/her thoughts in session could mean the difference between effectively treating a client or bringing a greater amount of distress into the client's life. For example, a therapist being aware of these earlier memories can screen these memories, and not react to the client in any harmful way. As noted, the importance of the therapist being aware of his/her thoughts, emotions, and feelings will give him/her a greater chance to control and change distress as it appears (Carmody and Baer 2008; Carmody et al. 2009).

Even though a therapist may be practicing self-care principles of various kinds, there still may be times when he/she is overwhelmed with distress. This is the time when a therapist might need to seek personal therapy.

Personal therapy

Various studies into personal therapy for mental health practitioners have shown positive results related to self-care (Daw and Joseph 2007; Macran and Shapiro 1998; Rake and Paley 2009). One aspect in which personal therapy can help therapists is the area of personal growth. Many therapists may ask how personal therapy can help them. After all, therapists are professionals who are trained and experienced in the area of psychological well-being and mental health. If the counselor can step back at this point and think about what therapy does for the client, it will be quite evident what personal therapy can do for the therapist.

Rake and Paley (2009) noted that personal therapy can be a process of discovering one's strengths, weaknesses, and limitations; and also in helping the therapist more fully understand his/her internal self and reshape himself/herself in a way that makes the psychotherapist more confident in treating resistant clients in stressful situations. In one research study consisting of 220 experienced psychotherapists who received personal therapy during their professional careers, Daw and Joseph (2007) discovered that personal therapy helped counselors to form an experiential learning experience about themselves, which improved the treatment outcome of their clients. In addition, this type of learning was also found to improve their socialization skills, knowledge of their stress limitations, understanding of the client's role in therapy, and sensitivity towards their own countertransferences. Similarly, Norcross (2005) noted that therapists who attended personal therapy reported improvements in self-esteem, social-life functioning, and emotional expression. In an interpretative phenomenological study of counseling psychologists, Rizq and Target (2008) reported that personal therapy helped psychologists develop greater emotional resilience, self-awareness, tolerating aspects of themselves, and an appreciation of the significance of self-reflexivity.

Some may not know what self-reflexivity is, or how it can help the mental health practitioner, but it has an important role in self-care. Archer (2003) defines self-reflexivity as a form of internal conversation where one can reflect back on past experiences, and determine how these experiences have shaped and determined one's present circumstances. In the case of mental health practitioners, Rizq and Target (2008) determined that psychotherapists use self-reflexivity to reflect back on early childhood experiences to try to make sense of how these experiences shaped their personalities and how they can further improve their lives. Attending personal therapy for a mental health practitioner is not only a time of personal growth and self-reflection, but also can help to relieve stress brought about by his/her job and lifestyle.

Most importantly, personal therapy can be most valuable to the mental health practitioner in times of emotional distress. As has been shown earlier in this book, counselors are especially vulnerable to the hazards of mental health practice and may need to seek help if they desire to stay psychologically healthy. Daw and Joseph (2007) state that personal therapy can help relieve symptoms associated with job burnout, STSS, and many other disturbances that may affect therapists' lives and may also increase their effectiveness in treating clients. In a qualitative study performed by Rake and Paley (2009), 16 psychotherapists reported that personal therapy helped to relieve symptoms associated with internal conflicts and/or traumatic events. O'Halloran and Linton's (2000) review of past literature on stressors that hinder the psychological well-being of psychotherapists reported that personal therapy brought about vast improvements in the relief of symptoms associated with job burnout and STSS. The symptoms associated with job burnout and STSS included insomnia, depression, and conflicts with family and friends (Arvay and Uhlemann 1996). Likewise, Norcross (2005) also discovered that personal therapy reduced symptom severity in therapists who experienced emotional distress in their workplace and personal lives. In addition, earlier in this book, it was shown that many individuals chose to become mental health practitioners because they suffered from some type of psychological distress earlier in their lives. Some of these counselors may still suffer from a chronic condition that may require personal therapy if they are to remain symptom free (Barnett 2007; DiCaccavo 2002).

So what kind of an individual is the therapist's therapist? Norcross, Bike, and Evans (2009) noted that mental health practitioners, who consisted of psychologists, psychiatrists, social workers, and counselors, selected their psychotherapists based on competence, warmth, caring, clinical experience, and openness. Theoretical orientations sought by the majority of these mental health practitioners were eclectic, integrative, cognitive, and psychodynamic. The main reasons for the selection of a specific therapist were personal competence and interpersonal qualities.

Many practitioners who attended therapy had good experiences, whereas others had bad experiences (Norcross *et al.* 2009). Norcross *et al.* mentioned several reasons why this is so.

Reasons given by many practitioners for their disturbing experiences were that their therapists were rigid in the application of their specific theoretical orientation in therapy, not considering the needs of the therapist being treated. Some practitioners attending therapy were happy just to talk and examine past experiences, yet some treating therapists were inflexible in changing their therapeutic approach accordingly. This conflict resulted in the practitioner leaving therapy prematurely. Another reason given was that some therapists were not empathic with the practitioner's situation, and seemed uncaring and harsh in their interactions during the counseling sessions. These were the major reasons given by therapists for premature termination of personal therapy. Although a therapist's self-awareness and attendance in personal therapy are important elements in maintaining his/her psychological well-being, another major element to self-care is developing and maintaining a positive attitude towards life.

Developing and maintaining a positive attitude

Developing and maintaining a positive attitude towards life is probably one of the most important aspects in a therapist's career. In years past, working on one's limitations and weaknesses was the major focus of both self-care and treating psychological distress (Carruthers and Hood 2004). Lately, there has been research showing that having a positive attitude towards life and events in one's life can have a more beneficial effect on maintaining one's psychological well-being (Cummins and Nistico 2001; MacLeod and Moore 2000).

A recently developing field of study called "positive psychology" has been getting increased attention during the past decade (Seligman and Csikszentmihalyi 2000). According to Seligman and Csikszentmihalyi, positive psychology is the scientific study of not only the distresses and symptoms associated with mental illness, but also includes the positive experiences, individual traits, and fulfilling life events that make one have a higher quality of life. Positive psychology examines what makes life pleasant, meaningful, and good. It seeks to apply meaningful and pleasant experiences from an individual's past to combat various distresses in an individual's present circumstances, such as depression, anxiety, and loneliness.

How does this apply to the psychotherapist? Many therapists treat their clients by knowing the client's strengths and weaknesses and observing how they have overcome past adversities. For many psychotherapists, treatment planning is focused on applying strengths to diminish the severity of the symptoms of the client's disorder (Seligman 2004). For instance, if a client has a diagnosis of major depression, but has a past of enjoying physical activities, then some type of physical activity can be applied as a treatment goal to help relieve the symptoms associated with the depression. Therapists can apply this principle to themselves. An example would be if a therapist is emotionally exhausted by his/her caseload and the therapist is an extrovert. In this case, the therapist can talk to a friend about something pleasant and get refocused on some enjoyable things in life. Being positive means more than doing things, it has to do with changing one's core beliefs and the way one thinks about people, events, and circumstances in one's life (Ingram and Snyder 2006). Beck talked much about examining one's core beliefs and changing them to a more realistic view (Beck *et al*. 1979).

Changing one's core beliefs leads to a change in one's attitude. According to Carruthers and Hood (2004), a positive change in attitude can help an individual overcome distress during and after stressful situations, and even improve his/her self-esteem and life satisfaction. For the practitioner this change can improve mood, buffer against job burnout and distress, and help to increase and maintain life satisfaction. In one study, Smedema, Catalano, and Ebener (2010) found that people who have an optimistic view of life events, even in distressful times, get more pleasure, happiness, and fulfillment in their lives than people who are generally pessimistic. In Carruthers and Hood's study, positive attitudes were related to having a sense of purpose in life. This sense of purpose can be associated with the therapist improving the behaviors of society. If an individual can imagine the effect he/she can have on society or even on his/her community for its betterment, then he/she might put this sense of purpose into action.

Having positive attitudes may not only give a counselor a sense of purpose, but it may also help to develop and/or maintain an individual's self-satisfaction and life-satisfaction. Cummins and Nistico (2001) discovered that individuals who have positive views about themselves develop a "satisfaction of self" that could be characterized as looking at themselves as worthy, able, and good. As a counselor, it is critical to focus on one's accomplishments rather than failures to help increase one's self-esteem (Smedema *et al.* 2010) and effectiveness in treating clients. There may be times where the therapist may have experienced a client committing suicide, physically harming someone, or even threatening to harm the therapist in some way. Refocusing one's thoughts, memories, and attitudes and observing how much good the mental health practitioner has done to help people can surely aid in improving one's self-esteem and integrity even in difficult situations.

Use of humor

Humor is another factor that has been shown to be beneficial to the psychological well-being of psychotherapists. In one study conducted by Stevanovic and Rupert (2004), 286 licensed psychologists rated maintaining a sense of humor among the top 3 of 34 items that were considered important to sustaining a satisfying and successful career.

In another study consisting of 595 clinicians who worked in solo independent practice, group practice, and in agencies, maintaining a sense of humor was ranked as the number one item in career-sustaining behaviors (Rupert and Kent 2007). The participants in this study found humor to be highly effective in combating stressors associated with professional duties, work demands, and job burnout. Furthermore, Kramen-Kahn and Hansen (1998) also noted that 82% of 208 psychotherapists endorsed maintaining a sense of humor as important in career-sustaining behaviors. However, a study conducted by Meissler-Daniels (1990) consisting of 144 mental health therapists who worked in a variety of settings including public schools, development centers, children's psychiatric centers, and adult psychiatric centers did not find any significant results between humor and job burnout.

In his research, Martin (2003) found a reason for the inconsistency of significant results between the correlation of humor and psychological distress in a variety of studies. Martin discovered that this inconsistency was due to the fact that many researchers view humor too broadly. During this time, Martin (2007) developed a theory that humor consists of two types: adaptive and maladaptive humor. Adaptive humor is made up of self-enhancing and affiliative humor, and maladaptive humor consists of aggressive and self-defeating humor. Martin described self-enhancing humor as having a humorous outlook on life while going through a distressing time in one's life. An example of this is thinking of a funny movie at a painful time in one's life. On the other hand, affiliative humor can be defined as that type of humor responsible in enhancing social relationships among individuals, such as telling jokes or saying something funny to amuse others. Martin (2007) noted self-defeating humor could be described as that type of humor that degrades oneself to make others laugh or to get the approval of others, and aggressive humor is used to make fun of others to attract attention. Research shows that both self-enhancing and affiliative humor have a positive relationship with psychological well-being (low levels of depression), whereas self-defeating humor has a negative relationship with psychological well-being (higher levels of depression) (Hugelsholfer at al. 2006; Kuiper *et al.* 2004). Aggressive humor was discovered to be neutral in many cases (Martin 2007).

A recent study (Malinowski 2013) into the effects of humor on job burnout of psychotherapists was performed using Martin's theory of humor. Malinowski found that self-enhancing humor contributed to a clinician's sense of personal accomplishment, whereas self-defeating humor contributed to depersonalization and emotional exhaustion. The results of this study seem to indicate that humor can either buffer against or contribute to job burnout, depending on how it is used.

In this chapter, the use of humor was discussed in the context of the therapist's life and work environment and not in the performance of therapy with clients. Although the use of humor with clients may be beneficial (Dewane 1978; Middleton 2007), its use is controversial and special training should be sought on the risks and advantages in its use with clients (Franzini 2001).

Summary

In summary, the psychological dimension is one of the most important dimensions for a therapist to address for his/her personal self-care. The therapist needs to be constantly aware of the internal environment within himself/herself, and the external world that seeks to disrupt his/her emotional well-being. Through self-awareness and self-care techniques such as MBSR, the therapist can maintain a healthy psychological well-being and reduce stress in his/her life. However, there may be times in the counselor's career, especially in his/her early career, when the therapist may be overwhelmed with his/her duties and responsibilities. During times such as these, the psychotherapist should seek help in the form of personal therapy. Personal therapy can be used to deal with problems of distress, and also as a preventative measure to improve and enhance one's psychological well-being. Finally, maintaining a positive attitude throughout one's career should not be underestimated. In this respect, the therapist like anyone else should look at situations and events in a positive light. The importance of being positive, even during stressful times, can help the therapist have an emotionally healthy outlook on life and his/her career. Finally, the theory and use of humor for therapists was examined to show its benefits in helping us protect against job burnout and stressors associated with the work environment. From discussing the benefits of the psychological dimension of self-care for the mental health practitioner, the discussion in the next chapter shifts to the spiritual dimension of self-care.

CHAPTER 8
The Spiritual Dimension

In the last chapter, the psychological dimension of self-care was examined. This dimension included a discussion of self-care strategies and a list of activities that the clinician should be practicing, such as self-awareness, developing and maintaining a positive attitude, the use of appropriate humor, and attending personal therapy to maintain his/her psychological well-being. The psychological dimension is not the only approach to self-care for the mental health practitioner. Another approach towards self-care is spirituality.

The importance of spirituality cannot, nor should not, be underestimated. Unfortunately, many therapists may not see much value in this area and leave it to the individuals who practice organized religion, even though Carlson, Erickson, and Seewald-Marquardt (2002) state that spirituality can be an important coping mechanism that a counselor can use in times of stress. In a review of nine studies of psychiatrists' religiosity in various countries, Cook (2011) found that psychiatrists were less likely to be affiliated with a religious institution than their clients. However, Cook did mention that the psychiatrists' faith might be related to a particular school of theory, a scientific method, or theoretical framework. Another study pertaining to psychologists that was conducted by Delaney, Miller, and Bisono (2013) discovered similar results. In that study, a large percentage of psychologists were found to be less religious than their clients. Nevertheless, it was noted that 82% of the participants acknowledged that religion was beneficial to an individual's psychological well-being. Nevertheless, Carlson *et al.* (2002)

found that many mental health practitioners in their study valued the principles of spirituality in their lives and noticed how these beliefs served to manage the stress encountered in their everyday lives.

The purpose of this chapter is to investigate the importance of spirituality as a coping resource for the mental health practitioner. This investigation will explore the many definitions of spirituality, the importance of spirituality in the life of the psychotherapist, and how religious practices play a part in spirituality.

Definitions

The term spirituality can mean different things to different people. According to Cashwell, Bentley, and Bigbee (2007), spirituality can be defined as "...a developmental process that is both active and passive wherein beliefs, disciplined practice, and experiences are grounded and integrated to result in increased *mindfulness* (nonjudgmental awareness of present experiences), *heartfulness* (experience of compassion and love), and *soulfulness* (connection beyond ourselves)" (p.67). Myers and Willard (2003) described spirituality as a way for individuals to find meaning in life and develop personal growth, responsibility, and relationships with others, whereas; Wills (2009) notes that spirituality suggests that every individual is a part of the greater whole and the actions of one person affects the greater whole. Atchley (2008), in his article, describes spirituality as "...an inner, subjective region of life that revolves around individual experiences of being, transcending the personal self, and connecting with the sacred" (p.12).

Many individuals may define "being spiritual" as different from "being religious" (Day 2010). Being religious may refer to a person's outward participation in a religious organization, such as attending services, masses, or charitable events, whereas being spiritual can be characterized as an individual's inward experience that may not be seen outwardly by other people, but indeed brings peace and a sense of meaning to his/her life (Myers and Willard 2003). Leseho (2007) mentions that, although spirituality and religion may have different meanings to a variety of people, it should produce peace and tranquility of mind. Unfortunately, there may be people who have experienced unpleasant events and feelings associated with institutionalized religions that have caused them to not want to be associated with any mention of religion, but do profess to be spiritual (Leseho 2007). In particular, Day (1994, 1999) found this distinction when studying and interviewing individuals on their views about being spiritual and being religious.

Nevertheless, many researchers found respondents who did not acknowledge that there were any differences between being religious and being spiritual (Cook *et al.* 2000; Corrigan *et al.* 2003; Shahabi *et al.* 2002). Day (2010) wrote that, although there are some individuals who view a distinction between these two terms, many people view themselves as both spiritual and religious and use these terms interchangeably to describe how they see themselves and their responsibility to society.

As has been discussed, spirituality is a broad term that can refer to many things, such as worshipping in a congregation, being mindful, or improving one's mental health through meditation (Schure, Christopher, and Christopher 2008). With regard to self-care, Hamilton and Jackson (1998) reported that people in the helping professions stated that their spirituality contributed to their quality of mental health, making them more self-aware of their limitations and weaknesses and motivating them to overcome them.

Although spirituality and religion may seem different to some people, several definitions of spirituality incorporate the practice of religion. Ellison (1983) found that finding meaning and purpose in one's life could come through connection to a higher power. This connection could be through God as this higher power is called by many religious organizations. This association has been shown to motivate many individuals to seek out religious organizations to find and learn meaning, peace, and purpose amongst a distressful society (Ellison 1983). Monroe and Schwab (2009) noted that spirituality could be a product of religion, which develops because of one's relationship with God and brings tranquility and meaning in every area of a one's life. However, Baker (2003a) notes that spirituality is something greater than traditional religion because it encompasses purpose, meaning, and direction in one's life.

Culture also plays an important part in defining spirituality. Wilson (2012) notes that spirituality is an innate property in which both culture and spirituality are interconnected; one's culture may often define how one finds meaning in life and determines one's health practices. Various cultures look at spirituality differently (Eichhorn 2011; Lun and Bond 2013) and this also encompasses the views of racial and ethnic groups (Frisby 1998). Sue and Sue (2003) state that in some cultures individuals believe that spirits can have an effect on the mental health of people, and mediums can intervene on behalf of those affected by these spirits. The American Indians practice a religious ritual known as a "vision quest" that is used as a religious renewal or a young man's rite of passage. It is used to access the spirit world through rituals, isolation, personal reflection, fasting, and prayers to the Great Spirit (Hammerschlag 1988; Heinrich, Corbin, and Thomas 1990).

From a psychotherapist's point of view, spirituality might mean something other than religion or being connected to a higher power. Spirituality may mean having a value system that is based on an awareness of oneself and others in one's environment, and how responsible an individual feels towards others in society (Cashwell *et al.* 2007). Cook (2011) makes note that some clinicians may state that their theoretical framework is the guiding principle for their behavior and way of life, whereas other psychotherapists might associate their spirituality with practices of traditional religious groups, such as attending church services and prayer (Case and McMinn 2001).

As one can see, spirituality can mean different things depending on many variables, but most would agree that it is a guide and blueprint to how one views life and how one interacts with the world. The next section of this chapter goes from defining what spirituality is to observing the importance of spirituality and the role it could play in the life of a psychotherapist.

Importance of spirituality

Spirituality has been shown to be a great asset to many psychotherapists. Numerous therapists have found spirituality can be used to prevent, as well as relieve distress associated with various stressors in their field (Carlson *et al.* 2002; Hernandez, Gangsei, and Engstrom 2007). Hernandez *et al.* have observed that psychotherapists could also develop their own spiritual dimension by simply observing how their clients have overcome trauma through faith. The effect of seeing this faith-based resilience in the lives of their clients could bring about a new appreciation of religion and the power to relieve distress. Just as many therapists' psychological well-being can be affected negatively by constantly hearing traumatized stories (Hesse 2002), therapists' mental and emotional functioning could also be affected positively by hearing stories of resilience (Hernandez *et al.* 2007).

Resisting distress is not the only benefit spirituality can bring. Miller (2001), in one research study, discovered that therapists who practiced spirituality reported moderate to high levels of happiness in their lives. Another study conducted by Fehring, Brennan, and Keller (1987) showed a positive relationship between an active and healthy type of spirituality and an ability to be optimistic when experiencing negative moods. Apparently, whether it is what many people call God, a higher power, or just purpose and meaning, spirituality gives an individual the ability to deal with negative and distressful events in life in greater ways and where many other people may fail (Temane and Wissing 2006). However, Powers, Cramer, and Grubka (2007) did not find any relationship between the integration of spirituality and its ability to prevent negative affect in individuals.

Nevertheless, Cashwell *et al.* (2007) emphasize that spirituality is an important coping resource for the holistic wellness of today's counselor. Purdy and Dupey (2005) noted that a holistic approach to spiritual wellness was composed of many variables, such as a belief in an organized universe, the ability to make meaning of death, the ability to make meaning of life, connectedness to others, a personal faith in the interpretation of one's world view, and a compassion for others who suffer.

Koenig (2004) found elements of spirituality that were important to an individual's psychological well-being, such as purpose and meaning, sense of control, guidance for decisions, social support, hope, and fostering a positive worldview. In Carlson *et al.*'s study (2002), mental health practitioners who valued the principles of spirituality used their belief system to successfully manage the stress encountered in their everyday lives. Other researchers such as Hernandez *et al.* (2007) emphasized that spirituality can be a major component towards prevention and reduction of symptoms including agitation, anxiety, and depression in the life of the psychotherapist. In addition, Cashwell *et al.* (2007) characterized the qualities of spiritual individuals as having a social conscience, non-hostile humor, intimate personal relations, and acceptance of self and others. However, Sulmasy (2002) notes that some individuals interpret spirituality as sharing a close relationship with family and friends, or enjoying simple pleasures such as the arts, music, and nature.

One of the most important self-care strategies one can perform as a clinician is reflecting on what one is doing, and how it is contributing to the whole. In this reflecting, it is important to look at the successes one has had in one's life, but even more, it is important to think about how each client one is treating could contribute to society when the client's distress is relieved (Rosenblatt 2009). Wills (2009) emphasizes that spirituality has to do with each individual contributing to the greater whole that changes society one person at a time.

Similarly, Erickson (1982) states that spirituality has to do with the individual seeing himself/herself as a part of the whole of society and his/her actions having the potential to affect society, and likewise society having the potential to affect the individual. This happens when individuals fully realize the effect they can have on people and the effect society can have on them (Van Dierendonck 2012). In this case, Rosenblatt (2009) mentions that, when clinicians think about how much their clients can contribute to society, this can motivate the practitioner to see his/her part in changing the quality of clients' lives. This, in turn, can bring about increased compassion satisfaction towards clients (Wee and Myers 2003).

Another type of reflecting is that of focusing and being aware of one's innermost world. This type of awareness can develop one's spirituality by self-exploration of the individual's thoughts and emotions through resources such as journaling, group discussions, and self-reflections (Neff 2003). When a therapist keeps a journal of his/her thoughts, actions, and behaviors, he/she can look back in the past and see how difficult situations and events were thought through and what actions resulted from it. Whether the resulting actions brought success or not is not the main point. The main point is learning how to build confidence in one's career by reflecting on one's past and present thought processes. The ability of a therapist to self-reflect and correct his/her thinking is critical to improving his/her life in a way that will make it happier and more productive. As one can see, spirituality can be a great asset in the life of a therapist.

Hodges (2002) shows that a truly spiritual individual, who is emotionally healthy, sees himself/herself as a part of a larger community that uses an intrinsic set of values to help society and finds meaning and purpose in life in everyday activities. Therapists will find this interaction in their daily lives with family, friends, co-workers and supervisors. The ability to take compliments with criticisms in a positive light to strengthen relationships and improve oneself is easier said than done. Additionally, therapists who were successful in preventing Vicarious Trauma (VT) in their lives noted that one aspect of this prevention was seeing their spiritual connectedness with society, their responsibility and accountability to take care of the whole (Harrison and Westwood 2009). The main point here is for the clinician to constantly self-reflect and change his/her thinking and behaviors as needed in order to be well rounded as a professional and an individual.

In addition, many people think therapists, whether they are counselors, psychotherapists, psychiatrists, or social workers, should never suffer from depression, anxiety, and/or other types of distress. However, the truth of the matter is therapists are human and emotional creatures who do have their breaking points. These breaking points can be reached and exceeded because of their caseload and/or work environment

(Lawson *et al.* 2007). That is why understanding oneself and one's strengths and weaknesses, and maintaining good emotional and psychological health are so important to self-care and being an effective therapist (Barnett *et al.* 2007).

Spirituality also helps the therapist relate to people in other ways. One way is something that has previously been mentioned. It is known as mindfulness. Cashwell *et al.* (2007) note that spirituality helps the counselor with focusing (mindfulness) a greater amount of attention on the client's thoughts and emotions, which in turn, brings about a close therapeutic relationship. This is part of empathizing with the client. The ability to be empathic is one of the greatest skills in treating a client. In this context, mindfulness refers to the therapist being fully alert and experiencing his/her thoughts and emotions in regards to the client. During this time, the counselor's self-awareness of his/her thoughts and those of the client is non-judgmental and non-critical, resulting in additional insight to strengthen the therapeutic relationship. The acceptance of one's thoughts and emotions as well as the client's in a non-critical way has been shown to improve cognitive functioning and one's state of psychological well-being (Brown and Ryan 2003; Fulton 2005).

Religion's part in spirituality

In this context, religion is defined as the teachings and doctrines of a religious organization. These organizations are known as Christianity, Islam, Buddhism, and Judaism among others. Most, if not all, of these organizations believe in a god or God and have theological practices of morality. In the United States, the Central Intelligence Agency (CIA 2008) reports that 51.3% of the population is Protestant, 23.9% Roman Catholic, 1.7% Mormon, 1.6% other Christian, 1.7% Jewish, 0.7% Buddhist, 0.6% Muslim, 2.5% other or unspecified, 12.1% unaffiliated, and 4% none. As the numbers show, the largest part of the population in the United States (78.5%) professes to be Christian.

How does the practice of organized religion help the mental health practitioner in the area of self-care? In many instances, religion has been shown to have positive effects on the psychological well-being of many individuals (Baetz and Toews 2009; Chatters 2000). Baetz and Toews noted that some qualities involved in the practice of religion, such as gratitude, forgiveness, and altruism, brought a sense of contentment, happiness, and peace. Peterson and Roy (1985) found that a religious belief system provided a source of comfort where many other people may become anxious, especially to those who firmly believed and practiced within that system. In Koenig's (2009) study, religious teaching was found to give individuals a sense of control, boost self-confidence, strengthen feelings of security, and instill a sense of comfort. Peterson and Roy (1985) noted individuals in their study acknowledged that this sense of comfort, especially during what most people would describe as anxious times, came because someone (God) greater than themselves watched over and cared for them. Similarly, Ellison (1998) informs that many individuals have acknowledged gaining a sense of self-worth and self-esteem by what they say is a personal relationship with the Divine, who cares and watches over them. Green and Elliott (2010) also discovered that people who proclaimed to be religious were found to be happy and in good health, regardless of socio-economic status, religious affiliation, employment status, or social support. In fact, one study showed that individuals who rated themselves as highly religious were better psychologically adjusted and with less distress than people who acknowledged having a low to moderate religiosity (Crawford, Handal, and Wiener 1989), although in Case and McMinn's (2001) study no differences in psychological well-being were noticed in those psychologists who reported being more religious than those who were less religious.

Various explanations are noted regarding how the practice of one's religion may produce such positive psychological effects. One of these explanations is prayer. Zondag and Van Uden (2011) state that the most common element of most types of religious prayers is the act of turning to a personal God and asking for an answer to some problem, which is known as petitionary prayer.

Of all types of prayers, meditative prayer has shown to reduce anxiousness and control anger, while increasing the ability to relax (Carlson *et al.* 2002). Case and McMinn (2001) found that meditative prayer has positive psychological properties to produce a sense of peace, control, and an ability to help in the prevention of stress and job burnout. Zondag and Van Uden (2011) describe the process of meditative prayer in this way:

> The characteristic element of meditative prayer is the act, which is of a cognitive nature. This type of prayer is mainly connected with reflection, contemplation, thought and taking stock of one's personal life and existence as a human being. The praying person withdraws into herself and hopes this will make her a better person. She longs for self-consciousness, insight and inner calm. To attain this she turns to a higher power and frequently also to herself, rather than to a concrete and personal God. (p. 23)

Lewis, Breslin, and Dein (2008) emphasize that of all types of prayer (such as petitionary prayer, meditative prayer, and religious prayer), meditative prayer had the greatest significant relationship to psychological well-being. This may be because meditative prayer provides a time of personal awareness of one's cognitive functioning that is important for self-regulation while other processes, such as worry and rumination, stop.

The practice of the use of forgiveness has also been shown to produce positive psychological effects. Several studies demonstrated that individuals who practiced forgiveness in their lives reported low levels of anxiety, depression, and hostility (Coyle and Enright 1997; Spilka *et al.* 2003; Worthington, Barry, and Parrott 2001) and an increase of happiness, contentment, and a sense of tranquility (Baetz and Toews 2009). In one study, religious participation was related to a greater type of forgiveness, which led to a reduction in hostility and an increase of subjective well-being (Aranda 2008; Lutjen, Silton, and Flannelly 2012). In another study, Konstam *et al.* (2000) found that 88% of 381 mental health counselors noted that forgiveness is an important component in maintaining an individual's psychological well-being and is highly relevant in their profession.

The act of forgiving goes much further than just "forgiving and forgetting" (Watts, Dutton, and Gulliford 2006). Worthington (1998) speaks of a five part process of forgiving and experiencing forgiveness:

1. recalling the hurt

2. empathizing with the one who hurt you

3. being altruistic

4. one's commitment to forgive

5. having a continually conscious decision to hold onto forgiveness towards that specific individual.

As has been discussed, forgiveness is an attitude, a decision, and a continual action.

Yet, a third reason as to how religion might produce qualities associated with psychological well-being in individuals is through social support. According to Ellison (1998), religious communities offer a different type of interaction than non-religious groups. This interaction is based on the teachings of the religious organization in which many stress unconditional love, care, and social support. Peterson and Roy (1985) emphasize that many people who participate in religious organizations come together because of common interests, values, and the satisfaction they receive from the interpersonal and affective bonds that develop. The benefits that develop because of these bonds have a positive effect because individuals give encouragement and sympathy to those in need, which reduce anxiety and distress and endow the giver with a sense of satisfaction that contributes to their psychological well-being. In addition, Ellison, Gay, and Glass (1989) found that the number of religious groups that an individual associated with and the strength of those ties predicted his/her psychological well-being, although those who had conflicts with members within their organization had greater distress (Krause *et al.* 2000). Nevertheless, religious events and activities do give members distraction from their worries and ruminations (Lee and Newberg 2005).

There are other reasons why religion affects one's psychological well-being in a positive way. Interestingly, Baetz and Toews

(2009) pointed out that it may be the understanding and strength of one's belief system that determines the individual's effectiveness to fight off stress. This area of understanding, mentioned above, pertains to comprehending the teachings and doctrines of one's faith. This may take some time to acquire, but it has been shown that a correct understanding is essential to produce a healthy psychological response (Baetz and Toews 2009). Additionally, these teachings and doctrines should produce a healthy psychological response within the individual.

Monroe and Schwab (2009) noted that many counselors found an inner healing from a personal knowledge and belief in the Scriptures (Christian Bible). This type of inner healing may help to prevent and/or reduce psychological distress. Similarly, in one research study, Case and McMinn (2001) found that psychologists who had a strong belief in God had a high level of psychological functioning during times of heightened stress. In fact, Case and McMinn discovered that spiritual practices such as attending religious services, meditation, and prayer played an important part in the prevention of emotional and psychological distress. Additionally, the psychologists in this study (Case and McMinn) pointed out that a strong belief in God was the main factor in coping during times of distress. In another study, Jones (2004) described various mediators responsible for religion having a positive effect on people's emotional well-being. These mediators included prayer, meditation, and social support and resulted in many individuals having a lower blood pressure, a lower heart rate, and a reduction in activity of the sympathetic nervous system. In other cases, religion has been demonstrated to have protective properties against mental disturbances such as suicidal ideation, depression, and anxiety (Koenig, McCullough, and Larson 2001), although this does not happen in every situation (Koenig 2009).

Psychological well-being, in many cases, has been shown to be dependent not only on religion alone, but on one's depth of religious commitment both in private and in public sectors Koenig 1995; Levin *et al.* 1995; Nelson 1989). Therefore, individuals who displayed the highest levels of religiosity and commitment were usually found to be the most psychologically well-adjusted.

To answer why mental health practitioners do not seek to be associated with religious organizations in greater numbers may be complicated. Some therapists might not relate to how participating in a religious organization can bring a positive psychological impact to their lives, even though they may have had a religious background (Kelly 1995; Worthington 1989). Furthermore, Diener, Tay, and Myers (2011) discovered that many individuals who fervently participated in religious practices were those who were experiencing hard times and/or came from undeveloped countries, whereas many who were educated and had mid- to upper socio-economic status may not have seen the importance in being involved with religious organizations.

Moreover, in some isolated cases, religion may seem to produce negative psychological effects. Lee and Newberg (2005) explained that there may be times when religious organizations may prohibit parishioners from seeking medical or psychological help, believing that all their followers need are a deeper belief in God (or a higher being) and in the Church's teachings. This type of advice may lead individuals to suffer needlessly, and in some cases, be fatal (Lee and Newberg 2005). In one study, Satterly (2001) mentions that some religious teachings may cause emotional anguish that may cause psychosomatic symptoms. This type of distress may seem to depend on many variables, such as an individual's psychological make-up, depth of commitment towards religious organization, and past life experiences (Himle *et al.* 2011; Pargament 2002; Rosmarin, Krumrei, and Andersson 2009). In another case, Smith, McCullough, and Poll (2003) discovered that individuals who used religion for their own purposes, such as status, self-justification, and/or security, recorded higher levels of depression than people who practiced their doctrinal teachings because of the faith they possessed. Additionally, people who may be naturally vulnerable to mental disorders can be open prey to individuals who want to or mistakenly take advantage of them by making them feel guilty, anxious, or depressed for not doing what they are instructed to do. However, religions that teach high moral standards, developing purpose and meaning in life, and being responsible for and caring for oneself and others have shown to create less distress and more peace than religions that do not (Diener *et al.* 2011; Jones 2004; Wills 2009).

Summary

In summary, this chapter has shown how spirituality can help the therapist in the area of self-care. First, spirituality was defined in many ways according to different authors, but it seems that purpose and meaning have a significant part to play in defining what spirituality means to the individual person. Second, in the life of the psychotherapist, the research does show that, in many cases, spirituality can create a sense of peace, tranquility, meaning, and purpose in one's life. Third, a review of how religion plays a part in spirituality was also discussed. It shows that faith and belief in god or God can have a beneficial effect on the psychological well-being of individuals. The spiritual dimension of self-care has indeed been shown to be advantageous for the therapist to practice. The next chapter will explore a well-researched dimension of self-care, known as the physical dimension.

CHAPTER 9

The Physical Dimension

The previous chapter examined spirituality and its effects on the psychological well-being of the psychotherapist. It was noted that spirituality is defined within the context of an individual's subjective beliefs. Spirituality was shown to play an important role in maintaining the clinician's psychological well-being and in helping to give relief during periods of stress. In addition, a review of the research into how religion can affect the clinician in times of distress and provide support was noted.

In this chapter, the physical dimension of self-care will be reviewed to determine the benefits it brings to the practitioner. There has been much research into how physical exercise can have a positive affect on the human body (Anunciacao, Casonatto, and Polito 2011; Garber *et al.* 2011; Sealey and Tope 2011). For example, it has been demonstrated that physical exercise performed at moderate to high levels of intensity can prevent heart attacks, and that a regular routine of physical activity is critical to maintaining proper cardiovascular health (Holtermann *et al.* 2009; Whyte and Laughlin 2010). In one study, Sealey and Tope (2011) discovered that the effects of exercise helped improve participants' blood pressure, flexibility, and cardiorespiratory health. It has also been shown how a change in one's lifestyle through exercise and diet could reduce one's chances of acquiring Type 2 diabetes (Walker *et al.* 2010).

In addition, the benefits of physical activities will be discussed as it pertains not only to the mental health practitioner, but also to the general public. The reason for this is to give the clinician a broad view of the research associated with the general population to help, not only themselves, but their clients as well. The focus of this chapter is not so much about how physical activity can help the counselor in the physical realm, but how it can help in the psychological realm. The objective of this chapter is to explore the benefits of physical activity on an individual's emotional and cognitive functioning, different types and intensities of exercise that are most beneficial to an individual's psychological well-being, probable causes of psychological improvements due to physical exercises, and the importance of leisure in one's life.

Benefits of physical activities on the emotional well-being

Research has shown that performing physical exercise of numerous types can be an asset to achieving and sustaining one's psychological well-being (Dubert 2002; Holmgren *et al*. 2010; Oaten and Cheng 2006). More specifically, there has been continued research into the potential benefits of physical activity on the emotional well-being of individuals. For example, Fox (1999) has noted how various forms of physical activity can improve symptoms associated with depression and decrease the risk of relapse. In one research study, Blumenthal *et al*. (1999) discovered that participants who suffered from chronic clinical depression and engaged in physical exercises such as walking or jogging had lower relapse rates than individuals who took antidepressants. Similarly, Rejeski *et al*. (1995) found that exercise could improve mood in women who exercised versus women who did not. Other studies have shown improvements in mood that were not specific to any one type of population, but were generalized across groups associated with gender, age, high risk, low risk, young, middle-aged, and elderly (Cairney *et al*. 2009; Dixon, Mauzey, and Hall 2003; Dubert 2002; Rejeski *et al*. 1992; Thogersen-Ntoumani and Fox 2005).

Although many studies into the psychological benefits of exercise had positive outcomes, there are some studies where no such correlation has been found, but these studies are limited.

One such study conducted by Cooper-Patrick *et al.* (1997) demonstrated that 973 physicians, evaluated from medical school to midlife, showed no evidence that physical exercise improved and/or maintained their emotional well-being. Such studies are from older research and may need investigations into a broader range of populations (King *et al.* 1989; Moses *et al.* 1989).

There are certain characteristics associated with the emotional well-being of individuals that may improve because of physical exercise. Self-esteem was shown to be one of these characteristics. In one such study, self-esteem was reported to have improved and psychological distress decreased in older adults who participated in physical activity (Cairney *et al.* 2009). Likewise, Fox (1999) revealed that physical exercise had an impact on enhancing self-esteem and self-worth in the general public. In Thogersen-Ntoumani and Fox's (2005) study, physical activities, such as sports and rigorous exercise, brought feelings of happiness, which enhanced perceptions of work performance. Another interesting study conducted by Valtonen *et al.* (2009) suggested that physical activities of various types had an inverse relationship to hopelessness in men who were middle-aged. Smits *et al.* (2008) showed that physical exercise not only improved the psychological well-being of people who suffered from depression, but also reduced symptoms associated with anxiety sensitivity (anxiety-related sensations). In another study, Hansen, Stevens, and Coast (2001) showed that exercising for at least 30 minutes could improve mood, vigor, and reduce or eliminate confusion.

Finally, Plante and Rodin (1990) performed a review of 41 studies to discover what association could be found between physical exercise and psychological well-being. Following this review, Plante and Rodin noted that physical exercise was related to improvements in individuals' psychological well-being, self-esteem, self-concept, and mood. Since the benefits of physical exercise have been shown to improve and maintain one's emotional well-being, physical exercise will be explored to discover what, if any, benefits it can bring to the cognitive functioning of individuals.

Benefits of physical activities on cognitive functioning

One may not be aware that physical exercise can be beneficial to improving one's mood, as well as improving cognitive functioning. It does seem that more and more research has been performed in the area of how physical exercise affects one's cognitive functioning. This research shows that physical activity performed by various age groups and at different intensities can be advantageous in improving and/or maintaining an individual's cognitive processes (Cruise *et al.* 2011; Motl, Sandroff, and Benedict 2011; Sibley and Etnier 2003). A meta-analysis of 44 research studies conducted by Sibley and Etnier (2003) demonstrated that a significant relationship exists between physical activity and academic performance in children aged 4–18 years of age. The areas related to academic performance in this study were intelligence quotient, mathematics, verbal tests, perceptual skills, and developmental level/academic readiness. Similarly, Tomporowski *et al.* (2008) examined a variety of studies related to exercise and executive functioning in children and concluded that physical exercise enhanced cognitive functioning in children and was an important aspect in their cognitive development. Physical exercise does not necessarily give children more intelligence than they would naturally have, but it does enhance the ability of children to use their cognitive abilities more efficiently.

Physical exercise was not only helpful in improving the executive functioning in children, but also was effective in maintaining cognitive performance in adults. In a meta-analysis of 15 studies of non-demented subjects whose ages were greater than 35 years old, results showed that physical exercise performed at low, moderate, or high intensity levels provided consistent and significant protection against cognitive decline (Sofi *et al.* 2010). Exercise was also advantageous for older adults (approximately 60 years of age) suffering from Parkinson's Disease in improving areas of the prefrontal lobe associated with verbal fluency and spatial working memory (Cruise at al. 2011). Additionally, Motl *et al.* (2011) noticed how exercise could help relieve symptoms of cognitive dysfunction associated with Multiple Sclerosis. In another study, physical exercise was also observed to be responsible for an increase in executive functioning and processing evidenced by electroencephalograms (EEGs) and functional MRIs (fMRIs) (Hillman, Erickson, and Kramer 2008). This increase in cognitive activity could most likely be due to the increase in neurotransmitter transmission activity in the brain while one is engaged in performing physical exercises (Meeusen and De Meirleir 1995). Now that the positive effects of physical exercise on the emotional well-being and cognitive functioning have been discussed, the beneficial effects from different types and intensities of physical exercises will be examined.

Types and intensity levels of physical exercise

One may ask, "What types of exercise and what intensity levels are best for promoting a healthy psychological well-being?" Many studies have been conducted that have determined the connection between various types of intensities of physical activity and psychological health. Kim and Kim (2007) demonstrated that intense exercises such as aerobics and hip-hop dancing had the ability to produce a sense of positive well-being and to lower psychological distress to a greater degree than activities involving body conditioning and ice-skating. In another study conducted by Smits *et al.* (2008), 60 individuals who suffered from symptoms related to anxiety and depression were asked to perform six 20-minute exercise sessions over a two-week period. To ensure participants reached a certain amount of physiological arousal and intensity, individuals were required to reach 70% of their maximum heart rate for their age at each session (.70 × [220 – age]). Results indicated a reduction of symptoms related to both depression and anxiety, with improvement to individuals' overall psychological functioning.

In several other research studies, rigorous aerobic exercise not only had the ability to improve mood but also produced physiological enhancements such as an improved heart rate, lower blood pressure, and increased lung capacity (Mihalko, McAuley, and Bane 1996; Rejeski *et al.* 1992). So, how might one define aerobics? Ledwidge (1980) defines aerobics as follows:

> Exercise which increases the endurance of the pulmonary and cardiovascular systems is known as aerobics (i.e. oxygen-consuming) exercise. Running, swimming, cycling, rowing, handball, cross-country skiing, and jogging all qualify as aerobic exercise; weight lifting, calisthenics, isotonics, and "stop and go" exercises like tennis, golf, and bowling do not. (p.127)

There does seem to be a connection between the intensity of the exercise and feelings of emotional health. As has been shown, rigorous physical activities in the form of aerobics can be a great asset in improving and maintaining one's emotional and psychological health.

Additionally, moderate exercise has been shown to be beneficial to an individual's psychological well-being. Valtonen *et al.* (2009) noted that individuals who exercised at a moderate level for at least two and a half hours per week were less likely to have depressed feelings than those who exercised less than one hour per week. However, in connection with the same study, those who maintained a high intensity workout for at least one hour were 37% less likely to display depressed feelings than those who exercised at a low level for less than an hour. Similarly, results of a study conducted by Hansen *et al.* (2001) showed that performing physical activities at a moderate intensity for 30 minutes was enough to produce improvements in positive feelings.

However, not all of the research produced similar results. Hall, Ekkekakis, and Petruzzello (2002) found that some exercises performed at a high intensity level over a period of time could have a negative effect on the psychological well-being of individuals. This may be due to the frustration of not meeting one's personal goal, because the goal was set too high, producing feelings of anxiety and frustration (Weinstein *et al.* 2010). In addition, if individuals do not have enough time to recover after high intensity workouts, then their psychological well-being could be affected in negative ways, such as changes in mood, sleep, energy levels, and depression (Caperuto *et al.* 2009).

As has been discussed, exercises of different varieties and intensities can be very beneficial in improving and maintaining one's psychological well-being. Rendi *et al.* (2008) discovered that the performance of some form of physical activity was needed in order to improve a person's psychological functioning, independent of the intensity of the exercise or workload. Research also shows that even low intensity activities can improve a person's psychological well-being (Dixon *et al.* 2003; Dubert 2002). The point here is that it is advantageous for everyone to start and maintain some type of exercise program. Although high intensity exercise such as aerobics seems to be the best in optimizing a person's emotional health and cognitive functioning, there is evidence that physical activity performed at any intensity level can help to maintain one's psychological well-being (Weinstein *et al.* 2010). The next section will explore probable causes for improvements in individuals' psychological functioning as a result of physical activities.

Probable causes for psychological improvements

There are many discussions but no consensus into the mechanisms responsible for exercise having such a positive effect on the psychological well-being of individuals (Lawlor and Hopker 2001). There may be multiple mechanisms with various interactions that are responsible for this phenomenon and just a few will be reviewed (Ng, Dodd, and Berk 2007; Stathopoulou *et al.* 2006). Plante and Rodin (1990) state that these mechanisms are psychologically and biologically based, and they provide various theories to explain the connection between exercise and emotional health. Some psychological theories say that exercise produces distraction from distress, feelings of mastery, a relaxed state of consciousness, social reinforcement, and a psychological buffer (Hughes 1984; Kobasa, Maddi, and Puccetti 1982; Ng *et al.* 2007; Raglin and Morgan 1985;

Simons *et al.* 1985; and Stathopoulou *et al.* 2006). Whereas, the biological-based theories focus on how exercise aids the increase of steroid production to counter stress, muscle tension release and relaxation, and also the release of certain neurotransmitters (Hughes 1984; Plante and Rodin 1990; Rocheleau *et al.* 2004; Wilfley and Kunce 1986).

One of the more popular theories is that exercise stimulates and enhances the production of certain neurotransmitters in the brain, which in turn, affects the psychological well-being of an individual in a positive way (McGovern 2012). According to Alloy *et al.* (1999) neurotransmitters are chemicals that transmit signals from one neuron to the next throughout the nervous system. This transmission starts from an electrical impulse within a neuron's body that travels down to the axon, which stimulates the release of neurotransmitters across the synapses (gaps) to adjacent neurons where these neurotransmitters are received by the neuron's dendrite. This successful electrochemical transmission from one neuron to the next is known as firing. Carter (1998) states that there are approximately 100 billion neurons in the brain, and it takes millions of these brain cells to fire in unison to produce just a single thought.

During exercise, four neurotransmitters, known as serotonin, dopamine, norepinephrine, and endorphins, are thought to increase and improve an individual's psychological functioning (Boeree 2009; Caperuto *et al.* 2009; Meeusen and De Meirleir 1995). These four neurotransmitters are classified as either inhibitory (those that create balance, calm the brain, and inhibit the tendency for neurons to fire) or excitatory (those that stimulate the brain and encourage neurons to fire). One of the inhibitory types of neurotransmitters known as serotonin is responsible for a stable mood and balances any excessive excitatory neurotransmitters from firing in the brain (Alloy *et al.* 1999). Carter notes that serotonin is also known as the "feel good" neurotransmitter because of its effect on mood and anxiety and its ability to regulate sleep, blood pressure, appetite, and pain.

Dopamine, on the other hand, can be considered either an excitatory or an inhibitory neurotransmitter, and is responsible for an individual's focus on tasks, motivation, creativity, and increased working memory (Boeree 2009). Known for its reward mechanisms in the form of pleasure, low levels of dopamine are responsible for Parkinson's Disease, whereas high levels seem to be responsible for hallucinations in individuals diagnosed with schizophrenia (Carter 1998; Flaherty 2011).

The third neurotransmitter, norepinephrine, is responsible for regulating mental and physical arousal (Carter 1998), and is also known as a contributor to enhancing mood (Goddard *et al.* 2010). Boeree (2009) writes that while stress seems to deplete this neurotransmitter, exercise appears to increase it. Similarly, Ledwidge (1980) found that norepinephrine levels within the brain increase dramatically during aerobic exercises.

The final neurotransmitter, endorphin, is an inhibitory neurotransmitter involved in pain reduction and pleasure (Alloy *et al.* 1999). Carter notes that endorphins are endogenous morphine-like chemicals produced in the pituitary gland that are similar to opioids. Endorphins released in response to pain or stress attach to receptors in neurons to block pain transmission to the brain (Goldfarb and Jamurtas 1997). One popular theory is that endorphins are released in response to physical exercise causing mood improvement, but for endorphins to be released the individual must exercise for a certain period of time at a moderate to high level of intensity (Rocheleau *et al.* 2004). McGovern (2012) notes that it takes approximately 30 minutes from the start of an exercise until endorphins are released, and endorphin release is related to a feeling of euphoria accompanied by minimization of discomfort associated with the physical activity (Goldfarb and Jamurtas 1997). After reviewing the various elements associated with improvements to an individual's psychological well-being, the research related to leisure will be explored in the next section of this chapter.

Leisure

So, what does leisure mean to you? Does it mean a walk at the beach during a hot summer afternoon, meeting with friends to share an evening meal, or just watching an interesting movie alone after an intense workday? The definition of leisure may mean different things to different people. Burch (2009) defines leisure as a subjective experience based on specific familial, friendship, and/or occupational settings. On the other hand, Heintzman (2008) describes leisure as a spiritual experience in which people can find meaning, purpose, and relief from life's daily hardships. One example may be taking a walk in the woods and observing the beauty of nature. Another example could be the refreshed feeling a person experiences after taking a week off from work on an enjoyable vacation. This feeling of being refreshed may come because of the distraction from the realties of one's work and the refocusing of the individual's mind to the pleasures of his/her personal experiences (Caldwell 2005). Leisure has also been explained as a way to develop creativity in times of anxiety and distress (Creek 2008). In this way, an individual is encouraged to develop some type of distraction that is enjoyable and pleasurable in seeking relief from his/her distress.

Most, if not all, people would not dispute the positive effect that leisure has on an individual's psychological well-being. Leisurely activities seem to quiet one's mind and improve an individual's outlook on life. In one study, Tinsley and Eldredge (1995) found that leisure could produce feelings of sensual enjoyment, cognitive stimulation, competition, novelty, and relaxation. In another study, Spiers and Walker (2009) discovered that leisure significantly improved many areas of an individual's life, which increased the amount of happiness, peace, and the quality of life that people were experiencing.

Participating in certain personal interests associated with leisure has also been shown to increase the coping abilities of most individuals, especially psychotherapists (Weiss 2004). In a qualitative study consisting of ten mental health professionals, composed of psychologists and counselors, aged 39–55, Grafanaki *et al.* (2005) reported:

(a) leisure improves the ability of counsellors and psychologists to cope with and improve performance at work, (b) attitude plays an important role in experiencing true leisure, (c) true leisure moments are often described in similar terms as spiritual moments, (d) leisure facilitates meaningful connections with others, (e) leisure in nature facilitates receptivity to spiritual experience, (f) one's choices of leisure and ways of approaching it reveal much about who the person is, and, (g) leisure is a major factor in promoting balance and integration. (p.31)

Research on recreational activities including crafts, hobbies, and outings with friends, showed how a continuous program of leisure could prevent the effects of depression from hindering an individual's emotional well-being (Dupuis and Smale 1995). Leisurely activities such as taking a slow walk in a park, participating in a humorous conversation, and/or meditation could have a tranquil effect when someone is going through a difficult or devastating time in his/her life (Hutchinson *et al.* 2008). In a like manner, Coster and Schwebel (1997) discovered that vacations served as an excellent way to achieve relaxation in a person's life. Vladut and Kallay (2010) also found that vacations were a way for a person to rejuvenate, buffer, and/or cope against the effects of burnout as well as reducing job stress. Vacations seem to be an outstanding method of refocusing an individual's mind from the distressing events encountered from one's past to the more pleasant experiences of a person's life (Coster and Schwebel 1997).

Leisure can also be used to create balance in one's life. In this context, leisure can be described as something in the life of an individual that is in opposition to work and that develops a sense of peace, restfulness, and happiness (Kelly 2009). In our society, much of our lives are dictated by our work schedules and work performance. As therapists, we strive for excellence, give of ourselves, and sacrifice our time to help others in distress. This sacrifice can bring added stress into one's life and cause one's psychological health to suffer. The answer is balance. In fact, a study conducted by Grafanaki *et al.* (2005) of practicing counselors and psychologists revealed leisure, when scheduled, brought about integration, balance, and prevention against job burnout. Similarly, Rodriguez, Latkova, and Sun (2008) found that people who have developed a balanced approach to work and leisure have been shown to have a greater life satisfaction than most other people.

Setting balance in one's life might not be as simple as one may think. One may be required to work a lot of overtime, both during the week and weekend. Some people might need extra money for their children's college expenses, catching up on bills, or paying for a long vacation. In addition, some people may have Type-A personality characteristics that compel them to put in a large amount of time at work and/or to take their work home. So what are some things that one can do to achieve balance in one's life? Lee, Reissing, and Dobson (2009) make some suggestions for achieving a work–life balance, especially among psychologists and counselors, such as setting goals, establishing priorities, and developing the ability to say "no."

Some therapists may have trouble with saying "no." The reluctance to say "no" may come because the therapist might feel he/she might hurt the feelings of the other person (Lee *et al.* 2009). This may happen if a client wants extra time in session, or if family, spouses, and/or friends want us to do something special for them, which may take away the time to relax and unwind. The reluctance to say "no" over time can lead to problems involving job burnout, resentments, and a cynical attitude (Maslach 1982).

Finding balance in a therapist's life is an imperative to achieving psychological well-being (Grafanaki *et al.* 2005). What this means is that if we are not taking care of ourselves and consciously creating balance, our effectiveness as psychotherapists will suffer. Maslach (1982) emphasizes that taking care of ourselves means that we clinicians need a proper balance between our work, home life, and leisurely activities. Psychotherapists all need proper balance and relaxation to rejuvenate themselves. A counselor usually advises his/her clients on the importance of balancing their lifestyles, but the most significant responsibility of a mental health practitioner is taking care of himself/herself (Wise, Hersh, and Gibson 2012).

Another aspect of balance in one's life is the ability to share a portion of one's leisure time with others. One of the greatest resources each of us has is the relationships we have with our families. Rupert *et al.* (2012) noted that when therapists take proper care of themselves in leisurely activities with their families, their psychological well-being is improved, and this increases their effectiveness at work and their life satisfaction is increased.

Our leisure time will not be pleasant and restful unless we are enjoying it. This is called leisure satisfaction (Rodriguez *et al.* 2008), and Rodriguez *et al.* noted that leisure satisfaction has to do with the amount of enjoyment and pleasure that an individual is receiving during the leisure activity. In a national survey consisting of 898 families, Agate *et al.* (2009) found that leisure satisfaction among families and couples significantly correlated with the families' quality of life. In other words, most, if not all, members of the family must get some satisfaction and enjoyment during the leisure activity or the leisure activity will not be gratifying.

Families and couples are not the only recipients of the psychological benefits of leisure activities. Individuals that do fun activities with friends and peers put themselves in a pleasant state of mind to take on stressful events in life (Voorpostel, Van der Lippe, and Gershung 2010). In this area, playing a game of basketball, going for a walk on the beach with someone special, or just going fishing with friends could relax the mind from a stressful week and allow bonding to take place. Samdahl (1992) noted that the best time for friends to get together for leisurely activities is the weekend. This is because most times there is no work for people to be concerned about and they can put their full attention into having fun and just relaxing.

Summary

In this chapter, many of the studies dealing with how the physical dimension promotes the psychological well-being of individuals have been discussed. These studies explored how the benefits of physical activity can maintain and/or increase the emotional and cognitive functioning of individuals. Furthermore, different types and intensity levels of physical exercise were examined to determine the most effective means of attaining the highest level of psychological well-being. In addition, the most probable causes for why physical exercises improve psychological functioning were explored, and theories that explain these causes were also reviewed. Finally, the importance of leisure was discussed, showing how leisure needs to be incorporated into the therapist's life. The next chapter of this book will investigate how social support can be of value in maintaining a therapist's psychological well-being in a stressful work environment.

CHAPTER 10

The Social Dimension

In the preceding chapter, the physical dimension of self-care was explored. This consisted of an examination on the effects that physical exercise had on the emotional and cognitive functioning of individuals. Additionally, various types of exercises and intensities were discussed to discover what potential benefits they can bring to maintain or improve an individual's psychological well-being. A review on how physical exercise stimulates and enhances neurotransmitter production in the brain was also explored. Finally, the importance of leisure activities was emphasized as a source of renewal for an individual's psychological functioning.

Throughout this book, various areas of self-care have been shown to affect the psychological well-being of the therapist in positive ways. The previous chapters documented the psychological, spiritual, and physical dimensions of self-care, and how they either maintained and/or increased the mental health capacities of practitioners who work in the mental health field. One may ask of all the dimensions discussed so far in this book, "Which dimension is most effective in maintaining the psychological well-being of individuals?" The answer is it would probably depend on the situation and may vary according to the type of population studied. In one study, where different types of self-care strategies were researched, Hansson, Hilleras, and Forsell (2005) found that social support had the strongest correlation to psychological well-being, followed by relaxation techniques and physical exercise. Furthermore, Meyer and Ponton (2006) emphasize that throughout the literature concerning self-care for counselors, relationships were a common element in helping to maintain an individual's mental health. Bell and Robinson III (2013) informed that developing and maintaining social relationships throughout a counselor's professional career is an important strategy for his/her psychological health and is an important factor in preventing disturbances such as Secondary Traumatic Stress. In respect to job burnout, Bradley *et al.* (2012) emphasize the importance of personal support from such sources as friends and family, and seeking out professional support from colleagues and/or supervisors when feelings of frustration and being overwhelmed are noticed. It must also be noted that there will be times when the clinician is in distress during the day. During this time, Skovholt (2001) stresses that the therapist should avoid the impulse to withdraw and isolate himself/herself, and instead actively seek emotional support from colleagues and supervisors.

In this chapter, the social aspect of self-care will be explored to see what steps can be applied to the life of the psychotherapist to maintain and/or increase his/her psychological well-being. The purpose of this chapter is to investigate how friends and family, peers, and supervisors can assist in maintaining one's psychological health even in the midst of a stressful work environment.

Friends and family

Hutchinson *et al.* (2008) reported that social support from friends in the form of participating in leisure activities is a great way to maintain one's emotional health. The maintenance and/or improvement of an individual's emotional health may be due not only to the distraction involved in an enjoyable activity but also to the bonding that develops between parties (Glover and Parry 2008). According to Coster and Schwebel (1997), psychologists rated stable relationships with friends as among the highest for maintaining their psychological well-being. Of course, this all depends on whether the therapist understands and believes that leisurely activities with friends will buffer him/her from stress and maintain his/her psychological well-being (Hutchinson *et al.* 2008). This refers to the subjective belief brought on from the objective evidence from research on relationships with other people.

Many times it has been shown that practitioners give advice to their clients, but do not follow that same advice for themselves (Miller 2001). Miller writes that there may be times when clinicians have had an intense day treating resistant clients, and the question may be asked, "What does the clinician do at this point?" Does the clinician seek out friends, get involved in an interesting discussion, do a fun activity with others, or withdraw and isolate himself/herself when he/she should be seeking emotional support (Norcross and Guy 2007)? This type of emotional support is different from being involved in a leisurely activity discussed in the last chapter. In this chapter, the psychological support is derived from the interaction with friends during the physical activity, not just the activity alone. In fact, Rodriguez *et al.* (2008) found that there was a stronger relationship between the interaction with friends during leisurely activities and life satisfaction than from leisurely activities alone.

Various studies have shown that having close relationships with friends highly correlates with maintaining an individual's psychological well-being. In one study, Fingerman and Hay (2002) discovered that adults of different ages believed their mental health was related to their social relationships with friends. In another study, individuals who had close friendships benefited by having less distress and a greater emotional well-being versus those people who did not have such relationships (Wrzus, Wagner, and Neyer 2011). Similarly, Lerias and Byrne (2003) found that close friendships were a significant factor in the prevention of Vicarious Traumatization (VT), whereas those who did not have close relationships tended to suffer from greater distress. In another study, Meyer and Ponton (2006) indicated that friendships can be a source of renewal, distraction, and enrichment where one can bond with others as well as give and get emotional support. Additionally, those individuals who had close relationships were less vulnerable to depression and reported having feelings of happiness with others (Pavot, Diener, and Fujita 1990). Finally, Perlman and Rook (1987) noted that people who have close friendships and receive a great amount of emotional support from such relationships have been shown to cope more effectively with a variety of stressors including job loss, illnesses, and even rape. Friends are not the only means of emotional support; support from family members has also been shown to be an asset in maintaining and improving one's psychological well-being (Lawson 2007).

When one thinks about it, families can be one of the best resources for providing and improving our psychological well-being. In a survey involving 506 professional counselors from the American Counseling Association (ACA) on career-sustaining behaviors, results showed that time spent with family ranked as the highest factor in maintaining a counselor's psychological well-being (Lawson and Myers 2011). Of all the social support resources that the counselor has, the family is the only one that is always there to draw upon. Of course, one must remember that quality time is the all-important element. Getting away with the family and enjoying each other can be refreshing and provide the critical bonding that is needed when an individual is going through stressful times. Kyle and Chick (2002) also discovered that sharing one's leisurely time with family members can enhance one's emotional well-being. In one longitudinal study that spanned over 23 years, family support demonstrated how effective it can be in reducing symptoms of several mental health disorders, especially depression (Kamen *et al.* 2011). Moreover, family members can be a great asset to the practitioner when there are decisions to be made concerning his/her life, including such events as moving or taking a new job (Day-Vines and Holcomb-McCoy 2007).

It must be noted that a practitioner's partner/spouse is one of the most important individuals that can help a psychotherapist maintain his/her psychological well-being. In two surveys (Kramen-Kahn and Hansen 1998; Stevanovic and Rupert 2004), counselors were asked what they believed to be their greatest sustaining behaviors that contributed to their positive attitudes and helped them function effectively. Spending time with their family/spouse was among the top five of 34 behaviors that counselors rated as highly satisfying, versus less satisfying. Most importantly, Norcross and Guy (2007) mention that a close relationship with his/her spouse/partner can help the clinician keep in touch with his/her feelings and needs, and provide understanding and unconditional love in times of distress.

Something that has shown to influence the effectiveness of family support in a negative way is conflict between work and family priorities. Rupert *et al.* (2009) discovered that additional work hours combined with the increased demand for high work performance placed an additional amount of strain on psychologists and took them away from family interaction. This, in turn, made these individuals more susceptible to emotional exhaustion. Administrative work, such as completing progress notes, treatment plans, attending meetings, and filling out specialized reports in addition to his/her normal caseload, could influence the practitioner to put in extra time at work and/or take his/her work home (Farber and Heifetz 1981; Kramen-Kahn and Hansen 1998; Rupert and Baird 2004; Stevanovic and Rupert 2004). This additional work can definitely cut into family time, which can place a strain on family relationships and increase the amount of stress endured by the therapist. The discussion now shifts from the influence friends and family can have on the psychological well-being of the practitioner to how peers at work can be an asset for the counselor.

Peer collaboration

Peer collaboration has also been shown to be associated with self-care (Barlow and Phelan 2007). Seeking peer support while dealing with highly emotional and intense clients can be beneficial in maintaining one's objectivity. What this means is that the therapist can take much pressure and stress off himself/herself by getting advice and recommendations on clients and situations that may be confusing. Examples include getting advice on how to motivate resistant clients who do not cooperate with treatment plan recommendations, and/or how to deal with clients who are not totally honest about their psychological well-being.

Peer support can be especially helpful early in one's career (Barlow and Phelan 2007). This is because therapists are highly vulnerable to job burnout very early in their career. Job burnout develops for a number of reasons already addressed in this book, such as the expectation that clients should improve quickly, underestimating individual differences among clients, and being unaware of organizational stressors (Azar 2000; Schaufeli *et al.* 1993). Ulman (2001) emphasizes that counselors in their early career may not have developed the ability to discern between transference and countertransference issues. In this context, the experienced therapist can provide critical advice and recommendations to help the younger and less experienced counselor avoid pitfalls associated with these issues. Colleagues can also advise young counselors on personal self-care techniques including what they may have learned earlier in their career, such as not to take the lack of improvement in clients personally, and also to take time off between clients for distraction and interaction with co-workers (Skovholt, Grier, and Hanson 2001).

Webb (2011) discusses how peer consultation is an imperative to maintaining one's psychological well-being and self-care, especially when working with suicidal clients. Peer consultation gives the counselor validation for the decisions he/she makes and helps maintain objectivity in other areas of his/her life. In this respect, whether a therapist is a novice or experienced, self-doubt and the feeling of incompetence are major concerns to mental health practitioners that can take a toll on their psychological well-being (Norcross and Guy 2007; Theriault and Gazzola 2010). In several studies, 42–83% of participants reported that self-doubt was a significant disturbance related to decision-making when treating clients (Mahoney 1991; Orlinsky *et al.* 1999). Theriault and Gazzola (2010) also noted that mental health practitioners who sought peer consultation with other colleagues in times of distress maintained and increased their psychological well-being.

Peer consultation provides various functions for the clinician's mental health. It gives insight into the interactions with clients that could increase his/her confidence and effectiveness (Coster and Schwebel 1997), and supports the therapist in times of confusion and self-doubt (Webb 2011). Spending time with peers and peer groups related to his/her profession has also been shown to maintain the clinician's psychological well-being from symptoms associated with job burnout (D'Souza, Egan, and Rees 2011) and VT (Sexton 1999).

So what can organizations do to prevent job burnout among their therapists? One solution is to provide their practitioners scheduled time for peer collaboration during various parts of the day (Maslach and Leiter 1997). This collaboration can be in the form of discussing difficult cases and/or just talking about events and fun things done during times off from work. As with any close relationship, trust is an important factor in establishing peer support. Being relaxed with one another and sharing one's thoughts and feelings is critical to receiving help from colleagues. Barlow and Phelan (2007) recommend meeting at specific times and specific locations at least once each week. This can be achieved by asking management to reserve a room in which therapists could discuss difficult cases and thereby obtain valuable advice or insight from other experienced clinicians. In this way, the sharing of difficulties and stressors of one's work can help to bring a new perspective to the therapist's problem and provide mutual comfort and support to buffer against different types of job burnout (Richards *et al.* 2010).

Practitioners who work in private practice are at a disadvantage concerning peer support (Zur 2008). This disadvantage is because most of the time they are isolated from their colleagues in their practice of psychotherapy. Clinicians who work in isolation do not have fellow colleagues near them for fellowship and to share their difficulties and problems. These therapists need to schedule time to meet with other counselors to ensure their objectivity in their profession. One of the advantages in working in private practice is that the therapist does not need to follow the rigid rules and policies of an agency. Unfortunately, there is no overseeing to prevent ethical violations while practicing psychotherapy in independent practice. Even more important than peer support, supervision is critical to maintaining self-care.

Supervision

Supervision is an important resource for ensuring the clinician's self-care and in maintaining his/her psychological well-being (Howard 2008). So how is supervision related to a clinician's self-care? Most, if not all, states require therapists to obtain a certain amount of hours under supervision for licensure. When one thinks about it, supervision is important not only for passing on valuable experience to younger practitioners, but also for the correction of mistakes that may harm clients or the therapist (Vasquez 1992). Good supervision usually brings confidence in one's abilities and a desire to pursue excellence in one's career. This refers to knowing how to take care of oneself and also applying this knowledge throughout one's career as a clinician.

Supervision can take much pressure and stress off the therapist, but the counselor needs to make a conscious effort to seek out supervision and use it. Supervision can be an important element of a therapist's psychological well-being, whether he/she is a student or an experienced professional (Skinstad 1993; Wheeler and Richards 2007). Schofield and Grant (2013) emphasize that clinical supervision can help develop students' and experienced therapists' awareness of stressors related to their work, as well as self-care principles. Although supervision is a requirement for coursework and licensure, Miller *et al.* (2011) recommend that experienced practitioners need to seek out supervision to ensure that they are not becoming overwhelmed with their responsibilities and thereby showing signs and symptoms related to job burnout or Secondary Traumatic Stress. Grant and Schofield (2007) noted that seeking out supervision promotes growth and psychological wellness in many clinicians. Similarly, Linley and Joseph (2007) indicated that therapists experienced greater levels of personal growth when they received formal supervision versus not receiving supervision. Ulmam (2001) writes that supervision provides the guidance and advice to help even experienced therapists when making critical decisions. These decisions might involve breaking confidentiality on issues involving a suicidal or a homicidal threat, or even a decision involving the notification to the proper authorities for suspected child neglect and/or abuse. In one study, Gibson *et al.* (2009) discovered that high levels of perceived supervisor support were related to low levels of depersonalization, low levels of emotional exhaustion, and higher levels of feelings of personal accomplishment compared to clinicians who had low levels of perceived supervisor support. Gibson *et al.* defined perceived supervisor support as the therapist's perception of the value the supervisor places on him/her as a worker. In other such studies, supervisors have been shown to help clinicians by monitoring and supporting therapists who treat trauma survivors against the harmful effects of Secondary Traumatic Stress (Sommer 2008; Sprang *et al.* 2007).

Research has shown that supervision can help therapists to maintain their psychological well-being in various ways. Supervisors can monitor and protect therapists' well-being in situations such as those involving erotic transference (Rodgers 2011), by encouraging self-awareness and self-efficacy, by providing support and challenges (Wheeler and Richards 2007), and by helping therapists to overcome their limitations and weaknesses (Beck *et al.* 2005). In one study where 345 psychologists were asked what contributed to their psychological well-being, supervision was rated highly (Coster and Schwebel 1997). One clinician in this study noted that it was the remembrance of helpful times when supervisors gave recommendations, suggestions, and feedback that got the therapist through difficult sessions.

Coster and Schwebel (1997) inform that one of the most important functions of a supervisor is to help the psychotherapist through tough times. This may involve consoling a clinician after a client's suicide or after an intense therapy session. In a research study consisting of 71 counselors from the American Mental Health Association (AMHA), Sterner (2009) noted that counselors who had good relationships with their supervisors had lower work-related stressors and greater work satisfaction. Supervisors can be one of the therapist's best assets because of the supervisor's experience and objectivity of not being involved in the treatment of the client or the therapist's emotionally charged situations. In a study conducted by Walker (2004), supervisors were shown to be beneficial to the therapist, especially those who work with clients who have been sexually abused as children. In this context, supervisors should be familiar with symptoms associated with Secondary Traumatic Stress and how to recognize these symptoms. Walker (2004) also emphasizes the importance of supervisors establishing relationships with those working under them and using this knowledge to determine if the therapists' effectiveness is degrading for some unknown reasons. Similarly, Howard (2008) notes that supervisors can further watch over the psychological well-being of their therapists by reviewing therapists' caseloads to ensure they are diverse and the clinician is not being overwhelmed. Barnett, Johnston, and Hillard (2006) describe some warnings that supervisors and clinicians should be aware of in respect to degradation of the therapist's ability to treat clients effectively. These warning signs may be decreased motivation, impatience, lack of focus, anger towards clients, increasing feelings of frustration, loss of enjoyment of his/her work, and increased fatigue.

As, like anyone else, supervisors cannot read thoughts and might not know that the clinician is encountering anxiety on the job, they should keep an open door policy with employees. Having said that, it is the duty and responsibility of the therapist to keep the lines of communication open with the supervisor to ensure his/her self-care. Of course, the supervisor must be perceived as approachable. In this respect, the supervisor should exhibit certain characteristics, skills, and talents related to interacting with others, including flexibility, understanding, authority to confront and challenge, compassion, being empathic, and displaying courage (Wheeler 2007). Barnett *et al.* (2007) mention that it is easier said than done for the therapist to open himself/herself, especially to his/her supervisor, and expose his/her vulnerabilities. Additionally, Greer (2002) notes that not all supervisors are helpful and effective in their observations, and in some cases they might be harmful. So far the discussion in this section has focused on clinicians who work in a public or group setting, but what about psychotherapists who work in independent or private practice?

Independent practice can have advantages in that one manages one's own professional life, but it also has disadvantages. One of the major disadvantages of private practice is isolation from colleagues (Brennan 2013). Hawkins and Shohet (2000) stress that the need for supervision for clinicians who work in independent practice cannot or should not be underestimated. Clinicians who work in independent practice do not have other peers and colleagues during the day with whom they can discuss difficult cases and feelings that arise and get objective advice as to how to handle the situation. Greenburg, Lewis, and Johnson (1985) note that without supervision the independent practitioner is cut off from most support and vulnerable to symptoms related to emotional distress and job burnout. In this situation, it would be in the best interest of the clinician to seek out supervision for support and to ensure his/her self-care and psychological well-being is being maintained (Savic-Jabrow 2010).

Supervision can be a great asset by noting any vulnerabilities and blind spots that the practitioner might not be aware of and observing if the clinician is becoming too emotionally involved in any particular case (Brennan 2013). Sometimes, when an independent practitioner is enduring some type of distress, possibly a divorce, it may be difficult to determine or to be aware if the therapist is impaired and to what degree (Williams *et al.* 2010). In this case, Vasquez (1992) describes how supervision can monitor a clinician's ethical behavior and give objective advice to a therapist who may not be aware of his/her condition. Again, a therapist's level of trust in discussing sensitive related information pertaining to his/her psychological well-being may take some time (Barnett *et al.* 2007).

Summary

In this chapter, the social aspect of self-care was explored. This consisted of examining three different areas of social support, which included support from family and friends, peers, and supervisors. All three sections of the social dimension of self-care have been shown to make a significant contribution to either maintaining and/or increasing the psychological well-being of the mental health practitioner. The first section of this chapter explored how family and friends help the therapist in the area of relaxation and distraction from his/her profession. Being with family and friends and planning activities grants the clinician emotional renewal and increased psychological well-being. The second section examined how consulting with peers and colleagues about client difficulties and feelings of doubt, inadequacies, and incompetence can instill confidence and knowledge about performing one's job effectively. Finally, the last section reviewed how supervision can monitor and advise the clinician concerning difficult ethical matters, cases concerning clients, and help in making critical decisions concerning his/her profession. The next and final chapter of this book will discuss the profession's and reader's ethical and professional responsibilities for reviewing and applying the principles related to self-care.

PART 4

What's Next?

CHAPTER 11

Awareness Through Education

This book has explored various topics pertaining to the hazards and self-care of the mental health practitioner. Some topics that have been examined are the role and responsibilities of the psychotherapist, general and specific disturbances that can affect a clinician's everyday functioning, and self-care strategies that can be practiced to maintain his/her psychological well-being.

In the beginning of this book, one question asked was "Why is self-care so important for the mental health practitioner?" Research has indicated that clinicians who work in the mental health field may be prone to developing symptoms related to various disturbances including depression (Gilroy *et al.* 2002; Pope and Tabachnick 1994), anxiety (Mahoney 1997), Compassion Fatigue (CF), Secondary Traumatic Stress (STS), job burnout and significant psychological distresses (Bell and Robinson III 2013; Figley 2002; Hannigan *et al.* 2004; Maslach 1982). Since clinicians are human and their type of work makes them vulnerable to psychological distresses—more so than the general public—additional and specialized measures need to be implemented into the life of the therapist to maintain his/her psychological well-being (Figley 2002; Maslach 1982).

This book has outlined various strategies that mental health practitioners can use to maintain and increase their psychological functioning. These self-care strategies were divided into four dimensions consisting of the psychological, spiritual, physical, and social. Each dimension discussed gave specific activities, based on research, to help psychotherapists function at their optimal level.

After reviewing the hazards and self-care principles in the preceding chapters, the question that must be asked is, "What is the mental health field, as a whole, going to do with this information?" One might even ask, "What is the reader of this book going to do with this material?" One answer might be to include this information and materials in graduate and PhD courses to make students who are studying to becoming psychotherapists more aware and sensitized to the pitfalls and self-care strategies of this profession. Another answer is to be continually committed to learning and practicing self-care principles and strategies throughout one's professional career.

The purpose of this final chapter is to examine and stress the need for additional education in graduate and PhD courses for self-care and to emphasize the need for experienced psychotherapists to continue researching, learning, and practicing self-care techniques to keep themselves psychologically healthy.

Graduate and PhD programs

As so many therapists know, one cannot correct a problem unless one is aware of it. Psychotherapists specialize in helping clients become aware of their problems, but are therapists aware and accepting that they, too, can suffer from symptoms and distresses associated with their line of work? The first step in helping mental health practitioners to be more aware of the hazards and self-care principles of their profession is through education. One important fact must be noted: that when self-care is taught in counseling programs, there tends to be a higher level of wellness reported compared to programs where it is not taught. A higher degree of wellness is shown when self-care strategies are discussed and re-emphasized in PhD programs (Myers and Willard 2003). In their research, Yager and Tovar-Blank (2007) found that for therapists to be effective in their profession they must know, be aware, and practice the principles of self-care. Unfortunately, many graduate programs, not all, provide a limited amount of information concerning self-care and focus mostly on the theory and practice of therapists' skills, theories, and therapies associated with the counseling profession (Hill 2004; Myers, Mobley, and Booth 2003; Roach 2005).

The consequences of not teaching and emphasizing principles of self-care may result in some therapists leaving the profession early in their career or developing symptoms associated with job burnout (Maslach 1982; Ross *et al.* 1989; Schaufeli *et al.* 1993). Some reasons why mental health practitioners may get burned out early in their careers are over-involvement with their clients (Koeske and Kelly 1995), over-empathizing (McKenzie Deighton *et al.* 2007), and an inability to note positive changes over a specific time in clients (McCarthy and Frieze 1999). Similarly, Schaufeli *et al.* (1993) pointed out that many mental health professionals may leave the field very early in their careers because of lack of progress in seeing their clients getting better quickly, thereby allowing discouragement to set in. In social work programs, Jones (2007) found that learning awareness of self, coping techniques and strategies very early in one's training could reduce job burnout symptoms and promote psychological health later in one's career. Likewise, Skovholt (2001), in his book, *The Resilient Practitioner: Burnout Prevention and Self-Care Strategies for Counselors, Therapists, Teachers, and Health Professionals* discusses how graduate student counseling programs need to develop and emphasize more of a counselor wellness approach in teaching students to reduce stress, especially during their internship programs.

Research supports the need for additional training for therapists in the area of self-care. In a survey consisting of 107 American Psychiatric Association (APA) program department heads, Schwebel and Coster (1998) discovered that these program leaders saw a lack of effort in instituting improvements in students' curriculum concerning self-care and hazards of the counseling profession. These department leaders commented that the main reason for the failure was the lack of funding and the time and space to include these items into the program curriculum. Furthermore, Kleespies *et al.* (2011) mention that:

Were psychology graduate and training programs to include education about the risks of professional impairment and the benefits of wellness practices in their curriculum, it seems plausible that future psychologists would be more likely to see the signs of impending personal difficulty and be more aware of the option of seeking assistance. (p.248)

In another study, Sommer and Cox (2005) interviewed nine crisis counselors who worked specifically with victims of sexual abuse. One out of nine clinicians reported having had academic training in the area of Vicarious Traumatization (VT). Similar studies conducted in clinical programs found therapists were lacking in training associated with VT (Adams and Riggs 2008; Trippany *et al.* 2004), education about dealing with the death of a client (Knox *et al.* 2006), or general distresses related to counseling (Case and McMinn 2001; Kleespies *et al.* 2011).

Research exists to show that there are academic programs which have instituted information about self-care principles into their curriculum. Sowa and May (1994) found that counselors who have had stress management courses during their academic training reported the greatest amount of coping resources in the area of relaxation techniques and self-care practices compared to those who have had other counseling programs. However, in one study, Roach and Young (2007) discovered that students who were involved in counseling programs that taught self-care principles did not make the needed improvements in the area of wellness. The students acquired knowledge of the hazards and self-care strategies, but did not apply these in their daily lives. In this case, Roach and Young recommended that, as part of the training curriculum, students should be encouraged to develop coping strategies in their daily lives and implement these as needed.

Whether an individual is preparing to become a professional working as a social worker, counselor, psychologist, or any other type of psychotherapist, all these individuals who are preparing to work performing psychotherapy are all vulnerable to job burnout, VT, and Compassion Fatigue (CF) (Bearse *et al.* 2013; Christopher and Maris 2010; Hesse 2002). Because of the devastating effects that these disturbances can bring into the therapist's career, family life, and psychological well-being there is an urgent need to incorporate self-care principles and techniques into the therapist's curriculum of each profession that practices psychotherapy.

There are several recommendations that are noted as ways of improving the counseling training curriculum. One recommendation that Christopher and Maris (2010) made to increase the psychological well-being of people who perform psychotherapy is to incorporate mindfulness training to help the student develop awareness as an action to maintain his/her psychological health against such disturbances as VT, job burnout, and CF. Christopher and Maris (2010) mention that mindfulness is a way to become aware and accept, moment by moment, one's own personal experiences, including the awareness of one's thoughts, emotions, and bodily sensations and through mindfulness make adjustments so one can relax and function as a professional at an optimal psychological level. Additionally, mediation, yoga, and physical exercise are also important components. In another recommendation, Sommer (2008) explains that the educational system should develop topics related to the professions' hazards and self-care principles and integrate these into the students' course materials.

Finally, Bearse *et al.* (2013) suggest that the training of future professionals could also include a requirement for students to attend personal therapy. In this way students can gain an understanding of their own psychological well-being and functioning. Setting and developing comprehensive graduate and PhD programs that address professional hazards and self-care is a must to provide therapists with resources that will be needed to maintain and increase their psychological health. But what happens when the student-therapist graduates and enters his/her chosen field. What should he/she do next?

Continuing education

A clinician's education, training, and practice of self-care skills should not stop after graduation from school. Myers and Sweeney (2005) stress that continually learning the latest information on self-care is an imperative for a therapist to maintain his/her psychological well-being. When one thinks about it, a counselor can become engrossed with focusing in on the needs of others so intently, that the clinician's well-being may be ignored to the point where he/she starts displaying symptoms related to those whom he/she is treating (Maslach 1982). In reference to this remark, Lawson and Venart (2005) found that clinicians may be more vulnerable to psychological disturbances than the general public. Meyer and Ponton (2006) compare a counselor's well-being to that of a tree. Meyer and Ponton (2006) describe how a clinician's psychological well-being should continually be watered with the knowledge of self-care techniques and cared for by continually participating in such things as leisure, meditation, personal therapy, socializing, additional schooling, and training.

One of the biggest differences between learning about self-care in graduate school versus professional practice is the freedom of choice and decisions to continue to learn and practice. In graduate school, the curriculum and details of the course are planned for the student counselor. In professional practice, there is nothing saying that practitioners should take specific continual educational courses. One thing that is in the mental health practitioner's control is the ability to examine research articles on the latest findings in helping therapists maintain their psychological well-being and attendance at seminars on self-care. Lawson and Myers (2011) noted that when counselors practiced career-sustaining behaviors, they reported higher levels of psychological well-being and life satisfaction. One of the requirements to sustain a therapist or counselor's license in most states is to accumulate so many continuing educational units for a period of one or two years. Many courses are up to the practitioner to select. It would behove the therapist to take courses specifically aimed at self-care. The reason for this is that the therapist has a sworn duty not only to keep himself/herself physically and psychologically healthy, but also to think how his/her condition, if degrading, might hurt the client. Whatever field and profession the reader is working in, he/she is ethically bound to keep the ethical code of his/her association. Breaking the requirements of one's code might lead to disciplinary action, but more important is the harm a clinician can do to the clients he/she is treating. After all, the practitioner is bound to keep the ethical principle he/she has sworn: "to do no harm."

The mental health field can implement a variety of recommendations to improve the psychological well-being of its workers. First, Hesse (2002) notes organizations can provide their workers with training to address the effects of Secondary Traumatic Stress and information on self-care principles so therapists' coping abilities increase. In fact, Bradley *et al.* (2012) wrote that organizational involvement in additional training of their clinicians was an important ingredient in professional competence and psychological functioning.

Ultimately, the mental health professional is responsible for maintaining his/her own psychological health. To ensure mental health practitioners can maintain their psychological well-being Cummins *et al.* (2007) have outlined a variety of self-assessment tools so the therapist can continually evaluate his/her psychological functioning. Some of the assessment instruments they mention are the Stress Reaction Inventory (Yassen 1995), the F.A.M.I.L.Y. self-care assessment inventory (Eckstein 2001), and the Professional Quality of Life Scale (Stamm 2005). In this regard, Venart, Vassos, and Pitcher-Heft (2007) stress that it is the responsibility of the mental health practitioner to not only care for his/her psychological well-being but also to constantly monitor his/her psychological functioning to ensure optimal performance in treating clients.

There are also ways the mental health practitioner can learn about the latest research on the hazards associated with the mental health field and educate himself/herself about self-care practices. Bradley *et al.* (2012) emphasize that reading professional articles, attending lectures, and seminars rated high as contributors to clinicians' feelings of competence, especially in the area of self-care. In fact, Bradley *et al.* discovered that therapists who attended lectures and seminars and actively participated in the form of role playing or group discussion had the highest feelings of competence in the area of maintaining their psychological well-being. Furthermore, Bell and Robinson III (2013) showed the advantages of educating and re-educating clinicians on the effects they could potentially suffer as a result of treating clients who experienced a similar type of traumatic event. When clinicians have self-awareness of their present and past experiences and are conscious of these thoughts and emotions while treating clients, then the therapist can take the appropriate steps to ensure that this does not affect his/her psychological well-being and the treatment of his/her clients.

Final thoughts

The main purpose of writing this book was to inform the mental health professional of the many potential hazards of the profession as well as the self-care practices that can be performed to improve and/or maintain his/her psychological well-being. From personal interviews with fellow colleagues and other research studies mentioned earlier in this book, many students, early career therapists, and experienced counselors may be unaware of the vulnerabilities that they are and will be exposed to while performing psychotherapy. This lack of knowledge may result in the clinician developing disturbances and symptoms similar to that of his/her clients. As professionals who specialize in the diagnosis and treatment of psychological disorders, they may think that they are immune to or even invincible against the stressors and disturbances of their profession. This type of attitude can leave the clinician open to developing disturbances that may not only affect his/her psychological well-being, but also to losing the ability to treat clients effectively. A trap such as this can lead the counselor to exhibit a variety of psychological problems such as job burnout, anxiety, depression, and even substance abuse issues (Collins and Long 2003; Freudenberger 1990; McKenzie Deighton *et al.* 2007; Rupert and Morgan 2005). The way of safeguarding one's mental health against these types of disturbances is by being aware of their existence and consistently applying the proper safe-care techniques throughout one's professional career.

References

Abu Baker, K. (1999) 'The importance of clinical sensitivity and therapist self-awareness when working with mandatory clients.' *Family Process, 8,* 55–67.

Ackerley, G. D., Burnell, J., Holder, D. C., and Kurdek, L. A. (1988) 'Burnout among licensed psychologists.' *Psychological Psychology: Research and Practice, 19,* 624–631.

Ackerman, S. J. and Hilsenroth, M. J. (2003) 'A review of the therapist characteristics and techniques positively impacting the therapeutic alliance.' *Clinical Psychology Review, 23,* 1, 1–33.

Adams, S. A. and Riggs, S. A. (2008) 'An exploratory study of vicarious trauma among therapist trainees.' *Training and Education in Professional Psychology, 2,* 1, 26–34. doi: 10.1037/1931-3918.2.1.26.

Agate, J. R., Zabriskie, R. B., Agate, S. T., and Poff, R. (2009) 'Family leisure satisfaction and satisfaction with family life.' *Journal of Leisure Research, 41,* 205–223.

Ainsworth, F. (2002) 'Mandatory reporting of child abuse and neglect: Does it really make a difference?' *Child & Family Social Work, 7,* 57–63.

Alleman, J. R. (2001) 'Personal, practical, and personal issues in providing managed mental health care: A discussion for new psychotherapists.' *Ethics & Behavior, 11,* 413–429.

Alloy, L. B., Jacobson, N. S., and Acocella, J. (1999) *Abnormal Psychology: Current Perspectives* (8th ed.). New York: McGraw-Hill College.

ACA (American Counseling Association) (2005) *ACA Code of Ethics.* Alexandria, VA: Author.

AMHCA (American Mental Health Counselors Association) (2010) *Principles of AMHCA code of Ethics.* Accessed on September 11, 2013 at www.amhca.org/about/codeia.aspx#commitment.

APA (American Psychiatric Association) (2000) *Diagnostic and Statistical Manual of Mental Disorders* (4th ed., text revision). Washington, DC: Author.

APA (American Psychological Association) (2002) 'Ethical Principles of Psychologists and Code of Conduct.' *American Psychologist, 57,* 12, 1060–1073. doi: 10.1037/0003-066X.57.12.1060.

APA (American Psychological Association) (2010) 'Survey findings emphasize the importance of self-care for psychologists'. Accessed on June 16, 2013 at www.apapracticecentral.org/update/2010/08-31/survey.aspx.

APAPO (American Psychological Association Practice Organization) (2013) 'What occupational hazards do psychologists in professional practice face?' Accessed on November 26, 2013 at www.apapracticecentral.org/ce/self-care/well-being.aspx.

Andresen, R., Oades, L., and Caputi, P. (2003) 'The experience of recovery from schizophrenia: Towards an empirically validated stage model.' *Australian and New Zealand Journal of Psychiatry, 37,* 586–594.

Angerer, J. M. (2003) 'Job burnout.' *Journal of Employment Counseling, 40,* 98–107.

Anunciacao , P. G., Casonatto, J., and Polito, M. D. (2011) 'Blood pressure responses and heart variability after resistance exercise with different intensities and same workload.' *International SportMed Journal, 12,* 53–67.

Appelbaum, S. A. (1992) 'Evils in the private practice of psychotherapy.' *Bulletin Of The Menninger Clinic, 56,* 2, 141.

Aranda, M. (2008) 'Relationship between religious involvement and psychological well-being: A social justice perspective.' *Health & Social Work, 33,* 1, 9–21.

Archer, M. S. (2003) *Structure, Agency, and The Internal Conversation.* New York: Cambridge University Press.

Armon, G., Shirom, A., and Melamed, S. (2012) 'The big five personality factors as predictors of chances across time in burnout and its facets.' *Journal of Personality, 80,* 2, 403–427. doi: 10.1111/j.1467-6494.2011.00731.x.

Arvay, M. J. and Uhlemann, M. R. (1996) 'Counsellor stress in the field: A preliminary study.' *Canadian Journal of Counselling, 30,* 193–210.

Atchley, R. C. (2008) 'Spirituality, meaning, and the experience of aging.' *Generations, 32,* 2, 12–16.

Austad, C. S. and Hoyt, M. F. (1992) 'The managed care movement and the future of psychotherapy.' *Psychotherapy, 29,* 109–118.

Austin, L. and Kortum, J. (2004) 'Self-injury: The secret language of pain for teenagers.' *Education, 124,* 3, 517–527.

Azar, S. T. (2000) 'Preventing burnout in professionals and paraprofessionals who work with child abuse and neglect cases: A cognitive behavioral approach to supervision.' *Journal of Clinical Psychology, 56,* 643–663.

Baetz, M. and Toews, J. (2009) 'Clinical implications of research on religion, spirituality, and mental health.' *Canadian Journal of Psychiatry, 54,* 292–301.

Baird, S. and Jenkins, S. (2003) 'Vicarious traumatization, secondary traumatic stress, and burnout in sexual assault and domestic violence agency staff.' *Violence and Victims, 18,* 71–86.

Baird, K. and Kracen, A. C. (2006) 'Vicarious traumatization and secondary traumatic stress: A research synthesis.' *Counselling Psychology Quarterly, 19,* 2, 181–188. doi: 10.1080/09515070600811899.

Baker, D. C. (2003a) 'Studies of the inner life: The impact of spirituality on the quality of life.' *Quality of Life Research, 12,* 1, 51–57.

Baker, E. K. (2003b) *The Therapist's Guide to Personal and Professional Well-Being.* Washington, DC: American Psychological Association.

Baker, E. K. (2007) 'Therapist self-care: Challenges within ourselves and within the profession.' *Professional Psychology: Research & Practice, 38,* 6, 607–608.

Baldwin, S. A., Wampold, B. E., and Imel, Z. E. (2007) 'Untangling the alliance-outcome correlation: Exploring the relative importance of therapist and patient variability in the alliance.' *Journal of Consulting and Clinical Psychology, 75,* 6, 842–852.

Ballenger-Browning, K. K., Schmitz, K. J., Rothacker, J. A., Hammer, P. S., Webb-Murphy, J. A., and Johnson, D. C. (2011) 'Predictors of burnout among military mental health providers. *Military Medicine, 176,* 253–260.

Barlow, C. A. and Phelan, A. M. (2007) 'Peer collaboration: A model to support counselor self-care.' *Canadian Journal of Counseling, 41,* 3–15.

Barnett, M. (2007) 'What brings you here? An exploration of the unconscious motivations of those who choose to train and work as psychotherapists and counselors.' *Psychodynamic Practice, 13,* 257–274. doi: 10.1080/14753 630701455796.

Barnett, J. E., Baker, E. K., Elman, N. S., and Schoener, G. R. (2007) 'In pursuit of wellness: The self-care imperative.' *Professional Psychology: Research and Practice, 38,* 6, 603–612. doi: 10.1037/0735-7028.38.6.603.

Barnett, J. E. and Hillard, D. (2001) 'Psychologist distress and impairment: The availability, nature, and colleague assistance programs for psychologists.' *Professional Psychology: Research and Practice, 32,* 2, 205–210.

Barnett, J. E., Johnston, L. C., and Hillard, D. (2006) 'Psychotherapist Wellness as an Ethical Imperative.' In L. VandeCreek, and J. B. Allen (eds) *Innovations in Clinical Practice: Focus on Health and Wellness.* Sarasota, FL: Professional Resources Press.

Bearse, J. L., McMinn, M. R., Seegobin, W., and Free, K. (2013) 'Barriers to psychologists seeking mental health care.' *Professional Psychology: Research and Practice, 44,* 3, 150–157. doi: 10.1037/a0031182.

Beck, E. S. (1994) 'Mental health counselors in private practice: Reflections of a full-time practitioner (a commentary).' *Journal of Mental Health Counseling, 16,* 4, 497–505.

Beck, R. and Buchele, B. (2005) 'In the belly of the beast: Traumatic countertransference.' *International Journal of Group Psychotherapy, 55,* 31–44.

Beck, B., Halling, S., McNabb, M., Miller, D., Rowe, J., and Schulz, J. (2005) 'On navigating despair: Reports from psychotherapists.' *Journal of Religion & Health, 44,* 2, 187–205.

Beck, A. T., Rush, A. J., Shaw, B. F., and Emery, G. (1979) *Cognitive Therapy of Depression.* New York: The Guilford Press.

Becker-Weidman, A. (2006) 'Treatment for children with trauma-attachment disorders: Dyadic development psychotherapy.' *Child and Adolescent Social Work Journal, 23,* 2, 147–172. doi: 10.1007/s10560-005-0039-0.

Beddoe, A. E. and Murphy, S. O. (2004) 'Does mindfulness decrease stress and foster empathy among nursing students?' *Journal of Nursing Education, 43,* 305–312.

Bell, C. H. and Robinson III, E. H. (2013) 'Shared trauma in counseling: Information and implications for counselors.' *Journal of Mental Health Counseling, 35,* 4, 310–323.

Bemister, T. B. and Dobson, K. S. (2012) 'A reply to Mills. Record keeping: Practical implications of ethical and legal issues.' *Canadian Psychology, 53,* 143–145. doi: 10.1037/a0027681.

Bernard, H. S. (2005) 'Countertransference: The evolution of a construct.' *International Journal of Group Psychotherapy, 55,* 1, 151–60.

Besharov, D. J. and Laumann, L. A. (1996) 'Child abuse reporting.' *Society, 33,* 40–46.

Bike, D. S., Norcross, J. C., and Schatz, D. (2009) 'Processes and outcomes of psychotherapists' personal therapy: Replication and extension 20 years later.' *Psychotherapy: Theory, Research, Practice, Training, 46,* 3, 19–31. doi: 10.1037/a0015139.

Blumenthal, J. A., Babyak, M. A., Moore, K. A., Craighead, E. *et al.* (1999) 'Effects of exercise training on older patients with major depression.' *Archives of Internal Medicine, 159,* 2349–2356.

Bober, T. and Regeher, C. (2005) 'Strategies for reducing secondary or vicarious trauma: Do they work?' *Brief Treatment and Crisis Intervention, 6,* 1–9.

Boellinghaus, I., Jones, F. W and Hutton, J. (2013) 'Cultivating self-care and compassion in psychological therapists in training: The experience of practicing loving-kindness meditation.' *Training and Education in Professional Psychology,* Advance online publication. doi: 10.1037/a0033092. Accessed on September 30, 2013 at http://psycnet.apa.org/psycinfo/2013-24405-001.

Boeree, C. G. (2009) *Neurotransmitters.* Accessed on December 20, 2013 at http://webspace.ship.edu/cgboer/genpsyneurotransmitters.html.

Bohnert P. and O'Connell. (2006) 'How to avoid burning out and keep your spark.' *Current Psychiatry, 5,* 1 39–42.

Bradley, S., Drapeau, M., and DeStefano, J. (2012) 'The relationship between continuing education and perceived competence, professional support, and professional value among clinical psychologists.' *Journal of Continuing Education in the Health Professions, 32,* 1, 31–38.

Brennan, C. (2013) 'Ensuring ethical practice: Guidelines for mental health counselors in private practice.' *Journal of Mental Health Counseling, 35,* 3, 245–261.

Bride, B. E. (2007) 'Prevalence of secondary traumatic stress among social workers.' *Social Work, 52,* 1, 63–70.

Bride, B. E., Robinson, M. M., Yegidis, B., and Figley, C. R. (2004) 'Development and validation of the secondary traumatic stress scale.' *Research on Social Work Practice, 14,* 1, 27–35. doi: 10.1177/1049731503254106.

Brockhouse, R., Msetfi, R. M., Cohen, K., and Joseph, S. (2011) 'Vicarious exposure to trauma and growth in therapists: The moderating effects of sense of coherence, organizational support, and empathy.' *Journal of Traumatic Stress, 24,* 6, 735–742. doi: 10.1002/jts.20704.

Brooks, J., Holttum, S., and Lavender, A. (2002) 'Personality style, psychological adaptation and expectations of trainee clinical psychologists.' *Clinical Psychology & Psychotherapy, 9,* 4, 253–270. doi: 10.1002/cpp.318.

Broskowski, A. (1991) 'Current mental health care environment: Why managed care is necessary.' *Professional Psychology: Research and Practice, 22,* 6–14.

Brown, K. W. and Ryan, R. M. (2003) 'The benefits of being present: Mindfulness and its role in psychological well-being.' *Journal of Personality and Social Psychology, 84,* 822–848.

Brown, R. and Kulik, J. (1977) 'Flashbulb memories.' *Cognition, 5,* 73–99.

Brucato, B. and Neimeyer, G. (2009) 'Epistemology as a predicator of psychotherapists' self-care and coping.' *Journal of Constructivist Psychology, 22,* 4, 269–282. doi: 10.1080/10720530903113805.

Burch, W. R. (2009) 'The social circles of leisure: Competing explanations.' *Journal of Leisure Research, 41,* 312–335.

Burwell-Pender, L. and Halinski, K. H. (2008) 'Enhanced awareness of countertransference.' *Journal of Professional Counseling: Practice, Theory, and Research, 36,* 38–51.

Busacca, L. A., Beebe, R. S., and Toman, S. M. (2010) 'Life and work value of counselor trainees: A national survey.' *The Career Development Quarterly, 59,* 2–18.

Cain, N. (2000) 'Psychotherapists with personal histories of psychiatric hospitalization: Countertransference in wounded healers.' *Psychiatric Rehabilitation Journal, 24,* 1, 22–28. doi: 10.1037/h0095127.

Cairney, J., Faulkner, G., Veldhuizen, S., and Wade, T. J. (2009) 'Changes over time in physical activity and psychological distress among older adults.' *Canadian Journal of Psychiatry, 54,* 160–169.

Caldwell, L. L. (2005) 'Leisure and health: Why is leisure therapeutic?' *British Journal of Guidance and Counseling, 33,* 7–23. doi: 10.1080/03069880 412331335939.

Canfield, J. (2005) 'Secondary traumatization, burnout, and vicarious traumatization: A review of the literature as it relates to therapists who treat trauma.' *Smith College Studies in Social Work, 75,* 2, 81–101. doi: 10.1300/J497v75n02_06.

Caperuto, E., Dos Santos, R., Mello, M., and Costa Rosa, L. (2009) 'Effect of endurance training on the hypothalamic serotonin concentration and performance.' *Clinical & Experimental Pharmacology & Physiology, 36,* 2, 189–191. doi: 10.1111/j.1440-1681.2008.05111.x.

Carlson, T. D., Erickson, M. J., and Seewald-Marquardt, A. (2002) 'The spiritualities of therapists' lives. Using therapists' spiritual beliefs as a resource for relational ethics.' *Journal of Family Psychotherapy, 13,* 215–236.

Carmel M. J. and Friedlander, M. L. (2009) 'The relation of secondary traumatization to therapists' perceptions of the working alliance with clients who commit sexual abuse.' *Journal of Counseling Psychology, 56,* 3, 461–467. doi: 10.1037/a0015422.

Carmody, J. and Baer, R. A. (2008) 'Relationships between mindfulness practice and levels of mindfulness, medical and psychological symptoms and well-being in a mindfulness-based stress reduction program.' *Journal of Behavioral Medicine, 31,* 23–33. doi: 10.1007/s10865-007-9130-7.

Carmody, J., Baer, R. A., Lykins, E. and Olendzki, N. (2009) 'An empirical study of the mechanisms of mindfulness in a mindfulness-based reduction program.' *Journal of Clinical Psychology, 65,* 613–626. doi: 10.1002/jclp.205579.

Carruthers, C. and Hood, C. (2004) 'The power of the positive: Leisure and well-being.' *Therapeutic Recreation Journal: Special Issue on Health and Health Promotion, 38,* 2, 225–245.

Carter, R. (1998) *Mapping the Mind.* Los Angeles: Weidenfield & Nicolson.

Case, P. W. and McMinn, M. R. (2001) 'Spiritual coping and well-functioning among psychologists.' *Journal of Psychology and Theology, 29,* 1, 29–40.

Cashwell, C. S., Bentley, D. P., and Bigbee, A. (2007) 'Spirituality and counselor wellness.' *Journal of Humanistic Counseling, Education, and Development, 46,* 66–81.

Casto, C., Caldwell, C., and Salazar, C. F. (2005) 'Creating mentoring relationships between female faculty and students in counselor education: Guidelines for potential mentees and mentors.' *Journal of Counseling & Development, 83,* 3, 331–336.

CDC (Centers for Disease Control and Prevention), National Center for Injury Prevention and Control (2010) *Web-based Injury Statistics Query and Reporting System (WISQARS).* Accessed on June 10, 2013 at www.cdc.gov/injury/wisqars/index.html.

CIA (Central Intelligence Agency) (2008) The CIA World Factbook 2009. New York: Skyhorse Publishing.

Chassman, L., Kotter, J., and Madison, J. (2010) 'An exploration of counselor experiences of adolescents with sexual behavior problems.' *Journal of Counseling & Development, 88,* 269–276.

Chatters, L. M. (2000) 'Religion and health: Public health research and practice.' *Annual Review of Public Health, 21,* 335–367.

Chemtob, C. M., Bauer, G. B., Hamada, R. S., Pelowski, S. R., and Muraoka, M. Y. (1989) 'Patient suicide: Occupational hazard for psychiatrists and psychologists.' *Professional Psychology: Research and Practice, 20,* 294–300.

Chemtob, C. M., Hamada, R. S., Bauer, G., and Torigoe, R. Y. (1988) 'Patient suicide: Frequency and impact on psychologists.' *Professional Psychology: Research and Practice, 19,* 416–420.

Chiesa, A. and Serretti, A. (2009) 'Mindfulness-based stress reduction management for healthy people: A review and meta-analysis.' *The Journal of Alternate and Complementary Medicine, 15,* 593–600. doi: 10.1089/acm.2008.0495.

Chrestman, K. R. (1999) 'Secondary Exposure to Trauma and Self Reported Distress among Therapists.' In B. H. Stamm (ed.) *Secondary Traumatic Stress: Self Care Issues for Clinicians, Researchers, and Educators.* Lutherville, MD: Sidran Press.

Christianson, C. L. and Everall, R. D. (2009) 'Breaking the silence: School counsellors' experiences of client suicide.' *British Journal of Guidance & Counselling, 37,* 157–168. doi: 10.1080/03069880902728580.

Christopher, J. C. and Maris, J. A. (2010) 'Integrating mindfulness as a self-care into counseling and psychotherapy training.' *Counselling and Psychotherapy Research, 10,* 114–125. doi: 10.1080./14733141003750285.

Cieslak, R., Shoji, K., Douglas, A., Melville, E., Luszcynska, A., and Benight, C. C. (2013) 'A meta-analysis of the relationship between job burnout and secondary traumatic stress among workers with indirect exposure to trauma.' *Psychological Services.* Advanced online publication. doi: 10.1037/a0033798.

Clarke, S., Oades, L., Crowe, T., Caputi, P., and Deane, F. (2009) 'The role of symptom distress and goal attainment in promoting aspects of psychological recovery for consumers with enduring mental illness. *Journal of Mental Health, 18,* 5, 389–397.

Cloninger, C. R., Pryzbeck, T. R., Svrakie, D. M., and Wetzel, R. D. (1994) *The Temperament and Character Inventory (TCI): A Guide to its Development and Use.* St. Louis, MO: Center for Psychobiology of Personality, Washington University.

Cohen, K. and Collens, P. (2012) 'The impact of trauma work on trauma workers: A metasynthesis on vicarious trauma and vicarious posttraumatic growth.' *Psychological Trauma: Theory, Research, Practice, and Policy, 5,* 6, 570–580. doi: 10.1037/a0030388.

Cohn, T. J. and Hastings, S. L. (2013) 'Building a practice in rural settings: Special considerations.' *Journal of Mental Health Counseling 35,* 3, 228–244.

Collins, G. R. (1995) *How to be a People Helper.* Wheaton, IL: Tyndale House Publishers Inc.

Collins, S. and Long, A. (2003) 'Working with the psychological effects of trauma: Consequences for mental healthcare workers – a literature review.' *Journal of Psychiatric and Mental Health Nursing, 10,* 417–424.

Cook, C. (2011) 'The faith of the psychiatrist.' *Mental Health, Religion & Culture, 14,* 1, 9–17. doi: 10.1080/13674671003622673.

Cook, S. H. (1999) 'The self in self-awareness.' *Journal of Advanced Nursing, 29,* 1292–1299.

Cook, S. W., Borman, P. D., Moore, M. A., and Kunkel, M. A. (2000) 'College students' perceptions of spiritual people and religious people.' *Journal of Psychology and Theology, 28,* 125–137.

Cooper-Patrick, L., Ford, D. E., Mead, L. A., Chang, P. P., and Klag, M. J. (1997) 'Exercise and depression in midlife: A prospective study.' *American Journal of Public Health, 87,* 670–673.

Cornille, T. A. and Meyers, T. W. (1999) 'Secondary traumatic stress among child protective service workers: Prevalence, severity and predictive factors.' *Traumatology, 5,* 1, 15–31.

Corrigan, P., McCorkle, B., Schell, B., and Kidder, K. (2003) 'Religion and spirituality in the lives of people with serious mental illness.' *Community Mental Health Journal, 39,* 6, 487–499.

Costa, L. and Altekruse, M. (1994) 'Duty-to-warn guidelines for mental health counselors.' *Journal of Counseling & Development, 72,* 4, 346–350.

Costa, P. T. Jr. and McCrae, R. (1987) 'Neuroticism, somatic complaints, and disease: Is the bark worse than the bite?' *Journal of Personality, 55,* 2, 299–316.

Costa, P. T. Jr. and McCrae, R. (1994) 'Stability and Change in Personality from Adolescence through Adulthood.' In C. F. Halverson, G. A. Kohnstamm and R. P. Martin (eds) *The Developing Structure of Temperament and Personality from Infancy to Adulthood.* Hillsdale, NJ: Lawrence Erlbaum Associates, Inc.

Coster, J. S. and Schwebel, M. (1997) 'Well-functioning in professional psychologists.' *Professional Psychology: Research and Practice, 28,* 1, 5–13.

Coyle, C. T. and Enright, R. D. (1997) 'Forgiveness intervention with postabortion men.' *Journal of Consulting and Clinical Psychology, 65,* 1042–1046.

Craig, C. D. and Sprang, G. (2010) 'Compassion satisfaction, compassion fatigue, and burnout in a national sample of trauma treatment therapists.' *Anxiety, Stress, & Coping, 23,* 3, 319–339. doi: 10.1080/10615800903085818.

Crawford, M. E., Handal, P. J., and Wiener, R. L. (1989) 'The relationship between religion and mental health/distress.' *Review of Religious Research, 31,* 1, 16–22.

Creamer, T. L. and Liddle, B. J. (2005) 'Secondary traumatic stress among disaster mental health workers responding to the September 11 attacks.' *Journal of Traumatic Stress, 18,* 1, 89–96. doi: 10.1002/jts.20008.

Creek, J. (2008) 'Creative leisure opportunities.' *Neuro Rehabilitation, 23,* 299–304.

Crenshaw, W. B. and Lichtenberg, J. W. (1993) 'Child abuse and limits of confidentiality: Forewarning practices.' *Behavioral Sciences and the Law, 11,* 181–192.

Crowell, K. and Levi, B. H. (2012) 'Mandated reporting thresholds for community professions.' *Child Welfare, 91,* 35–53.

Cruise, K. E., Bucks, R. S., Loftus, A. M., Newton, R. U., Pegoraro, R. R., and Thomas, M. G. (2011). 'Exercise and Parkinson's: Benefits for cognition and quality of life.' *Acta Neurologica Scandinavica, 123,* 13–19.

Cummins, P. N., Massey, L., and Jones, A. (2007) 'Keeping ourselves well: Strategies for promoting and maintaining counselor wellness.' *Journal of Humanistic Counseling, Education & Development, 46,* 1, 35–49.

Cummins, R. A. and Nistico, H. (2001) 'Maintaining life satisfaction: The role of the positive cognitive bias.' *Journal of Happiness Studies, 3,* 37–69.

Cunningham, M. (2003) 'Impact of trauma work on social work clinicians: Empirical findings.' *Social Work, 48,* 4, 451–459.

Dam, A., Keijsers, G., Verbraak, M., Eling, P., and Becker, E. (2012) 'Burnout patients primed with success did not perform better on a cognitive task than burnout patients primed with failure.' *Psychology, 3,* 583–589. doi: 10.4236/psych.2012.38087.

Dannenfelser, R. (2007) 'Mentors needed.' *Contemporary Sexuality, 41,* 5.

Danzinger, P. R. and Welfel, E. R. (2001) 'The impact of managed care on mental health counselors: A survey of perceptions, practices, and compliances with ethical standards.' *Journal of Mental Health Counseling, 23,* 137–150.

Darden, A. A. (2011) 'Psychologists' experiences of grief after client suicide: A qualitative study.' *Omega: Journal of Death & Dying, 63,* 4, 317–342.

Davidson, J. and Davidson, T. (1996) 'Confidentiality and managed care: Ethical and legal concerns.' *Health & Social Work, 21,* 208–216.

Daw, B. and Joseph, S. (2007) 'Qualified therapists' experiences of personal therapy.' *Counseling and Psychotherapy, 7,* 227–232. doi: 10.1080./14733140701709064.

Day, J. (1994) 'Narratives of "Belief" and "Unbelief" in Young Adult Accounts of Religious Experience and Moral Development.' In D. Hutsebaut and J. Corveleyn (eds) *Belief and Unbelief: Psychological Perspectives.* Amsterdam: Rodopi.

Day, J. (1999) 'Exemplary Sierrans: Moral Influences.' In R. Mosher, D. Connor, K. Kalliel, J. Day, N. Yakota, M. Porter, and J. Whiteley (eds) *Moral Action in Young Adulthood.* Columbia, SC: National Resource Center for the First-Year Experience and Students in Transition, University of South Carolina Press.

Day, J. M. (2010) 'Religion, spirituality, and positive psychology in adulthood: A developmental view.' *Journal of Adult Development, 17,* 4, 215–229.

Day-Vines, N. L. and Holcomb-McCoy, C. (2007) 'Wellness among African American counselors.' *Journal of Humanistic Counseling, Education and Development, 46,* 82–97.

Delaney, H. D., Miller, W. R., and Bisono, A. M. (2013) 'Religiosity and spirituality among psychologists: A survey of clinician members of the American Psychological Association.' *Spirituality in Clinical Practice, 1,* S, 95–106.

DeLettre, J. L. and Sobell, L. C. (2010) 'Keeping psychotherapy notes separate from the patient record.' *Clinical Psychology and Psychotherapy, 17,* 160–163. doi: 10.1002/cpp.654.

Devilly, G. J., Wright, R., and Varker, T. (2009) 'Vicarious trauma, secondary traumatic stress or simply burnout? Effect of trauma therapy on mental health professionals.' *Australian and New Zealand Journal of Psychiatry, 43,* 4, 373–385.

Dewane, C. M. (1978) 'Humor in therapy.' *Social Work, 23,* 6, 508–510.

DiCaccavo, A. (2002) 'Investigating individuals' motivations to become counselling psychologists: The influence of early caretaking roles within the family.' *Psychology and Psychotherapy: Theory, Research and Practice, 75,* 4, 463–472. doi: 10.1348/147608302321151943.

DiCaccavo, A. (2006) 'Working with parentification: Implications for clients and counselling psychologists.' *Psychology and Psychotherapy: Theory, Research and Practice, 79,* 3, 469–478.

Diener, E., Tay, L., and Myers, D. G. (2011) 'The religion paradox: If religion makes people happy, why are so many dropping out?' *Journal of Personality and Social Psychology, 6,* 1278–1290.

DiMarco, M. and Zoline, S. S. (2004) 'Duty to warn in the context of HIV/AIDS-related psychotherapy: Decision making among psychologists.' *Counseling & Clinical Psychology Journal, 1,* 68–85.

Dirmaier, J., Harfst, T., Koch, U., and Schulz, H. (2006) 'Therapy goals in inpatient psychotherapy: Differences between diagnostic groups and psychotherapeutic orientations.' *Clinical Psychology and Psychotherapy, 13,* 34–46. doi: 10.1002/cpp.470.

Dixon, W., Mauzey, E., and Hall, C. (2003) 'Physical activity and exercise: Implications for Counselors.' *Journal of Counseling & Development, 81,* 502–505.

Dorn, F. J. (1984) 'The social influence model: A social psychological approach to counseling.' *The Personnel and Guidance Journal, 62,* 342–345.

Drogin, E. Y., Connell, M., Foote, W. E., and Sturm, C. A. (2010) 'The American Psychological Association's revised "record keeping guidelines": Implications for the practitioner.' *Professional Psychology: Research and Practice, 41,* 236–243. doi: 10.1037/a0019001.

D'Souza, F., Egan, S., and Rees, C. (2011) 'The relationship between perfectionism, stress and burnout in clinical psychologists.' *Behaviour Change, 28,* 1, 17–28. doi: 10.1375/bech.28.1.17.

Dubert, P. M. (2002) 'Physical activity and exercise: Recent advances and current challenges.' *Journal of Consulting and Clinical Psychology, 70,* 526–536. doi: 10.1037/0022-006X.70.3.526.

Dubrow, M. L. (2011) 'Healthcare professionals: Commission your own self-care quality.' *Healthcare Counseling & Psychotherapy, 11,* 4–11.

Dupuis, S. L. and Smale, B. J. (1995) 'An examination of the relationship between psychological well-being and depression and leisure activity participation among adults.' *Society and Leisure, 18,* 67–92.

Dutton, M. A. and Rubinstein, F. L. (1995) 'Working with People with PTSD: Research Implications.' In C. R. Figley (ed.) *Compassion Fatigue: Secondary Traumatic Stress Disorder in Helpers.* New York: Brunner/Mazel.

Dycian, A., Fishman, G., and Bleich, A. (1994) 'Suicide and self-inflicted injuries.' *Aggressive Behavior, 20,* 9–16.

Dyckman, J. (1997) 'The impatient therapist: Managed care and countertransference.' *American Journal of Psychotherapy, 51,* 329–403.

Dyer, W. W. and Vriend, J. (1977) 'A goal-setting checklist for counselors.' *Personnel and Guidance Journal, 55,* 469–471.

Eby, M. D., Chin, J. L., Rollock, D., Schwartz, J. P., and Worrell, F. C. (2011) 'Professional psychology training in the era of a thousand flowers: Dilemmas and challenges for the future.' *Training and Education in Professional Psychology, 5,* 57–68. doi: 10.1037/a0023462.

Eckstein, D. (2001) 'A F.A.M.I.L.Y. approach to self-care: Creating a healthy balance.' *The Family Journal, 9,* 327–338.

Edmundson, M. (2007) *The Death of Sigmund Freud: The Legacy of his Last Days.* New York: Bloomsbury.

Egan, G. (1998) *The Skilled Helper: A Problem Approach to Helping* (6th ed.). Pacific Grove, CA: Brooks/Cole Publishing.

Egan, G. (2013) *The Skilled Helper: A Problem-Management and Opportunity-Developmental Approach to Helping* (10th ed.). Belmont, CA: Brooks/Cole.

Eichhorn, J. (2011) 'Happiness for believers? Contextualizing the effects of religiosity on life-satisfaction.' *European Sociological Review, 28,* 583–593. doi: 10.1093/esr/jcr027.

El-Ghoroury, N. H., Galper, D. L., Sawaqdeh, A., and Bufka, L. F. (2012) 'Stress, coping, and barriers to wellness among psychology graduate students.' *Training and Education in Professional Psychology, 6,* 122–134. doi: 10.1037/a0028768.

Elliot, A. J. and Church, M. A. (2002) 'Client-articulated avoidance goals in the therapy context.' *Journal of Counseling Psychology, 2,* 243–254.

Elliott, D. M. and Guy, J. D. (1993) 'Mental health professionals versus non-mental-health professionals: Childhood trauma and adult functioning.' *Professional Psychology: Research and Practice, 24,* 1, 83–90. doi: 10.1037/0735-7028.24.1.83.

Ellis, A. (2005) 'Why I (really) became a therapist.' *Journal of Clinical Psychology, 61,* 8, 945–948. doi: 10.1002/jclp.20166.

Ellison, C. (1983) 'Spiritual well-being: Conceptualization and measurement.' *Journal of Psychology and Theology, 11,* 330–340.

Ellison, C. G. (1998) 'Introduction to symposium: Religion, health, and well-being.' *Journal for the Scientific Study of Religion, 37,* 692–694.

Ellison, C. G., Gay, D. A., and Glass, T. A. (1989) 'Does religious commitment contribute to individual life satisfaction.' *Social Forces, 68,* 1, 100–123.

Emerson, S. and Markos, P. A. (1996) 'Signs and symptoms of the impairment counselor.' *Journal of Humanistic Education & Development, 34,* 108–117.

Emery, S., Wade, T. D., and McLean, S. (2009) 'Associations among therapist beliefs, personal resources and burnout in clinical psychologists.' *Behaviour Change, 26,* 83–96.

Erden, N. S., Toplu, D., and Yashoglu, M. M. (2013) 'Mediating effects of job demands on the relationship between type A personality and workaholism: A study on Turkish workers.' *Journal of Organizational Behavior, 12,* 2, 7–9.

Erickson, R. (1982) *The Life Cycle Completed: A Review.* New York: Norton.

Erlangsen, A., Bille-Brahe U., and Jeune, B. (2003) 'Differences in suicide between the old and the oldest old.' *Journal of Gerontology, 58,* 314–322.

Everall, R. D. and Paulson, B. T. (2004) 'Burnout and secondary traumatic stress: Impact on ethical behaviour.' *Canadian Journal of Counseling, 38,* 1, 25–35.

Fang, F., Kemp, J., Jawandha, A., Juros, J. *et al.* (2007) 'Encountering patient suicide: A resident's experience.' *Academic Psychiatry, 31,* 340–44.

Fagan, T. J., Ax, R. K., Liss, M., Resnick, R. J., and Moody, S. (2007) 'Professional education and training: How satisfied are we? An exploratory study.' *Training and Education in Professional Psychology, 1,* 13–25.

Farber, B. A. and Heifetz, L. J. (1981) 'The satisfactions and stresses of psychotherapeutic work: A factor analysis study.' *Professional Psychology, 12,* 621–630.

Farber, B. A., Manevich, I., Metzger, J., and Saypol, E. (2005) 'Choosing psychotherapy as a career: Why did we cross that road?' *Journal of Clinical Psychology, 61,* 8, 1009–1031. doi: 10.1002/jclp.20174.

Fauth, J. and Hayes, J. A. (2006) 'Counselors' stress appraisals as predictors of countertransference behavior with male clients.' *Journal of Counseling and Development: JCD, 84,* 4, 430–439. doi: 1122832241.

Fehring, R. J., Brennan, P. F., and Keller, M. L. (1987) 'Psychological and spiritual well-being in college students.' *Research in Nursing and Health, 10,* 391–398.

Feist, J. and Feist, G. J. (1998) *Theories of Personality* (4th ed.). New York: McGraw Hill.

Feldman-Summers, S. and Jones, G. (1984) 'Psychological impacts of sexual contact between therapists or other health care practitioners and their clients.' *Journal of Consulting and Clinical Psychology, 52,* 6, 1054–1061. doi: 10.1037/0022-006X.52.6.1054.

Feller, C. P. and Cottone, R. R. (2003) 'The importance of empathy in the therapeutic alliance. *Journal of Humanistic Counseling, Education, & Development, 42,* 1, 53–61.

Figley, C. R. (1995) 'Compassion Fatigue as Secondary Traumatic Stress Disorder: An Overview.' In C. R. Figley (ed.) *Compassion Fatigue: Coping with Secondary Traumatic Stress Disorder in Those Who Treat the Traumatized.* New York: Brunner/Mazel.

Figley, C. R. (1999) 'Compassion Fatigue: Toward a New Understanding of the Cost of Caring.' In B. H. Stamm (ed.) *Secondary Traumatic Stress: Self-Care Issues for Clinicians, Researchers, and Educators* (2nd ed.). Lutherville, MD: Sidran Press.

Figley, C. R. (2002) 'Compassion fatigue: Psychotherapists' chronic lack of care.' *Journal of Clinical Psychology, 58,* 11, 1433–1441. doi: 10.1002/jclp.10090.

Fingerman, K. L. and Hay, E. L. (2002) 'Searching under the streetlight? Age biases in the personal and family relationships literature.' *Personal Relationships, 9,* 415–433.

Flaherty, A. W. (2011) 'Brain illness and creativity: Mechanisms and treatment.' *Canadian Journal of Psychiatry, 56,* 3, 132–143.

Follette, V. M., Polusny, M. M., and Milbeck, K. (1994) 'Mental health and law enforcement professionals: Trauma history, psychological symptoms, and impact of providing services to child sexual abuse survivors.' *Professional Psychology: Research and Practice, 25,* 275–282.

Fox, K. (1999) 'The influence of physical activity on mental well-being.' *Public Health Nutrition, 2,* 411–418.

Fox, R. and Cooper, M. (1998) 'The effects of suicide on the private practitioner: A professional and personal perspective.' *Clinical Social Work Journal, 26,* 143–157.

Franzini, L. R. (2001) 'Humor in therapy: The case for training therapists in its uses and risks.' *Journal of General Psychology, 128,* 2, 170–193.

Freshwater, D. (2002) 'The Therapeutic Use of Self.' In D. Freshwater (ed.) *Therapeutic Nursing: Improving Patient Care Through Self-Awareness and Reflection.* London: Sage.

Freud, S. (1958) 'Remembering, Repeating, and Working-Through.' In J. Strachey (ed. and trans.) *The Standard Edition of the Complete Psychological Works of Sigmund Freud, Vol. 12.* London: Hogarth Press. (Original work published 1914.)

Freud, S. (1959) 'Future Prospects of Psychoanalytic Psychotherapy.' In J. Strachey (ed. and trans.) *The Standard Edition of the Complete Psychological Works of Sigmund Freud: Vol.11.* London: Hogarth Press. (Original work published 1910.)

Freudenberger, H. J. (1974) 'Staff burn-out.' *Journal of Social Issues, 30,* 159–165.

Freudenberger, H. J. (1975) 'The staff burnout syndrome in alternative institutions.' *Psychotherapy: Theory, Research, and Practice, 12,* 73–82.

Freudenberger, H. J. (1977) 'Burn-out: Occupational hazards of the child care worker.' *Journal of Research and Practice in Children's Services, 6,* 90–99.

Freudenberger, H. J. (1990) 'Hazards of psychotherapeutic practice.' *Psychotherapy in Private Practice, 8,* 31–34.

Friedman, M. and Ulmer, D. (1984) *Treating Type A Behavior and Your Heart*. New York: Alfred A. Knopf.

Frisby, C. L. (1998) 'Culture and Cultural Differences.' In J. H. Sandoval, C. L. Frisby, K. F. Geisinger, J. D. Scheuneman, and J. R. Grenier (eds) *Test Interpretation and Diversity: Achieving Equity in Assessment*. Washington, DC: American Psychological Association. doi: 10.1037/10279-003.

Fujimura, L. F., Weis, D. M., and Cochran, J. R. (1985) 'Suicide: Dynamics and implications for counseling.' *Journal of Counseling & Development, 63*, 612–615.

Fulton, P R. (2005) 'Mindfulness as Clinical Training.' In C. K. Germer, R. D. Siegel and P. R. Fulton (eds) *Mindfulness and Psychotherapy*. New York: Guilford Press.

Galantino, M. L., Baime, M., Maguire, M., Szapary, P. O., and Farrar, J. T. (2005) 'Short communication: Association of psychological and physiological measures of stress in healthcare professionals during an 8-week mindfulness meditation program: Mindfulness in practice.' *Stress and Health, 21*, 255–261. doi: 10.1002/smi.1062.

Gammelgaard, J. (2003) 'The unconscious: A re-reading of the Freudian concept.' *The Scandinavian Psychoanalytic Review, 26*, 1, 11–21.

Garber, C. E., Blissmer, B., Deschenes, M. R., Franklin, B. A. *et al.* (2011) 'Quantity and quality of exercise for developing and maintaining cardiorespiratory, musculoskeletal, and neuromotor fitness in apparently healthy adults: Guidance for prescribing exercise.' *Medicine & Science in Sorts & Exercise, 43*, 1334–1359.

Gass, C. S. (1984) 'Therapeutic influence as a function of therapist attire and the seating arrangement in an initial interview,' *Journal of Clinical Psychology, 40*, 52–57.

Geller, J. D., Norcross, J. C., and Orlinsky, D. E. (eds) (2005) *The Psychotherapist's Own Psychotherapy: Patient and Clinician Perspectives*. New York: Oxford University Press.

Gelso, C. J. and Hayes, J. A. (2001) 'Countertransference management.' *Psychotherapy, 38*, 418–422.

Gendlin, E. T. (1996) *Focusing Oriented Psychotherapy: A Manual of the Experiential Method*. New York: Guilford Press.

Gentile, S. R., Asamen, J. K., Harmell, P. H., and Weathers, R. (2002) 'The stalking of psychologists by their clients.' *Professional Psychology: Research and Practice, 33*, 490–494. doi: 10.1037/0735-7028.33.5.490.

Gibson, D. M., Dollarhide, C. T., and Moss, J. M. (2010) 'Professional identity development: A grounded theory of transformational tasks of new counselors.' *Counselor Education & Supervision, 50*, 10, 21–38.

Gibson, J. A., Grey, I. M., and Hastings, R. P. (2009) 'Supervisor support as a predictor of burnout and therapeutic self-efficacy in therapists working in ABA schools.' *Journal of Autism & Developmental Disorders, 39*, 7, 1024–1030. doi: 10.1007/s10803-009-0709-4.

Gibson, F., McGrath, A., and Reid, N. (1989) 'Occupational stress in social work.' *British Journal of Social Work, 19*, 1, 1–16.

Gilroy, P., Carroll, L., and Murra, J. (2002) 'A preliminary survey of counseling psychologists' personal experiences with depression and treatment.' *Professional Psychology: Research and Practice, 33*, 4, 402–407.

Gitlin, M. G. (1999) 'A psychiatrist's reaction to a patient's suicide.' *The American Journal of Psychiatry, 156*, 1630–1640.

Gitlin, M. G. (2007) 'Aftermath of a tragedy: Reaction of psychiatrists to patient suicides.' *Psychiatric Annals, 37*, 684–687.

Glaser, R. D. and Thorpe, J. S. (1986) 'Unethical intimacy: A survey of sexual contact and advances between psychology educators and female graduate students.' *American Psychologist, 41*, 1, 43–51.

Glosoff, H., Garcia, J., Herlihy, B., and Remley, T. (1999) 'Managed care: Ethical considerations for counselors.' *Counseling & Values, 44*, 8–17.

Glover, T. D. and Parry, D. C. (2008) 'Friendships developed subsequent to a stressful life event: The interplay of leisure, social capital, and health.' *Journal of Leisure Research, 40*, 208–230.

Goddard, A. W., Ball, S. G., Martinez, J., Robinson, M. J. *et al.* (2010) 'Current perspectives of the roles of the central norepinephrine system in anxiety and depression.' *Depression and Anxiety, 27*, 339–350.

Goldfarb, A, H. and Jamurtas, A. Z. (1997) 'B-Endorphin response to exercise.' *Sports Medicine, 24*, 1, 8–16.

Goncher, I. D., Sherman, M. F., Barnett, J. E., and Haskins, D. (2013) 'Programmatic perceptions of self-care emphasis and quality of life among graduate trainees in clinical psychology: The mediational role of self-care utilization.' *Training and Education in Professional Psychology, 7*, 1, 53–60.

Good, G. E. and Beitman, B. D. (2006) *Counseling and Psychotherapy Essentials: Integrating Theories, Skills, and Practices.* New York: W. W. Norton & Company, Inc.

Goodman, T. A. (1985) 'From Tarasoff to Hopper: The evolution of the therapist's duty to protect third parties.' *Behavioral Sciences & the Law, 3*, 195–225. Accessed on January 17 at http://ezproxy.library.capella.edu/login?url=http://search.ebscohost.com/login.aspx?direct =true&db=a2h&AN=12584420&site=ehost-live.

Gostin, L. O. (2002) *Public Health Law and Ethics: A Reader* (chapter 10). Accessed on July 28, 2013 at www.publichealthlaw.net/Reader/docs/Tarasoff.pdf.

Grafanaki, S., Pearson, D., Cini, F., Godula, D. *et al.* (2005) 'Sources of renewal: A qualitative study on the experience and role of leisure in the life of counselors and psychologists.' *Counseling Psychology Quarterly, 18*, 31–40.

Granello, D. (2010) 'A suicide crisis intervention model with 25 practical strategies for implementation.' *Journal of Mental Health Counseling, 32*, 3, 218–235.

Grant, J. and Schofield, M. (2007) 'Career-long supervision: Patterns and perspectives.' *Counselling & Psychotherapy Research, 7*, 1, 3–11.

Green, L. (1993) 'Containing and the patient's observation of the therapist's countertransference.' *Clinical Social Work Journal, 21*, 375–383.

Green, M. and Elliott, M. (2010) 'Religion, health, and psychological well-being.' *Journal of Religion and Health, 49*, 2, 149–163.

Green, A. G. and Hawley, G. C. (2009) 'Early career psychologists: Understanding, engaging, and mentoring tomorrow's leaders.' *Professional Psychology: Research and Practice, 40*, 2, 206–212. doi: 10.1037/a0012504.

Greenburg, S. L., Lewis, G. J. and Johnson, M. (1985) 'Peer consultation groups for private practitioners.' *Professional Psychology: Research and Practice, 16*, 3, 437–447.

Greer, J. A. (2002) 'Where to turn for help: Responses to inadequate clinical supervision.' *The Clinical Supervisor, 21*, 1, 135–143.

Grossman, L. R. and Koocher, G. P. (2010) 'Privacy, confidentiality, and privilege of health records and psychotherapy notes in custody cases.' *American Journal of Family Law, 24*, 1, 41–50.

Gulfi, A., Dransart, A. A., Heeb, J., and Gutjahr, E. (2010) 'The impact of patient suicide on the professional reactions and practices of mental health caregivers and social workers.' *Crisis, 31,* 202–210. doi: 10.1027/0227-5910/a000027.

Hall, E. E., Ekkekakis, P., and Petruzzello, S. J. (2002) 'The affective beneficence of vigorous exercise revisited.' *British Journal of Health Psychology, 7,* 47–66.

Hamilton, D. M. and Jackson, M. H. (1998) 'Spiritual development: Paths and processes.' *Journal of Instructional Psychology, 25,* 262–270.

Hammerschlag, C. A. (1988) *The Dancing Healers.* San Francisco: Harper & Row.

Hannan, C. (2010, April) 'Samantha Kuberski, six years old, youngest suicide victim in Oregon State history.' Accessed on November 12, 2012 at www.seattleweekly.com/dailyweekly/2010/04/samantha_kuberski_six-years-ol.php.

Hannigan, B., Edwards, D., and Burnard, P. (2004) 'Stress and stress management in clinical psychology: findings from a systematic review.' *Journal of Mental Health, 13,* 3, 235–245.

Hansen, J. T. (2009) 'Self-awareness revisited: Reconsidering a core value of the counseling profession.' *Journal of Counseling & Development, 87,* 186–193.

Hansen, C. J., Stevens, L. C., and Coast, J. R. (2001) 'Exercise duration and mood: How much is enough to feel better?' *Health Psychology, 20,* 4, 267–275.

Hansson, A., Hilleras, P., and Forsell, Y. (2005) 'What kind of self-care strategies do people report using and is there an association with well-being?' *Social Indicators Research, 73,* 133–139. doi: 10.1007/s11205-004-0995-3.

Harris, S. M. and Busby, D. M. (1998) 'Therapist physical attractiveness: An unexplored influence on client disclosure.' *Journal of Martial & Family Therapy, 24,* 251–257.

Harrison, R. L. and Westwood, M. J. (2009) 'Preventing vicarious traumatization of mental health therapists: Identifying protective practices.' *Psychotherapy: Theory, Research, Practice, Training, 46,* 2, 203–219. doi: 10.1037/a0016081.

Hart, N., McGowan, J., Minati, L., and Critchley, H. D. (2013) 'Emotional regulation and bodily sensation: Interoceptive awareness is intact in borderline personality disorder.' *Journal of Personality Disorders, 27,* 4, 506–518.

Hatcher, S. L., Kipper-Smith, A., Waddell, M., Uhe, M. *et al.* (2012) 'What therapists learn from psychotherapy clients: Effects on personal and professional lives.' *The Qualitative Report, 17,* 95, 1–21.

Hauck, E. L., Synder, L. A., and Cox-Fuenzalida, L. (2008) 'Workload variability and social support: Effects on stress and performance.' *Current Psychology, 27,* 112–125. doi: 10.1007/s12144-008-9026-x.

Hawkins, P. and Shohet, S. (2000) *Supervision in the Helping Professions.* Philadelphia: Open University Press.

Hawton, K. and James, A. (2005) 'Suicide and deliberate self-harm in young people.' *British Medical Journal, 330,* 891–894.

Hawton, K. and Harriss, L. (2008) 'How often does deliberate self-harm occur relative to suicide: A study of variations by gender and age.' *Suicide & Life–Threatening Behavior, 38,* 650–660. Accessed on January 15, 2010 at http://proquest.umi.com/pqdweb?did=1634411391&sid=1&Fmt=4&clientId=86884&RQT=309&VName=PQD

Hayes, J. A., Yeh, Y. and Eisenberg, A. (2007) 'Good grief and not-so-good grief: Countertransference in bereavement therapy.' *Journal of Clinical Psychology, 63,* 4, 345–355. doi: 10.1002/jclp.20353.

Heilbrun, A. B. Jr. and Friedberg, E. B. (1988) 'Type A personality, self-control, and vulnerability to stress.' *Journal of Personality Assessment, 52,* 3, 420–433.

Heinrich, R. K., Corbin J. L., and Thomas, K. R. (1990) 'Counseling Native Americans.' *Journal of Counseling and Development , 69,* 128–133.

Heintzman, P. (2008) 'Leisure-spiritual coping: A model for therapeutic recreation and leisure services.' *Therapeutic Recreation Journal, 42,* 56–73.

Hellman, I. D. and Morrison, T. L. (1987) 'Practice setting and type of caseload as factors in psychotherapist stress.' *Psychotherapy, 24,* 3, 427–433.

Hendin, H., Haas, A. P., Maltsberger, J. T., Koestner, B., and Szanto, K. (2006) 'Problems in psychotherapy with suicidal patients.' *Journal of American Psychiatry, 163,* 67–72.

Hendin, H., Haas, A. P., Maltsberger, J. T., Szanto, K., and Rabinowicz, H. (2004) 'Factors contributing to therapists' distress after the suicide of a patient.' *Journal of American Psychiatry, 161,* 1442–1446.

Henry, W. E., Sims, J. H., and Spray, S. L. (1971) *The Fifth Profession: Becoming a Psychotherapist.* San Francisco: Jossey-Bass.

Henry, W. E., Sims, J. H., and Spray, S. L. (1973) *Public and Private Lives of Psychotherapists.* San Francisco: Jossey-Bass.

Herman, J. L. (1992) *Trauma and Recovery: The Recovery of Violence: From Domestic Abuse to Political Terror.* New York: Basic Books.

Hernandez, P., Gangsei, D., and Engstrom, D. (2007) 'Vicarious resilience: A new concept in work with those who survive trauma.' *Family Process, 46,* 229–241.

Hesse, A. R. (2002) 'Secondary trauma: How working with trauma survivors affects therapists.' *Clinical Social Work Journal, 30,* 293–309.

Hibel, J. and Polanco, M. (2010) 'Tuning the ear: Listening in narrative therapy.' *Journal of Systemic Therapies, 29,* 51–66.

Hill, N. R. (2004) 'The challenges experienced by pretenured faculty members in counselor education: A wellness perspective.' *Counselor Education and Supervision, 44,* 135–146.

Hillman, C. H., Erickson, K., I., and Kramer, A. F. (2008) 'Be smart, exercise your heart: Exercise effects on brain and cognition.' *Nature Reviews Neuroscience, 9,* 58–65.

Himle, J. A., Chatters, L. M., Taylor, R. J., and Nguyen, A. (2011) 'The relationship between obsessive-compulsive disorder and religious faith: Clinical characteristics and implications for treatment.' *Psychology of Religion and Spirituality, 3,* 241–258. doi: 10.1037/a0023478.

Hitch, D. (2012) 'Better access to mental health: Mapping the evidence supporting participation in meaningful occupations.' *Advances in Mental Health, 10,* 181–189.

Hodges, S. (2002) 'Mental health, depression, and dimensions of spirituality and religion.' *Journal of Adult Development, 9,* 2, 109–115.

Hoffman, R. (1995) 'Sexual dual relationships in counseling: Confronting the issues.' *Counseling and Values, 40*, 1, 15–23. doi: 10.1002/j.2161-007X.1995.tb00383.x.

Holmgren, E., Gosman-Hedstrom, G., Lindstrom, B., and Wester, P. (2010) 'What is the benefit of a high-intensive exercise program on health-related quality of life and depression after stroke? A randomized controlled trial.' *Advances in Physiotherapy, 2010,* 125–133.

Holmqvist, R. (2001) 'Patterns of consistency and deviation in therapists' countertransference feelings.' *The Journal of Psychotherapy Practice and Research, 10*, 2, 104–117.

Holtermann, A., Mortensen, O. S., Burr, H., Sogaard, K., Gyntelberg, F., and Suadicani, P. (2009) 'The interplay between physical activity at work and during leisure time–risk of ischemic heart disease and all-cause mortality in middle-aged Caucasian men.' *Scandinavian Journal of Work, Environment & Health, 35*, 466–474.

Hooper, L. M., DeCoster, J., White, N., and Voltz, M. L. (2011) 'Characterizing the magnitude of the relation between self-reported childhood parentification and adult psychopathology: A meta-analysis.' *Journal of Clinical Psychology, 67*, 10, 1028–1043. doi: 10.1002/jclp.20807.

Horn, P. J. (1994) 'Therapists' psychological adaption to client suicide.' *Psychotherapy, 31,* 190–195.

Horowitz, R. (2008) 'Hope and expectation in the psychotherapy of the long-term mentally ill.' *Bulletin of the Menninger Clinic, 72,* 237–258.

Hotelling, K. (1988) 'Ethical, legal, and administrative options to address sexual relationships between counselor and client.' *Journal of Counseling & Development, 67*, 4, 233–237. doi: 10.1002/j.1556-6676.1988.tb02589.x.

Howard, F. (2008) 'Managing stress or enhancing wellbeing? Positive psychology's contributions to clinical supervision.' *Australian Psychologist, 43*, 2, 105–113. doi: 10.1080/00050060801978647.

Howe, D. (1993) *One Being a Client: Understanding the Process of Counseling and Psychotherapy.* London: Sage.

Hugelshofer, D. S., Kwon, P., Reff, R. C., and Olson, M. L. (2006) 'Humour's role in the relation between attributional style and dysphoria.' *European Journal of Personality, 20,* 325–336.

Hughes, J. R. (1984) 'Psychological effects of habitual aerobic exercise: A critical review.' *Preventive Medicine, 13,* 66–78.

Hutchinson, S. L., Bland, A. D., and Kleiber, D. A. (2008) 'Leisure and stress-coping: Implications for the therapeutic recreation practice.' *Therapeutic Recreation Journal, 42*, 1, 9–23.

Hutchinson, M., Casper, P., Harris, J., Orcutt, J., and Trejo, M. (2008) *The Clinician's Guide to Writing Treatment Plans and Progress Notes.* Accessed on January 19, 2014 at www.sccgov.org/sites/dads/Adult%20System%20of%20Care%20Policy%20-%20Procedure/Documents/Clinician_Gde_toolkit.pdf.

Hutchinson, L. R. and Skinner, N. F. (2007) 'Self-awareness and cognitive style: Relationships among adaption-innovation, self-monitoring, and self-consciousness.' *Social Behavior and Personality, 35, 551–560.*

Hutchinson, A. K., Stuart, A. D., and Pretorius, H. G. (2010) 'Biological contributions to well-being: The relationships amongst temperament, character strengths, and resilience.' *South American Journal of Industrial Psychology, 36*, 2, 1–10.

Ilies, R., Dimotakis, N., and DePater, I. E. (2010) 'Psychological and physiological reactions to high workloads: Implications for well-being.' *Personnel Psychology, 63,* 407–436.

Ilies, R., Schwind, K. M., Wagner, D. T., Johnson, M. D., DeRue, D. S., and Ilgen, D. R. (2007) 'When can employees have a family life? The effects of daily workload and affect on work–family conflict and social behaviors at home.' *Journal of Applied Psychology, 92,* 1368–1379. doi: 10.1037/0021-9010.92.5.1368.

Inbar, J. and Ganor, M. (2003) 'Trauma and compassion fatigue: Helping the helpers.' *Journal of Jewish Communal Service, 79,* 109–111.

Ingram, R. E. and Snyder, C. R. (2006) 'Blending the good with the bad: Integrating positive psychology and cognitive psychotherapy.' *Journal of Cognitive Psychotherapy: An International Quarterly, 20, 2,* 117–122.

Ivey, G. (2000) 'A listening-formulating model for psychoanalytic psychotherapy.' *Psychotherapy, 37,* 22–34.

Iwaniec, D., Larkin, E., and McSherry, D. (2007) 'Emotionally harmful parenting.' *Child Care in Practice, 13,* 203–220. doi: 10.1080/135752707 01353531.

Jackson, H. and Nuttall, R. (2001) 'A relationship between childhood sexual abuse and professional sexual misconduct.' *Professional Psychology: Research and Practice, 32, 2,* 200–204. doi: 10.1037/0735-7028.32.2.200.

Jenkins, S. R. and Baird, S. (2002) 'Secondary traumatic stress and vicarious trauma: A validational study.' *Journal of Traumatic Stress, 15, 5,* 423–432. doi: 10.1023/A:1020193526843.

Johansen, K. H. (1993) 'Countertransference and Divorce in the Therapist.' In J. H. Gold. & J. C. Nemiah (eds) *Beyond Transference: When the Therapist's Real Life Intrudes.* Washington, DC: American Psychiatric Press.

Johnson, B. W. (2002) 'The intentional mentor: Strategies and guidelines for the practice of mentoring.' *Professional Psychology: Research and Practice, 33, 1,* 88–96.

Johnson, S. L. (1997) *The Therapist's Guide to Clinical Intervention: The 1-2-3's of Treatment Planning.* New York: Academic Press.

Johnson, W. B., Digiuseppe, R., and Ulven, J. (1999) 'Albert Ellis as mentor: National survey results.' *Psychotherapy, 36, 3,* 305–312.

Jones, J. W. (2004) 'Religion, health, and the psychology of religion: How the research on religion and health helps us understand health.' *Journal of Religion and Health, 43,* 317–328.

Jones, S. H. (2007, January) 'Secondary trauma and burnout in child protective workers: Implications for preparation of social workers.' Paper presented at the 11th Annual Conference of the Society for Social Work and Research, San Francisco.

Jordaan, I., Spangenberg, J. J., Watson, M. B., and Fouche, P. (2007) 'Emotional stress and coping strategies in South African clinical and counseling psychologists.' *African Journal of Psychology, 37, 4,* 835–855.

Joyce, P. R., McKenzie, J. M., Luty, S. E., Mulder, R. T. *et al.* (2003) 'Temperament, childhood environment and psychopathology as risk factors for avoidant and borderline personality disorders.' *Australian & New Zealand Journal of Psychiatry, 37,* 756–764. doi: 10.1111/j.1440-1614.2003.01263.x.

Kabat-Zinn, J. (2003) 'Mindfulness-based stress reduction (MBSR).' *Constructivism in the Human Sciences, 8,* 73–107.

Kadambi, M. A., and Truscott, D. (2004) 'Vicarious trauma among therapists working with sexual violence, cancer and general practice.' *Canadian Journal of Counselling, 38*, 4, 260–276.

Kamen, C., Cosgrove, V., McKellar. J., Cronkite, R., and Moos, R. (2011) 'Family support and depressive symptoms: A 23-year follow-up.' *Journal of Clinical Psychology, 67*, 215–223.

Kampf, A., McSherry, B., Thomas, S., and Abrahams, H. (2008) 'Psychologists' perceptions of legal and ethical requirements for breaching confidentiality.' *Australian Psychologist, 43*, 3, 194–204.

Karel, M. J. and Stead, C. D. (2011) 'Mentoring geropsychologists-in-training during internship and postdoctoral fellowship years.' *Educational Gerontology, 37*, 5, 388–408. doi: 10.1080/03601277.2011.553560.

Karon, B. P. (1995) 'Provision of psychotherapy under managed health care: A growing crisis and national nightmare.' *Professional Psychology: Research and Practice, 26*, 5–9.

Kaslow, N. J. and Rice, D. G. (1985) 'Developmental stresses of psychology internship training: What training staff can do to help.' *Professional Psychology: Research and Practice, 16*, 253–261.

Kassam-Adams, N. (1999) 'The Risks of Treating Sexual Trauma: Stress and Secondary Trauma in Psychotherapists.' In B.H. Stamm (ed.) *Secondary Traumatic Stress: Self-Care Issues for Clinicians, Researchers, and Educators* (2nd ed.) Baltimore: Sidran Press.

Kell, C. (1999) 'Confidentiality and the counsellor in general practice.' *British Journal of Guidance & Counselling, 27*, 431.

Kelly, E. W. Jr. (1995) *Spirituality and Religion in Counseling and Psychotherapy: Diversity in Theory and Practice*. Alexandria, VA: American Counseling Association.

Kelly, J. R. (2009) 'Work and leisure: A simplified paradigm.' *Journal of Leisure Research, 41*, 439–451.

Kim, E. (2007) 'Occupational stress: A survey of psychotherapists in Korea and the United States.' *International Journal of Stress Management, 14*, 111–120. doi: 10.1037/1072-5245.14.1.111.

Kim, S. and Kim, J. (2007) 'Mood after various brief exercise and sport modes: Aerobics, hip-hop dancing, ice skating, and body conditioning.' *Perceptual and Motor Skills, 104*, 1265–1270. doi: 10.2466/pms.104.4.1265-1270.

King, T. and Bannon, E. (2002, March) *The Burden of Borrowing: A Report on the Rising Rates of Student Debt*. Washington, DC: The State PIRGs' Higher Education Project.

King, A. C., Taylor, C. B., Haskells, W. L., and DeBush, R. F. (1989) 'Influence of regular aerobic exercise on psychological health.' *Health Psychology, 8*, 305–324.

Kirk-Brown, A. and Wallace, D. (2004) 'Predicting burnout and job satisfaction in workplace counselors: The influence of role stressors, job challenge, and organizational knowledge.' *Journal of Employment Counseling, 41*, 29–37.

Kitchener, K. S. (1992) 'Psychologist as teacher and mentor: Affirming ethical values throughout the curriculum.' *Professional Psychology: Research and Practice, 23*, 3, 190–195.

Kleespies, P. M. (1993) 'The stress of patient suicidal behavior: Implications for interns and training programs in psychology.' *Professional Psychology: Research and Practice, 24*, 4, 477–482. doi: 10.1037/0735-7028.24.4.477.

Kleespies, P. M., Van Orden, K. A., Bongar, B., Bridgeman, D. *et al.* (2011) 'Psychologist suicide: Incidence, impact, and suggestions for prevention, intervention, and prevention.' *Professional Psychology: Research & Practice, 42,* 3, 244–251. doi: 10.1037/a0022805.

Kniveton, B. H. (2004) 'The influence and motivations on which students base their choice of career.' *Research in Education, 72,* 47–57.

Knox, S., Burkard, A. W., Jackson, J. A., Schaack, A. M., and Hess, S. A. (2006) 'Therapists-in-training who experience a client suicide: Implications for supervision.' *Professional Psychology: Research & Practice, 37,* 5, 547–557. doi: 10.1037/0735-7028.37.5.547.

Kobasa, S. C., Maddi, S. R., and Puccetti, M. C (1982) 'Personality and exercise as buffers in the stress–illness relationship.' *Journal of Behavioral Medicine, 5,* 391–404.

Koenig, H. G. (1995) 'Religion and older men in prison.' *International Journal of Geriatric Psychiatry, 10,* 219–23.

Koenig, H. G. (2004) 'Spirituality, wellness, and quality of life.' *Sexuality, Reproduction, & Menopause, 2,* 2, 76–82.

Koenig, H. G. (2009) 'Research on religion, spirituality, and mental health: A review.' *The Canadian Journal of Psychiatry, 54,* 283–291.

Koenig, H. G., McCullough, M. E., and Larson, D. B. (2001) *Handbook of Religion and Health.* New York: Oxford University Press.

Koeske, G. F. and Kelly, T. (1995) 'The impact of overinvolvement in burnout and job satisfaction.' *American Journal of Orthopsychiatry, 65,* 282–292.

Konstam, V., Marx, F., Schurer, J., Harrington, A., Lombardo, N. E., and Deveney, S. (2000) 'Forgiving: What mental health counselors are telling us.' *Journal Of Mental Health Counseling, 22,* 3, 253–267.

Koosowa, A. J. (2009) 'Psychiatrist availability, social disintegration, and suicide deaths in U. S. counties, 1990–1995.' *Journal of Community Psychology, 37,* 1, 73–87.

Kramen-Kahn, B. and Hansen, N. D. (1998) 'Rafting the rapids: Occupational hazards, rewards, and coping strategies of psychotherapists.' *Professional Psychology: Research and Practice, 29,* 130–134.

Kraus, V. I. (2005) 'Relationship between self-care and compassion satisfaction, compassion fatigue, and burnout among mental health professionals working with adolescent sex offenders.' *Counseling and Clinical Psychology Journal, 2,* 1, 81–88.

Krause, N., Chatters, L. M., Meltzer, T., and Morgan, D. L. (2000) 'Negative interaction in the church: Insights from focus groups with older adults.' *Review of Religious Research, 41,* 510–533.

Kuiper, N. A., Grimshaw, M., Leite, C., and Kirsh, G. (2004) 'Humor is not always the best medicine: Specific components of sense of humor and psychological well-being.' *Humor: International Journal of Humor Research, 17,* 135–168.

Kummer, A. (2006) 'The Power of Mentoring: More than teaching.' *ASHA Leader, 11,* 39.

Kyle, G. and Chick, G. (2002) 'The social nature of leisure involvement.' *Journal of Leisure Research, 4,* 426–448.

Lacewing, M. (2005) 'Emotional self-awareness and ethical deliberation.' *Ratio, 18,* 65–81. doi: 10.1111/j.1467-9329.2005.00271.x.

Lahey, B. B. (2009) 'Public health significance of neuroticism.' *American Psychologist, 64,* 241–256. doi: 10.1037/a0015309.

Landry, L. P. (1999) 'Secondary traumatic stress disorder in the therapists from the Oklahoma city bombing.' (Order No. 9981105, University of North Texas). *ProQuest Dissertations and Theses.* Accessed on January 21, 2013 at http://search.proquest.com/docview/304513883?accountid=36783. (304513883).

Laungani, P. (2002) 'Stand up, speak out and talkback. The counselling interview: First impressions.' *Counselling Psychology Quarterly, 15,* 1, 107–113.

Lawless, L., Ginter, E., and Kelly, K. (1999) 'Managed care: What mental health counselors need to know.' *Journal of Mental Health Counseling, 21, 50–66.*

Lawlor, D. A. and Hopker, S. W. (2001) 'The effectiveness of exercise as an intervention in the management of depression: Systematic review and meta-regression analysis of randomised controlled trials.' *BMJ, 322, 1–8.*

Lawson, G. (2007) 'Counselor wellness and impairment: A national survey.' *Journal of Humanistic Counseling, Education & Development, 46,* 1, 20–34.

Lawson, G. and Myers, J. E. (2011) 'Wellness, professional quality of life, and career-sustaining behaviors: What keeps us well?' *Journal of Counseling and Development, 89,* 163–171.

Lawson, G. and Venart, E. (2005) 'Preventing Counselor Impairment: Vulnerability, Wellness, and Resilence.' In G. R. Walz & R. Yep (eds) *VISTAS: Perspectives on Counseling 2005.* Alexandria, VA: American Counseling Association.

Lawson, G., Venart, E., Hazler, R. J., and Kottler, J. A. (2007) 'Toward a culture of counselor wellness.' *Journal of Humanistic Counseling, Education, and Development, 46, 5–19.*

Layman, M. J. and McNamara, J. R. (1997) 'Remediation for ethics violations: Focus on psychotherapists' sexual contact with clients.' *Professional Psychology: Research and Practice, 28,* 3, 281–292.

Lazarus, A. (2012) 'Achieving success through mentors.' *Physician Executive, 38,* 1, 42–46.

Ledwidge, B. (1980) 'Run for your mind: Aerobic exercise as a means of alleviating anxiety and depression.' *Canadian Journal of Behavioural Science, 12,* 126–140.

Lee, S. M., Baker, C. R., Cho, S. H., Heckathorn, D. E. *et al.* (2007) 'Development and initial psychometrics of the burnout inventory.' *Measurement and Evaluation in Counseling and Development, 40,* 142–154.

Lee, S. M., Cho, S. H., Kissinger, D., and Ogle, N. T. (2010) 'A typology of burnout in professional counselors.' *Journal of Counseling & Development, 88,* 131–138.

Lee, B. Y. and Newberg, A. B. (2005) 'Religion and health: A review and critical analysis.' *Journal of Religion & Science, 40,* 443–468.

Lee, C. M., Reissing, E. D., and Dobson, D. (2009) 'Work-life balance for early career Canadian psychologists in professional programs.' *Canadian Psychology, 50,* 74–82. doi: 10.1037./a0013871.

Leiper, R. and Casares, P. (2000) 'An investigation of the attachment organization of clinical psychologists and its relationships to clinical practice.' *British Journal of Medical Psychology, 73,* 4, 449–464.

Leitner, L. A. (1973) 'Role modeling as an assessment of counselor interpersonal skills.' *Journal of Clinical Psychology, 29,* 1, 110–111.

Lent, J. and Schwartz, R. C. (2012) 'The impact of work setting, demographic characteristic, and personality factors related to burnout among professional counselors.' *Journal of Mental Health Counseling, 34,* 4, 355–372.

Lerias D. and Byrne, M. K. (2003) 'Vicarious traumatization: Symptoms and predictors. *Stress and Health, 19,* 129–138.

Lesage, A. D. (2005) 'Can psychiatrists prevent suicide? Yes, in collaboration.' *Canadian Journal of Psychiatry, 50,* 9, 507–508.

Leseho, J. (2007) 'Spirituality in counsellor education: A new course.' *British Journal of Guidance & Counselling, 35,* 4, 441–454. doi: 10.1080/03069880701594803.

Levi, B. H. and Portwood, S. G. (2011) 'Reasonable suspicion of child abuse: Finding a common language.' *Journal of Law, Medicine, & Ethics, 39,* 62–69.

Levin, J. S., Chatters, L. M., and Taylor, R. J. (1995) 'Religious effects on health status and life satisfaction among Black Americans.' *Journal of Gerontology (Social Sciences), 50B,* S154–S163.

Levinson, D. J., Darrow, C. N., Klein, E. B., Levinson, M. H., and McKee, B. (1978) *The Seasons of a Man's Life.* New York: Ballantine.

Lewis, C. A., Breslin, M. J., and Dein, S. (2008) 'Prayer and mental health: An introduction to this special issue of mental health, religion, and culture.' *Mental Health, Religion & Culture, 11,* 1, 1–7

Lim, N., Kim, E. K., Kim, H., Yang, E., and Lee, S. M. (2010) 'Individual and work-related factors influencing burnout of mental health professionals: A meta-analysis.' *Journal of Employment Counseling, 47,* 86–96.

Lind, E.W. (2000) 'Secondary traumatic stress: Predictors in psychologists.' Dissertation Abstracts International, 61, 3283.

Linley, P. A. and Joseph, S. (2007) 'Therapy work and therapists' positive and negative well-being.' *Journal of Social and Clinical Psychology, 26,* 3, 385–403. doi: 10.1521/jscp.2007.26.3.385.

Littauer, H., Sexton, H., and Wynn, R. (2005) 'Qualities clients wish for in their therapists.' *Scandinavian Journal of Caring Sciences, 19,* 28–31. doi: 10.1111/j.1471-6712.2005.00315.x.

Lloyd, C., McKennan, K., and King, R. (2005) 'Sources of stress experienced by occupational therapists and social workers in mental health settings.' *Occupational Therapy International, 12,* 81–94.

Lun, V. and Bond, M. (2013) 'Examining the relation of religion and spirituality to subjective well-being across national cultures.' *Psychology of Religion and Spirituality, 5,* 4, 304–315. doi: 10.1037/a0033641.

Lutjen, L. J., Silton, N. R., and Flannelly, K. J. (2012) 'Religion, forgiveness, hostility and health: A structural equation analysis.' *Journal of Religion and Health, 51,* 2, 468–478.

Mackrill, T. (2011) 'Differentiating life goals and therapeutic goals: Expanding our understanding of the working alliance.' *British Journal of Guidance & Counselling, 39,* 1, 25–39. doi: 10.1080/03069885.2010.531382.

MacLeod, A. K. and Moore, R. (2000) 'Positive thinking revisited: Positive cognitions, well-being and mental health.' *Clinical Psychology and Psychotherapy, 7,* 1–10.

Macran, S. and Shapiro, D. (1998) 'The role of personal therapy for therapists: A review.' *British Journal of Medical Psychology, 71,* 13–25.

Maheu, M. M., McMenamin, J. P., Pulier, M. L., and Posen, L. (2012) 'Future of telepsychology, telehealth, and various technologies in psychological research and practice.' *Professional Psychology: Research & Practice, 43,* 6, 613–621. doi: 10.1037/a0029458.

Mahoney, M. (1991) *Human Change Process: The Scientific Foundation of Psychotherapy*. New York: Basic Books.

Mahoney, M. (1997) 'Psychotherapists' personal problems and self-care patterns.' *Professional Psychology: Research and Practice, 28,* 1, 14–16. doi: 10.1037/0735-7028.28.1.14.

Malinowski, A. J. (2013) 'Characteristics of job burnout and humor among psychotherapists.' *Humor: International Journal of Humor Research, 26,* 1, 117–133.

Markus, H. (1977) 'Self-schemata and processing information about the self.' *Journal of Personality and Social Psychology, 35,* 63–78.

Martin, R. A. (2003) 'Sense of Humor.' In S. J. Lopez and C. R. Snyder (eds) *Positive Psychological Assessment: A Handbook of Models and Measures.* Washington, DC: American Psychological Association.

Martin, R. A. (2007) *The Psychology of Humor: An Integrative Approach.* New York: Elsevier Academic Press.

Martin, C., Godfrey, M., Meekums, B., and Madill, A. (2011) 'Managing boundaries under pressure: A qualitative study of therapists' experiences of sexual attraction in therapy.' *Counselling and Psychotherapy Research, 11,* 4, 248–256.

Maslach, C. (1982) *Burnout—The Cost of Caring.* New York: Prentice-Hall, Inc.

Maslach, C. (1993) 'Burnout: A Multidimensional Perspective.' In W. B. Schaufeli, C. Maslach, and T. Marek (eds) *Professional Burnout: Recent Developments in Theory and Research.* Philadelphia: Taylor & Francis.

Maslach, C. (2003) 'Job burnout: New directions in research and intervention.' *Current Directions in Psychological Science, 12,* 189–192.

Maslach, C. and Jackson, S. E. (1981) 'The measurement of experienced burnout.' *Journal of Occupational Behaviour, 2,* 99–113.

Maslach, C., Jackson, S. E., and Leiter, M. P. (1996) *Maslach Burnout Inventory Manual* (3rd ed.). Palo Alto, CA: Consulting Psychologists Press.

Maslach, C. and Leiter, M. P. (1997) *The Truth About Burnout.* San Francisco: John Wiley & Sons.

Maslach, C. and Leiter, M. P. (2008) 'Early predictors of job burnout and engagement.' *Journal of Applied Psychology, 93,* 498–512. doi: 10.1037/0021-9010.93.3.3.498.

Maslach, C., Schaufeli, W. B., and Leiter, M. P. (2001) 'Job burnout.' *Annual Review of Psychology, 52,* 397–422.

McAdams III, C. R. and Foster, V. A. (2000) 'Client suicide: Its frequency and impact on counselors.' *Journal of Mental Health Counseling, 22,* 2, 107–121.

McAdams III, C. R. and Foster, V. A. (2002) 'An assessment of resources for counselor coping and recovery in the aftermath of client suicide.' *Journal of Humanistic Counseling, Education and Development, 41,* 2, 232–241.

McCann, L. and Pearlman, L. A. (1990) 'Vicarious traumatization: A framework for understanding the psychological effects of working with victims.' *Journal of Trauma Stress, 3,* 1, 131–149.

McCann, I. L. and Saakvitne, K. W. (1995) 'Treating Therapists with Vicarious Traumatization and Secondary Traumatic Stress Disorders.' In C. R. Figley (ed.) *Compassion Fatigue: Coping with Secondary Traumatic Stress Disorder in Those Who Treat the Traumatized.* New York: Brunner/Mazel.

McCarthy, W. C. and Frieze, I. H. (1999) 'Negative aspects of therapy: Client perceptions of therapists' social influence, burnout, and quality of care.' *Journal of Social Issues, 55,* 33–50.

McConnaughy, E. A. (1987) 'The person of the therapist in psychotherapeutic practice.' *Psychotherapy: Theory, Research, Practice, Training, 24,* 3, 303–314. doi: 10.1037/h0085720.

McGlasson, T. D. (2012) 'Listening clearly: Alternative treatments for adolescent depression.' *The Preventative Researcher, 19,* 18–20.

McGovern, M. K. (2012) 'The effects of exercise on the brain.' *Serendip.* Accessed on December 21, 2013 at http://serendip.brynmawr.edu/bb/neuro/neuro05/web2/mmcgovern.html.

McKenzie Deighton, R., Gurris, N., and Traue, H. (2007) 'Factors affecting burnout and compassion fatigue in psychotherapists treating torture survivors: Is the therapist's attitude to working through trauma relevant?' *Journal of Traumatic Stress, 20,* 1, 63–75. doi: 10.1002/jts.20180.

McLeod, S. A. (2008) *Person Centred Therapy—Simply Psychology.* Accessed on October 21, 2013 at www.simplypsychology.org/client-centred-therapy.html.

Meadors, P., Lamson, A., Swanson, M., White, M., and Sira, N. (2009) 'Secondary traumatization in pediatric healthcare providers: Compassion fatigue, burnout, and secondary traumatic stress.' *OMEGA—Journal of Death and Dying, 60,* 2, 103–128.

Meek, H. W. (2005) 'Promoting self-awareness: Infant observation training as a model.' *Smith College Studies in Social Work, 75,* 33–58.

Meeusen, R. and De Meirleir, K. (1995) 'Exercise and brain transmission.' *Sports Medicine, 20,* 3, 160–188.

Meissler-Daniels, S. (1990) 'Burnout, humor and narcissism in psychologists.' (Order No. 9027828, St. John's University (New York)). *ProQuest Dissertations and Theses,* p. 143. Accessed on December 1, 2013 at http://search.proquest.com/docview/303861463?accountid=36783. (303861463).

Melamed, Y., Szor, H., and Bernstein, E. (2001) 'The loneliness of the therapist in the public outpatient clinic.' *Journal of Contemporary Psychotherapy, 31,* 103–112. doi: 0022-0116/01/0600-0103.

Messari, S. and Hallam, R. (2003) 'CBT for psychosis: A qualitative analysis of clients' experiences.' *British Journal of Clinical Psychology, 42,* 171–188.

Meyer, D. and Ponton, R. (2006) 'The healthy tree: A metaphorical perspective of counselor well-being.' *Journal of Mental Health Counseling, 28,* 3, 189–201.

Meyers, T. W. and Cornille, T. Z. (2002) 'The Trauma of Working with Traumatized Children.' In C. R. Figley (ed.) *Treating Compassion Fatigue.* New York: Brunner-Routledge.

Middleton, W. (2007) 'Gunfire, humour and psychotherapy.' *Australasian Psychiatry, 15,* 2, 148–155. doi: 10.1080/10398560601148358.

Mihalko, S. L., McAuley, E., and Bane, S. M. (1996) 'Self-efficacy and affective responses to acute exercises in middle-aged adults.' *Journal of Social Behavior and Personality, 11,* 375–385.

Miller, G. (2001) 'Finding happiness for ourselves and our clients.' *Journal of Counseling & Development, 79,* 382–385.

Miller, J. K. (2008) 'Exploring self-awareness in mental health practice.' *Mental Health Practice, 12,* 31–35.

Miller, M., Hempstead, K., Nguyen, T., Barber, C., and Rosenberg-Wohl, S. (2013) 'Method choice in non-fatal self-fatal as a predictor of subsequent episodes of self-harm and suicide: Implications for clinical practice.' *American Journal of Public Health, 103,* 61–68.

Miller, G. D., Iverson, K. M., Kemmelmeter, M., MacLane, C. *et al.* (2011) 'A preliminary examination of burnout among counselor trainees treating clients with recent suicidal ideation and borderline traits.' *Counselor Education & Supervision, 50,* 5, 344–359.

Miller, R. D. and Weinstock, R. (1987) 'Conflict of interest between therapist–patient confidentiality and the duty to report sexual abuse of children.' *Behavioral Sciences & the Law, 5,* 161–174.

Mir, S. S. (2011) 'HIPAA privacy rule: Maintaining the confidentiality of medical records, part 2.' *Journal of Health Care Compliance, 13,* 3, 35–78.

Mogudi-Carter, M. (2001) 'Challenges experienced by a therapist working with multicultural families: Case studies.' *International Journal for the Advancement of Counselling, 23,* 237–243.

Monroe, P. G. and Schwab, G. M. (2009) 'God as healer: A closer look at biblical images of inner healing with guiding questions for counselors.' *Journal of Psychology and Christianity, 28,* 121–129.

Moses J., Steptoe, A., Matthews, A., and Edwards, S. (1989) 'The effects of exercise training on mental well-being in the normal population.' *Journal of Psychosomatic Research, 33,* 47–61.

Motl, R. W., Sandroff, B. M., and Benedict, R. B. (2011) 'Cognitive dysfunction and multiple sclerosis.' *Multiple Sclerosis, 17,* 1034–1040. doi: 10.1177/1352458511409612.

Motta, R., Kefer, J., Hertz, M., and Hafeez, S. (1999) 'Initial evaluation of the secondary trauma questionnaire.' *Psychological Reports, 85,* 997–1002.

Munsey, C. (2006) 'Helping colleagues to help themselves.' *Monitor on Psychology, 37,* 7, 35. Accessed on September 16, 2013 at www.apa.org/monitor/julaug06/colleagues.aspx.

Myers, S. (2000) 'Empathic listening: Reports on the experience of being heard.' *Journal of Humanistic Psychology, 40,* 148–173.

Myers, J. E., Mobley, A. K., and Booth, C. S. (2003) 'Wellness of counseling students: Practicing what we preach.' *Counselor Education and Supervision, 42,* 264–274.

Myers, J. E., and Sweeney, T. J. (eds) (2005) *Counseling for Wellness: Theory, Research, and Practice.* Alexandria, VA: American Counseling Association.

Myers, J. E., Sweeney, T. J., and Witmer, J. M. (2000) 'The wheel of wellness counseling for wellness: A holistic model for treatment planning.' *Journal of Counseling and Development, 78,* 3, 251–266.

Myers, J. E. and Willard, K. (2003) 'Integrating spirituality into counseling and counselor training: A developmental, wellness approach.' *Counseling & Values, 42,* 2, 142–155.

Nasar, J. L. and Devlin, A. S. (2011) 'Impressions of psychotherapists' offices.' *Journal of Counseling Psychology, 58,* 310–320. doi: 10.1037/a0023887.

Neff, K. (2003) 'Self-compassion. An alternative conceptualization of a healthy attitude towards oneself.' *Self and Identity, 2,* 85–101.

Nelson, P. B. (1989) 'Ethnic differences in intrinsic/extrinsic religious orientation and depression in the elderly.' *Archives of Psychiatric Nursing, 3,* 4, 199–204.

Nelson, K. W. and Jackson, S. A. (2003) 'Professional counsellor identity development: A qualitative study of Hispanic student interns.' *Counselor Education and Supervision, 43,* 1, 2–14. doi: 10.1002/j.1556-6978.2003.tb01825.x.

Nesbitt, P. D. (1995) 'First and second-career clergy: Influences of age and gender on the career-stage paradigm.' *Journal of the Scientific Study of Religion, 34,* 2, 152–172.

Newell, J. M. and MacNeil, G. (2010) 'Professional burnout, secondary traumatic stress, and compassion fatigue: A review of theoretical terms, risk factors, and preventive methods for clinicians.' *Best Practices in Mental Health: An International Journal, 6, 2, 57–68.*

Newman, B. S., Dannenfelser, P. L., and Pendleton, D. (2005) 'Child abuse investigations: Reasons for using child advocacy centers and suggestions for improvement.' *Child & Adolescent Social Work Journal, 22,* 165–181. doi: 10.1007/s10560-005-3416-9.

Ng, F., Dodd, S., and Berk, M. (2007) 'The effects of physical activity in the acute treatment of bipolar disorder: A pilot study.' *Journal of Affective Disorders, 101,* 259–262.

Nikcevic, A. V., Kramolisova-Advani, J., and Spada, M. M. (2007) 'Early childhood experiences and current emotional distress: What do they tell us about aspiring psychologists?' *The Journal of Psychology: Interdisciplinary and Applied, 141,* 1, 25–34.

Nock, M. K. and Photos, V. A. (2006) 'Parent motivation to participate in treatment: Assessment and prediction of subsequent participation.' *Journal of Child and Family Studies, 15,* 345–358. doi: 10.1007/s10826-006-9022-4.

Norcross, J. C. (2005) 'The psychotherapist's own psychotherapy: Educating and developing psychologists.' *American Psychologist, 60,* 840–850.

Norcross, J. C., Bike, D. H., and Evans, K. L. (2009) 'The therapist's therapist: A replication and extension 20 years later.' *Psychotherapy Theory, Research, Practice, Training, 46,* 32–41.

Norcross, J. C. and Guy, J. D. (2007) *Leaving It at the Office: A Guide to Psychotherapist Self-Care.* New York: The Guilford Press.

Nuttall, A. K., Valentino, K., and Borkowski, J. G. (2012) 'Maternal history of parentification, maternal warm responsiveness, and children's externalizing behavior.' *Journal of Family Psychology, 26,* 5, 767–775. doi: 10.1037/a0029470.

Oaten, M. and Cheng, K. (2006) 'Longitudinal gains in self-regulation from regular physical exercise.' *British Journal of Health Psychology, 11,* 717–733.

O'Connor, M. F. (2001) 'On the etiology and effective management of professional distress and impairment among psychologists.' *Professional Psychology: Research and Practice, 32,* 345–350.

O'Halloran, T. O. and Linton, J. M. (2000) 'Stress on the job: Self-care resources for counselors.' *Journal of Mental Health Counseling, 22,* 354–364.

Okun, B. F. and Kantrowitz, R. E. (2008) *Effective Helping: Interviewing and Counseling Techniques* (7th ed.). Belmont, CA: Brooks/Cole.

Orlinsky, D., Ambuhl, H., Ronnestad, M. H., Davis, J., *et al.* (1991) 'Development of psychotherapists: Concepts, questions, and methods of a collaborative international study.' *Psychotherapy Research, 9,* 2, 127–153.

Orlinsky, D., Hansruedi, A., Botermans, J.C., Davis, J., Ronnestad, M., Willuttzki, U., *et al.* (1999) Psychotherapists' assessments of their development at different career levels. *Psychotherapy, 36,* 203–215.

Orlinsky, D. E. and Ronnestad, M. H. (2005) *How Psychotherapists Develop: A study of Therapeutic Work and Professional Growth.* Washington, DC: American Psychological Association.

Osborn, C. J. (2004) 'Seven salutary suggestions for counselor stamina.' *Journal of Counseling & Development, 82,* 319–328.

Owen, J., Imel, Z., Adelson, J., and Rodolfa, E. (2012) '"No-show": Therapist racial/ethnic disparities in client unilateral termination.' *Journal of Counseling Psychology, 59,* 314–320. doi: 10.1037/a0027091.

Pargament, K. L. (2002) 'Is religion nothing but …? Explaining religion versus explaining religion away.' *Psychological Inquiry, 13,* 239–244.

Parkinson, F. (1997) *Critical Incident Debriefing: Understanding and Dealing with Trauma.* London: Souvenir Press.

Pavot, W., Diener, E., and Fujita, F. (1990) 'Extraversion and happiness.' *Personality and Individual Differences, 11,* 1299–1306.

Pearlman, L. A. and Saakvitne, K. W. (1995) 'Treating Therapists with Vicarious Traumatization and Secondary Traumatic Stress Disorders.' In C. R. Figley (ed.) *Compassion Fatigue: Coping with Secondary Traumatic Stress Disorder in Those Who Treat the Traumatized.* New York: Brunner/Mazel.

Perlman, D. and Rook, K. S. (1987) 'Social Support, Social Deficits, and the Family: Toward the Enhancement of Well-Being.' In S. Oskamp (ed.) *Family Processes and Problems: Social Psychological Aspects.* Newbury Park, CA: Sage.

Perseius, K., Kaver, A., Ekdahl, S., Asberg, M., and Samuelsson, M. (2007) 'Stress and burnout in psychiatric professionals when starting to use dialectical behavioural therapy in the work with young self-harming women showing borderline personality symptoms.' *Journal of Psychiatric and Mental Health Nursing, 14,* 635–643.

Peterson, U., Demerouti, E., Bergstrom, G., Samuelsson, M., Asberg, M., and Nygren, A. (2008) 'Burnout and physical and mental health among Swedish health care workers.' *Journal of Advanced Nursing, 62,* 84–95.

Peterson, L. R. and Roy, A. (1985) 'Religiosity, anxiety, and meaning and purpose: Religion's consequences for psychological well-being.' *Review of Religious Research, 27,* 1, 49–62.

Pettifor, J., McCarron, M. C., Schoepp, G., Stark, C., and Stewart, D. (2011) 'Ethical supervision in teaching, practice, and administration.' *Canadian Psychology, 52,* 3, 198–205. doi: 10.1037/a0024549.

Phelps, R., Eisman, E. J., and Kohut, J. (1998) 'Psychological practice and managed care: Results of the CAPP practitioner's survey.' *Professional Psychology: Research and Practice, 29,* 31–36.

Philips, B. (2009) 'Comparing apples and oranges: How do patient characteristics and treatment goals vary between different forms of psychotherapy.' *Psychology and Psychotherapy: Theory, Research and Practice, 82,* 323–336.

Pillay, A, and Johnston, E. R. (2011) 'Intern clinical psychologists' experiences of their training and internship placements.' *South African Journal of Psychology, 41,* 1, 74–82.

Pinto, R. M. (2003) 'The impact of secondary traumatic stress on novice and expert counselors with and without a history of trauma.' *Dissertation Abstracts International, 63* (9-A), 3117.

Pistorius, K., Feinauer, L., Harper, J., Stahmann, R., and Miller, R. (2008) 'Working with sexually abused children.' *American Journal of Family Therapy, 36,* 3, 181–195.

Plante, T. G. and Rodin, J. (1990) 'Physical fitness and enhanced psychological health.' *Current Psychology: Research & Reviews, 9,* 1, 3–24.

Pope, K. S. (1988) 'How clients are harmed by sexual contact with mental health professionals: The syndrome and its prevalence.' *Journal of Counseling & Development, 67,* 4, 222–226. doi: 10.1002/j.1556-6676.1988.tb02587.x.

Pope, K. S. and Bouhoutsos, J. C. (1986) *Sexual Intimacy between Therapist and Patients.* New York: Praeger.

Pope, K. S. and Feldman-Summers, S. (1992) 'National survey of psychologists' sexual and physical abuse history and their evaluation of training and competence in these areas.' *Professional Psychology: Research and Practice, 23, 5, 353–361.*

Pope, K. S., Keith-Spiegel, P., and Tabachnick, B. G. (1986) 'Sexual attraction to clients: The human therapist and the (sometimes) inhuman training system.' *American Psychologist, 41, 147–158.*

Pope, K. S., Keith-Spiegel, P., and Tabachnick, B.G. (2006) 'Sexual attraction to clients: The human therapist and the (sometimes) inhuman training system.' *Training and Education in Professional Psychology, S, 2, 96–111.* doi: 10.1037/1931-3918.S.2.96.

Pope, K. S. and Tabachnick, B. G. (1993) 'Therapists' anger hate, fear, and sexual feelings: National survey of therapist responses, client characteristics, critical events, formal complaints, and training.' *Professional Psychology: Research & Practice, 24, 142–145.*

Pope, K., and Tabachnick, B. (1994) 'Therapists as patients: A national survey of psychologists' experiences, problems, and beliefs.' *Professional Psychology: Research and Practice, 25, 3, 247–258.* doi: 10.1037/0735-7028.25.3.247.

Pound, P. and Duchac, N. (2009) 'Driven by goals: Choice theory and the HELP method.' *International Journal Of Reality Therapy, 28, 2, 36–39.*

Powers, D. V., Cramer, R. J., and Grubka, J. M. (2007) 'Spirituality, life stress, and affective well-being.' *Journal of Psychology and Theology, 35, 3, 235–243.*

Pulido, M. (2007) 'In their words: secondary traumatic stress in social workers responding to the 9/11 terrorist attacks in New York City.' *Social Work, 52, 3, 279–281.* doi: 10.1093/sw/52.3.279.

Purcell, R., Powell, M. B., and Mullen, P. E. (2005) 'Clients who stalk psychologists: Prevalence, methods, and motives.' *Professional Psychology: Research & Practice, 36, 537–543.*

Purdy, M. and Dupey, P. (2005) 'Holistic flow model of spiritual wellness.' *Counseling and Values, 49, 2, 95–106.*

Praissman, S. (2008) 'Mindfulness-based stress reduction: A literature review and clinician's guide.' *Journal of the American Academy of Nurse Practitioners, 20, 4, 212–216.* doi: 10.1111/j.1745-7599.2008.00306.x.

Raglin, J. S. and Morgan, W. P. (1985) 'Influence of vigorous exercise on mood states.' *The Behavior Therapist, 8, 179–183.*

Raiya, H. A. and Pargament, K. I. (2010) 'Religiously integrated psychotherapy with Muslim clients: From research to practice.' *Professional Psychology: Research & Practice, 41, 181–188.* doi: 10.1037/a0017988.

Rake, C. and Paley, G. (2009) 'Personal therapy for psychotherapists: The impact on therapeutic practice. A qualitative study using interpretative phenomenological analysis.' *Psychodynamic Practice, 15, 275–294.* doi: 10.1080/14753630903024481.

Rambo, A. H., Heath, A., and Chenail, R. J. (1993) *Practicing Therapy: Exercises for Growing Therapists.* New York: W. W. Norton & Company.

Rashotte, L. S. (2006) 'Social Influence.' In G.Ritzer & J. M. Ryan (eds) *The Blackwell Encyclopedia of Sociology* (Vol. 9). Oxford: Blackwell Publishing.

Reeves, D. B. (2009) 'Model teachers.' *Educational Leadership, 66, 5, 85–86.*

Reid, Y., Johnson, S., Morant, N., Kuipers, E. *et al.* (1999) 'Improving support for mental health staff: A qualitative study.' *Social Psychiatry and Psychiatric Epidemiology, 34, 6, 309–315.*

Regan, J., Burley, H. L., Hamer, G., and Wright, A. (2006) 'Secondary traumatic stress in mental health professionals.' *Tennessee Medicine, 99,* 4, 39–40.

Rejeski, W. J., Gauvin, L., Hobson, M. L., and Norris, J. L. (1995) 'Effects of baseline responses, in-task feelings, and duration of activity on exercise-induced feeling states in women.' *Health Psychology, 14,* 350–359.

Rejeski, W. J., Thompson, A., Brubaker, P. H., and Miller, H. S. (1992) 'Acute exercise: Buffering psychosocial stress responses in women.' *Health Psychology, 11,* 355–362.

Rendi, M., Szabo, A., Szabo, T., Velenczei, A., and Kovacs, A. (2008) 'Acute psychological benefits of aerobic exercise: A field study into the effects of exercise.' *Psychology, Health, & Medicine, 13,* 2, 180–184.

Richards, B. M. (2000) 'Impact upon therapy and the therapist when working with suicidal patients: Some transference and countertransference aspects.' *British Journal of Guidance & Counseling, 28,* 3, 325–337.

Richards, K. C., Campenni, C. E., and Muse-Burke, J. L. (2010) 'Self-care and well-being in mental health professionals: The mediating effects of self-awareness and mindfulness.' *Journal of Mental Health Counseling, 3,* 247–264.

Risin, L. I. and McNamara, J. (1989) 'Validation of child abuse: The psychologist's role.' *Journal of Clinical Psychology, 45,* 175–184.

Rizq, R. and Target, M. (2008) '"The power of being seen": An interpretative phenomenological analysis of how experienced counseling psychologists describe the meaning and significance of personal therapy in clinical practice.' *British Journal of Guidance & Counseling, 36,* 131–1153. doi: 10.1080/03069880801926418.

Roach, L. F. (2005) 'The influence of counselor education programs on counselor wellness.' *Dissertation Abstracts International, A66-06,* 2117–2133.

Roach, L. F. and Young, M. E. (2007) 'Do counselor education programs promote wellness in their students?' *Counselor Education & Supervision, 47,* 29–45.

Rober, P. (2005) 'The therapist's self in dialogical family therapy: Some ideas about not-knowing and the therapist's inner conversation.' *Family Process, 44,* 4, 477–495. doi: 10.1111/j.1545–5300.2005.00073.x.

Robiner, W. N., Ax, R. K., Stamm, B. H., and Harowski, K. (2002) 'Addressing the supply of psychologists in the workplace: Is focusing principally on demand sound economics?' *Journal of Clinical Psychology in Medical Settings, 9,* 273–285.

Robinson, W. and Reid, P. T. (1985) 'Sexual intimacies in psychology revisited.' *Professional Psychology: Research and Practice, 16,* 4, 512–520. doi: 10.1037/0735-7028.16.4.512.

Rocheleau, C. A., Webster, G. D., Bryan, A., and Frazier, J. (2004) 'Moderators of the relationship between exercise and mood changes: Gender, exertion level, and workout duration.' *Psychology and Health, 19,* 4, 491–506.

Rodgers, N. M. (2011) 'Intimate boundaries: Therapists' perception and experience of erotic transference within the therapeutic relationship.' *Counselling & Psychotherapy Research, 11,* 4, 266–274. doi: 10.1080/14733145.2011.557437.

Rodolfa, E., Hall, T., Holms, V., and Davena, A. (1994) 'The management of sexual feelings in therapy.' *Professional Psychology: Research and Practice, 25,* 2, 168–172. doi: 10.1037/0735-7028.25.2.168.

Rodolfa, E., Kraft, W. A., and Reilley, R. R. (1988) 'Stressors of professionals and trainees at APA-approved counseling and VA medical center internship sites.' *Professional Psychology: Research and Practice, 19*, 43–49.

Rodriguez, A., Latkova, P., and Sun, Y. (2008) 'The relationship between leisure and life satisfaction: Application of activity and need theory.' *Social Indicators Research, 86*, 163–175. doi: 10.1007/s11205-007-9101-y.

Rogers, C. R. (1980) *A Way of Being*. Boston: Houghton Mifflin.

Rogers, C. R. (2007) 'The necessary and sufficient conditions of therapeutic personality change.' *Psychotherapy: Theory, Research, Practice, Training, 44*, 240–248. doi: 10.1037/0033-3204.44.3.240.

Ronnestad, M. H. and Skovholt, T. M. (2003) 'The journey of the counselor and therapist: Research findings and perspectives on development.' *Journal of Career Development, 30*, 1, 5–44.

Rosenberger, E. W. and Hayes, J. A. (2002) 'Therapist as subject: A review of the empirical countertransference literature.' *Journal of Counseling & Development, 80*, 3, 264–270. doi: 10.1002/j.1556-6678.2002.tb00190.x.

Rosenblatt, P. C. (2009) 'Providing therapy can be therapeutic for a therapist.' *American Journal of Psychotherapy, 63*, 169–181.

Rosmarin, D. H., Krumrei, E. J., and Andersson, G. (2009) 'Religion as a predictor of psychological distress in two religious communities.' *Cognitive Behaviour Therapy, 38*, 54–64. doi: 10.1080/16506070802477222.

Ross, R. R., Altmaier, E. M., and Russell, D. W. (1989) 'Job stress, social support, and burnout among counseling center staff.' *Journal of Counseling Psychology, 36*, 464–470.

Rupert, P. A. and Baird, K. A. (2004) 'Managed care and the independent practice of psychology.' *Professional Psychology: Research and Practice, 35*, 185–193. doi: 10.1037/0735-7028.35.2.185.

Rupert, P. A. and Kent, J. (2007) 'Gender and work setting differences in career-sustaining behaviors and burnout among professional psychologists.' *Professional Psychology: Research & Practice, 38*, 1, 88–96. doi: 10.1037/0735-7028.38.1.88.

Rupert, P. A. and Morgan, D. J. (2005) 'Work setting and burnout among psychologists.' *Professional Psychology: Research and Practice, 36*, 544–550. doi: 10.1037/0735-7028.36.5.544.

Rupert, P. A., Stevanovic, P., Hartman, E. R., Bryant, F. B., and Miller, A. (2012) 'Predicting work-family conflict and life satisfaction among professional psychologists.' *Professional Psychology: Research and Practice, 43*, 341–348. doi: 10.1037/a0026675.

Rupert, P. A., Stevanovic, P., and Hunley, H. A. (2009) 'Work-family conflict and burnout among practicing psychologists.' *Professional Psychology: Research and Practice, 40*, 54–61. doi: 10.1037/a0012538.

Ruskin, I., Sakinofsky, R. M., Bagby, S., Dickens, S., and Sousa, G. (2004) 'Impact of patient suicide on psychiatrists and psychiatric trainees.' *Academic Psychiatry, 28*, 104–110.

Saakvitne, K. W. (2002) 'Shared trauma: The therapist's increased vulnerability.' *Psychoanalytic Dialogues, 12*, 443–449.

Saarnio, P. (2010) 'Big five personality traits and interpersonal functioning in female and male substance abuse therapists.' *Substance Abuse & Misuse, 45*, 10, 1463–1473. doi: 10.3109/10826081003749963.

Salston, M. D. and Figley, C. R. (2003) 'Secondary traumatic stress effects of working with survivors of criminal victimization.' *Journal of Traumatic Stress, 16*, 2, 167–175.

Samdahl, D. M. (1992) 'Leisure in our lives: Exploring the common leisure occasion.' *Journal of Leisure Research, 24,* 19–32.

Samstag, L. W. (2007) 'The necessary and sufficient conditions of therapeutic personality change: Reactions to Rogers' 1957 article.' *Psychotherapy: Theory, Research, Practice, Training, 44,* 295–299. doi: 10.1037/0033-3204.44.3.295.

Sanders, S., Jacobson, J., and Ting, L. (2005) 'Reactions of mental health social workers following a client suicide completion: A qualitative investigation. *Omega, 51,* 197–216.

Sanyal, N. (2011) 'Client-centered therapy: The interior decorator of mind.' *Amity Journal of Applied Psychology, 2,* 49–53.

Sarasohn, M. K. (2005) 'The use of shame and dread in countertransference.' *Clinical Social Work Journal, 33,* 4, 445–453. doi: 10.1007/s10615-005-7037-8.

Satterly, L. (2001) 'Guilt, shame, and religious and spiritual pain.' *Holistic Nursing Practice, 15,* 30–39.

Saulsburg, F. T. and Campbell, R. E. (1985) 'Evaluations of child abuse reporting by physicians.' *American Journal of Diseases of Children, 139,* 393–489.

Savic-Jabrow, P. (2010) 'Where do counsellors in private practice receive their support? A pilot study.' *Counselling & Psychotherapy Research, 10,* 3, 229–232. doi: 10.1080/14733140903469889.

Sawyer, A. (2011) 'Let's talk: a narrative of mental illness, recovery, and the psychotherapist's personal treatment.' *Journal of Clinical Psychology, 67,* 8, 776–788. doi: 10.1002/jclp.20822.

Scaife, J. M. and Pomerantz, M. (1999) 'A survey of the record keeping practices of clinical psychologists.' *Clinical Psychology & Psychotherapy, 6,* 3, 210–226.

Scaturo, D. J. (2002) 'Fundamental dilemmas in contemporary psychotherapy: A transtheoretical concept.' *American Journal of Psychotherapy, 56,* 115–133.

Schauben, L. J. and Frazier, P. A. (1995) 'Vicarious trauma: The effects on female counselors of working with sexual violence survivors.' *Psychology of Women Quarterly, 19,* 1, 49–64.

Schaufeli, W. B., Maslach, C., and Marek, T. (eds) (1993) *Professional Burnout: Recent Developments in Theory and Research.* Washington, DC: Taylor & Francis.

Schoener, R. R. (2007) 'Do as I say, not as I do.' *Professional Psychology: Research & Practice, 38,* 6, 610–612.

Schofield, M. J. and Grant, J. (2013) 'Developing psychotherapists' competence through clinical supervision: Protocol for a qualitative study of supervisory dyads.' *BMC Psychiatry, 13,* 1, 1–9.

Schure, M. B., Christopher, J., and Christopher, S. (2008) 'Mind–body medicine and the art of selfcare: Teaching mindfulness to counseling students through yoga, meditation, and qigong.' *Journal of Counseling and Development, 86,* 47–56.

Schwartz, B. K. (1992) 'Effective treatment techniques for sex offenders.' *Psychiatric Annals, 22,* 6, 315–319.

Schwebel, M. and Coster, J. (1998) 'Well-functioning in professional psychologists: As program heads see it.' *Professional Psychology: Research and Practice, 29,* 284–292.

Schwebel, M., Skorina, J. K., and Schoener, G. (1996) *Assisting Impaired Psychologists* (rev. ed.) Washington DC: American Psychological Association.

Sealey, R. M. and Tope, S. B. (2011) 'Effects of exercise interventions on physical condition and health of Vietnam veterans.' *International Journal of Therapy and Rehabilitation, 18,* 438–448.

Seikkula, J. and Trimble, D. (2005) 'Healing elements of the therapeutic conversation: Dialogue as an embodiment of love.' *Family Process, 44,* 461–475.

Seligman, L. (2004) *Diagnosis and Treatment Planning in Counseling* (3rd ed.). New York: Springer.

Seligman, M. E. and Csikszentmihalyi, M. (2000) 'Positive psychology: An Introduction.' *American Psychologist, 55,* 5–14. doi: 10.1037/0003-066X.55.1.5.

Senour, M. N. (1982) 'How counselors influence clients.' *The Personnel and Guidance Journal, 60,* 345–349.

Sexton, L. (1999) 'Vicarious traumatisation of counselors and effects on their workplaces.' *British Journal of Guidance & Counseling, 27,* 3, 393–403.

Shahabi, I., Powell, L., Musick, M., Pargament, K., Thoresen, C., Williams, D. *et al.* (2002) 'Correlates of self-perceptions of spirituality in American adults.' *Annals of Behavioral Medicine, 24,* 59–68.

Shallcross, L. (2011) 'Taking care of yourself as a counselor.' *Counseling Today,* Accessed on November 27, 2013 at http://ct.counseling.org/2011/01/taking-care-of-yourself-as-a-counselor.

Shapiro, S. L., Brown, K. W., and Biegel, G. M. (2007) 'Teaching self-care to caregivers: Effects of mindfulness-based stress reduction on the mental health of therapists in training.' *Training and Education in Professional Psychology, 1,* 2, 105–115. doi: 10.1037/1931-3918.1.2.105.

Sharma, V. P. (2003) 'Type A behaviors.' *Mind Publications.* Accessed on September 21, 2013 at www.mindpub.com/art502.htm.

Sharry, J., Darmody, M., and Madden, B. (2002) 'A solution-focused approach to working with clients who are suicidal.' *British Journal of Guidance & Counselling, 30,* 4, 383–399. doi: 10.1080/0306988021000025690.

Sherman, M. and Thelen, M. H. (1998) 'Distress and professional impairment among psychologists in clinical practice.' *Professional Psychology: Research and Practice, 29,* 1, 79–85.

Sibley, B. A. and Etnier, J. L. (2003) 'The relationship between physical activity and cognition in children: A meta-analysis.' *Pediatric Exercise Science, 15,* 243–256.

Simons, A. D., McGowan. C. R., Epstein, L. H., Kupfer, D. J., and Robertson, R. J. (1985) 'Exercise as a treatment for depression: An update.' *Clinical Psychology Review, 5,* 553–568.

Singer, J. B. and Slovak, K. (2011) 'School social workers' experiences with youth suicidal behavior: An exploratory study.' *Children & Schools, 33,* 4, 215–228.

Skinstad, A. (1993) 'Practicum supervision in Norway and the United States.' *Journal of Counseling & Development, 71,* 4, 406–408.

Skovholt, T. M. (2001) *The Resilient Practitioner: Burnout Prevention and Self-Care Strategies for Counselors, Therapists, and Health Professionals.* Needham Heights, MA: Allyn & Bacon.

Skovholt, T. M., Grier, T. L., and Hanson, M. R. (2001) 'Career counseling for longevity: Self-care and burnout prevention strategies for counselor resilience.' *Journal of Career Development, 27,* 167–176.

Skovholt, T. M. and Ronnestad, M. H. (2003) 'Struggles of the novice counselor and therapist.' *Journal of Career Development, 30,* 1, 45–58.

Smedema, S. M., Catalano, D., and Ebener, D. J. (2010) 'The relationship of coping, self-worth, and subjective well-being: A structural equation model.' *Rehabilitation Counseling Bulletin, 53,* 131–142. doi: 10.1177/0034355209358272.

Smith, T. B., McCullough, M. E., and Poll, J. (2003) 'Religiousness and depression: Evidence for a main effect and the moderating influence of stressful life events.' *Psychological Bulletin, 129,* 614–636.

Smits, J. A., Berry, A. C., Rosenfield, D., Powers, M. B., Behar, E., and Otto, M. W. (2008) 'Reducing anxiety sensitivity with exercise.' *Depression and Anxiety, 25,* 689–699.

Smolyansky, B. H., Stark, L. J., Pendley, J., Robins, P. M., and Price, K. (2013) 'Confidentiality and electronic medical records for behavioral health records: The experience of pediatric psychologists at four children's hospitals.' *Clinical Practice in Pediatric Psychology, 1,* 1, 18–27. doi: 10.1037/cpp0000009.

Sofi, F., Valecchi, D., Bacci, D., Abbate, R. *et al.* (2010) 'Physical activity and risk of cognitive decline: A meta-analysis of prospective studies.' *Journal of Internal Medicine, 269,* 107–117. doi: 10.1111/j.1365-2796.2010.02281.x.

Sommer, C. A. (2008) 'Vicarious traumatization, trauma-sensitive supervision, and counselor preparation.' *Counselor Education & Supervision, 48,* 1, 61–71.

Sommer, C. A. and Cox, J. A. (2005) 'Elements of supervision in sexual violence counselors' narratives: A qualitative analysis.' *Counselor Education and Supervision, 45,* 2, 119–134.

Sonne, J. L. and Pope, K. S. (1991) 'Treating victims of therapist–patient sexual involvement.' *Psychotherapy: Theory, Research, Practice, Training, 28,* 1, 174–187. doi: 10.1037/0033-3204.28.1.174.

Sowa, C. J. and May, K. M. (1994) 'Occupational stress within the counseling profession: Implications for counselor training.' *Counselor Education & Supervision, 34,* 1, 19–30.

Spiers, A. and Walker, G. J. (2009) 'The effects of ethnicity and leisure satisfaction on happiness, peacefulness, and quality of life.' *Leisure Sciences, 31,* 84–99. doi: 10.1080/01490400802558277.

Spilka, B., Hood, R., Hunsberger, B., and Gorsuch, R. (2003) *The Psychology of Religion: An Empirical Approach.* New York: Guilford.

Sprang, G., Clark, J. J., and Whitt-Woosley, A. (2007) 'Compassion fatigue, compassion satisfaction, and burnout: Factors impacting a professional's quality of life.' *Journal of Loss and Trauma, 12,* 3, 259–280. doi: 10.1080/15325020701238093.

Stamm, B. H. (1995) *Secondary Traumatic Stress: Self-Care Issues for Clinicians, Researchers and Educators.* Lutherville, MD: Sidran Press.

Stamm, B. H. (2005) *The ProQOL Manual.* Accessed on January 11, 2014 at www.compassionfatigue.org/pages/ProQOLManualOct05.pdf.

Stamm, B. H. (2009) *Professional Quality of Life: Compassion Satisfaction and Fatigue Version 5 (ProQOL).* Accessed on November 19, 2013 at www.proqol.org.

Stamm, B. H. (2010) *The Concise ProQOL Manual.* Accessed on November 19, 2013 at http://proqol.org/uploads/ProQOL_Concise_2ndEd_12-2010.pdf.

Stathopoulou, G., Powers, M. B., Berry, A. C., Smits, A. J., and Otto, M. W. (2006) 'Exercise interventions for mental health: A quantitative and qualitiative review.' *Clinical Psychology Science Practice, 13,* 179–193.

Steed, L. G. and Downing, R. (1998) 'A phenomenological study of vicarious traumatisation amongst psychologists and professional counsellors working in the field of sexual abuse/assault.' *The Australasian Journal of Disaster and Trauma Studies.* Accessed on November 19, 2013 at www.massey.ac.nz/~trauma/issues/1998-2/steed.htm.

Sterner, W. R. (2009) 'Influence of the supervisory working alliance on supervisee work satisfaction and work-related stress: A national survey.' *Journal of Humanistic Counseling, Education, and Development, 46,* 20–34.

Stevanovic, P. and Rupert, P. A. (2004) 'Career-sustaining behaviors, satisfactions, and stresses of professional psychologists.' *Psychotherapy: Theory, Research, Practice, Training, 41,* 3, 301–309. doi: 10.1037/0033-3204.41.3.301.

Strong, S. R. (1968) 'Interpersonal influence process.' *Journal of Counseling Psychology, 15,* 215–224.

Sue, D. W. and Sue, D. (2003) *Counseling the Culturally Diverse: Theory and Practice* (4th ed.). New York: John Wiley & Sons.

Sugimoto, C. R. (2012) 'Are you my mentor? Identifying mentors and their roles in LIS doctoral education.' *Journal of education for Library and Information Science, 53,* 1, 2–19.

Sulmasy, D. P. (2002) 'A biopsychosocial-spiritual model for the care of patients at the end of life.' *The Gerontologist, 42,* 24–33.

Swearingen, C. (1990) 'The impaired psychiatrist.' *Psychiatric Clinics of North American, 13,* 1, 1–11.

Synder, M. (1987) *Public Appearances, Private Realities: The Psychology of Self-Monitoring.* New York: Freeman.

Taber, B. J., Leibert, T. W., and Agaskar, V. R. (2011) 'Relationships among client-therapist personality congruence, working alliance, and therapeutic outcome.' *Psychotherapy, 48,* 4, 376–380. doi: 10.1037/a0022066.

Tang, C. S. (1990) 'Effect of student therapists' interpersonal competence on an initial interview.' *The Journal of Social Psychology, 131,* 147–149.

Tara, D. (2007) 'The relevance of the Freudian concept on "transference" to existential psychotherapy.' *Journal of the Society for Existential Analysis, 18,* 2, 348–357.

Temane, Q. M. and Wissing, M. P. (2006) 'The role of spirituality as a mediator for psychological wellbeing across different contexts.' *South African Journal of Psychology, 36,* 3, 582–597.

Terracciano, A., Costa, P. T. Jr, and McCrae, R. R. (2006) 'Personality plasticity after age 30.' *Personality and Social Psychology Bulletin, 32,* 8, 999–1009. doi: 10.1177/0146167206288599.

Theriault, A. and Gazzola, N. (2005) 'Feelings of inadequacy, insecurity, and incompetence among experienced therapists.' *Counseling and Psychotherapy Research, 5,* 11–18. doi: 10.1080/14733140512331343840.

Theriault, A., and Gazzola, N. (2010) 'Therapist feelings of incompetence and suboptimal processes in psychotherapy.' *Journal of Contemporary Psychotherapy, 40,* 4, 233–243.

Thogersen-Ntoumani, C. and Fox, K. (2005) 'Physical activity and mental well-being typologies in corporate employees: A mixed methods approach.' *Work & Stress, 19,* 50–67. doi: 10.1080/02678370500084409.

Thomas, S. P. (2009) 'Neuroticism: A construct that deserves the attention of mental health researchers and clinicians.' *Issues in Mental Health Nursing, 30,* 727. doi: 10.3109/01612840903263520.

Thomas, S. E., Werner-Wilson, R. J., and Murphy, M. J. (2005) 'Influence of the therapist and client behaviors on therapy alliance.' *Contemporary Family Therapy, 27,* 19–35. doi: 10.1007/s10591-004-1968-z.

Thomyangkoon, P. and Leenaars, A. (2008) 'Impact of death by suicide of patients on Thai psychiatrists.' *Suicide & Life-Threatening Behavior, 38,* 728–740.

Ting, L., Jacobson, J. M., and Sanders, S. (2011) 'Current levels of perceived stress among mental health social workers who work with suicidal clients.' *Social Work, 56,* 327–336.

Ting, L., Jacobson, J. M., Sanders, S., Bride, B. E., and Harrington, D. (2005) 'The secondary traumatic stress scale (STSS): Confirmatory factor analyses with a national sample of mental health social workers.' *Journal of Human Behavior in the Social Environment, 11,* 177–194.

Tinsley, H. E. and Eldredge, B. D. (1995) 'Psychological benefits of leisure participation: A taxonomy of leisure activities based on their need-gratifying properties.' *Journal of Counseling Psychology, 42,* 123–132.

Tomporowski, P. D., Davis, C. L., Miller, P. H., and Naglieri, J. A. (2008) 'Exercise and children's intelligence, cognition, and academic achievement.' *Educational Psychology Review, 20,* 111–131. doi: 10.1007/s10648-007-9057-0.

Trippany, R. L., Kress, V. E., and Wilcoxon, S. A. (2004) 'Preventing vicarious trauma: What counselors should know when working with trauma survivors.' *Journal of Counseling & Development, 82,* 1, 31–37.

Tucker, L. and Lubin, W. (1994) *National Survey of Psychologists* (Report from Division 39). Washington, DC: American Psychological Association.

Tuisku, V., Pelkonen, M., Karlsson, L., Kiviruusu, O. *et al.* (2006) 'Suicidal ideation, deliberate self-harm behaviour and suicide attempts among adolescent outpatients with depressive mood disorders and comorbid axis I disorders.' *European Child & Adolescent Psychiatry, 15,* 199–206. doi: 10.1007/s00787-005-0522-3.

Ulman, K. H. (2001) 'Unwitting exposure of the therapist.' *The Journal of Psychotherapy Practice and Research, 10,* 14–22.

Valtonen, M., Laaksonen, D. E., Laukkanen, J., Tolmunen, T. *et al.* (2009) 'Leisure-time physical activity, cardiorespiratory fitness and feelings of hopelessness in men.' *BMC Public Health, 9,* 1–7. doi: 10.1186/1471-2458-9-204.

VandenBos, G. R. (2007) *APA Dictionary of Psychology.* Washington, DC: American Psychological Association.

Van Den Bosch, L. C., Verheul, R., Langeland, W., and Van Den Brink, W. (2003) 'Trauma, dissociation, and posttraumatic stress disorder in female borderline patients with and without substance abuse problems.' *Australian & New Zealand Journal of Psychiatry, 37,* 5, 549–555.

Van Den Hurk, P., Giommi, F., Gielen, S. C., Speckens, A. E., and Barendregt, H. P. (2010) 'Greater efficiency in attentional processing related to mindfulness and meditation.' *The Quarterly Journal of Experimental Psychology, 63,* 1168–1180. doi: 10.1080./17470210903249365.

Van Dierendonck, D. (2012) 'Spirituality as an essential determinant for the good life, its importance relative to self-determinant psychological needs.' *Journal of Happiness Studies, 13,* 685–700.

Van Wagoner, S. L., Gelso, C. J., Hayes, R. A., and Diemer, R. A. (1991) 'Countertransference and the reputedly excellent therapist.' *Psychotherapy: Theory, Research, Practice, Training, 28*, 411–421.

Vasquez, M. J. T. (1992) 'Psychologist as clinical supervisor: Promoting ethical practice.' *Professional Psychology: Research and Practice, 23*, 3, 196–202.

Veilleux, J. C. (2011) 'Coping with client death: Using a case study to discuss the effects of accidental, undetermined, and suicidal deaths on therapists.' *Professional Psychology: Research and Practice, 42*, 222–228. doi: 10.1037/a0023650.

Venart, E., Vassos, S., and Pitcher-Heft, H. (2007) 'What individual counselors can do to sustain wellness.' *Journal of Humanistic Counseling, Education & Development, 46*, 1, 50–65.

Vladut, C. I. and Kallay, E. (2010) 'Work stress, personal life, and burnout. Causes, consequences, and possible remedies.' *Cognition, Brain, Behavior: An Interdisciplinary Journal, 3*, 261–280.

Voorpostel, M., Van der Lippe, T., and Gershung, J. (2010) 'Spending time together–changes over four decades in leisure time spent with a spouse.' *Journal of Leisure Research, 42*, 243–265.

Voss Horrell, S. C., Holohan, D. R., Didion, L. M., and Vance, G. (2011) 'Treating Traumatized OEF/OIF Veterans: How Does Trauma Treatment Affect the Clinician?' *Professional Psychology: Research & Practice, 42*, 1, 79–86. doi: 10.1037/a0022297.

Vredenburgh, L. D., Carlozzi, A. F., and Stein, L. B. (1999) 'Burnout in counseling psychologists: Type of practice setting and pertinent demographics.' *Counseling Psychology Quarterly, 12*, 3, 293–302.

Wagner, B. M., Wong, S. A., and Jobes, D. A. (2002) 'Mental health professionals' determinations of adolescent suicide attempts.' *Suicide & Life-Threatening Behavior, 32*, 284–300.

Walfish, S., Barnett, J. E., Marlyere, K., and Zielke, R. (2010) '"Doc, there's something I have to tell you": Patience disclosure to their psychotherapist of unprosecuted murder and other violence.' *Ethics & Behavior, 20*, 311–323. doi: 10.1080/105084222010491743.

Walker, M. (2004) 'Supervising practitioners working with survivors of childhood abuse: counter transference; secondary traumatization and terror.' *Psychodynamic Practice, 10*, 2, 173–193. doi: 10.1080/1475363 0410001686753.

Walker, K. Z., O'Dea, Gomez, M., Girgis, M., and Colagiuri, R. (2010) 'Diet and exercise in the prevention of diabetes.' *Journal of Human Nutrition and Dietetics, 23*, 344–352.

Walsh, B. and Walsh, S. (2002) 'Caseload factors and the psychological well-being of community mental health staff.' *Journal of Mental Health, 11*, 67–78. doi: 10.1080/0963823012000041470.

Walters, D. (1995) 'Mandatory reporting of child abuse: Legal, ethical, and clinical implications within a Canadian context.' *Canadian Psychology, 36*, 163–182. doi: 10.1037/0708-5591.36.3.163.

Wang, S. and Kim, B. S. (2010) 'Therapist multicultural competence, Asian American participants' cultural values, and counseling process.' *Journal of Counseling Psychology*, Advanced online publication. doi: 10.1037/a0020359.

Watts, F., Dutton, K., and Gulliford, L. (2006) 'Human spiritual qualities: Integrating psychology and religion.' *Mental Health, Religion and Culture, 9*, 3, 277–289.

Webb, K. B. (2011) 'Care of others and self: A suicidal patient's impact on the psychologist.' *Professional Psychology: Research and Practice, 42,* 3, 215–221.

Wee, D. and Myers, D. (2003) 'Compassion satisfaction, compassion fatigue, and critical incident stress management.' *The International Journal of Emergency Mental Health, 5,* 1, 33–37.

Weinstein, A. A., Deuster, P. A., Francis, J. L., Beadling, C., and Kop, W. J. (2010) 'The role of depression in short-term mood and fatigue responses to acute exercise.' *International Journal of Behavioral Medicine, 17,* 51–57.

Weiss, L. (2004) *Therapist's Guide to Self-Care.* New York: Brunner-Routledge.

Wheeler, S. (2002) 'Nature or nurture: Are therapists born or trained?' *Psychodynamic Practice, 8,* 4, 427–441. doi: 10.1080/13533330210000388.

Wheeler, S. (2007) 'What shall we do with the wounded healer? The supervisor's dilemma.' *Psychodynamic Practice, 13,* 3, 245–256. doi: 10.1080/14753630701455838.

Wheeler, S. and Richards, K. (2007) 'The impact of clinical supervision on counsellors and therapists, their practice and their clients: A systematic review of the literature.' *Counselling & Psychotherapy Research, 7,* 1, 54–65.

White, D. (2006) 'The hidden costs of caring: What managers need to know.' *Health Care Manager, 25,* 4, 341–347.

Whyte, J. J. and Laughlin, M. H. (2010) 'The effects of acute and chronic exercise on the Vasculature.' *Scandinavian Physiological Society, 199,* 441–450. doi: 10.1111/j.1748-1716.201002127.x.

Widom, A. S., Marmorstein, N. R., and White, H. R. (2006) 'Childhood victimization and illicit drug use in middle adulthood.' *Psychology of Addictive Behaviors, 20,* 4, 394–403.

Wilfley, D. and Kunce, J. (1986) 'Differential physical and psychological effects of exercise.' *Journal of Counseling Psychology, 63,* 337–342.

Wilkerson, K. (2009) 'An examination of burnout among school counselors guided by stress-management theory.' *Journal of Counseling and Development, 87,* 429–437.

Wilkins, P. (2000) 'Unconditional positive regard reconsidered.' *British Journal of Guidance & Counseling, 28,* 23–36.

Wilkinson-Tough, M., Bocci, L., Thorne, K., and Herlihy, J. (2010) 'Is mindfulness-based therapy an effective intervention for obsessive-intrusive thoughts: A case series.' *Clinical Psychology and Psychotherapy, 17,* 250–268. doi: 10.10002/cpp.665.

Williams, E. N. (2003) 'The relationship between momentary states of therapist self-awareness and perceptions of the counseling process.' *Journal of Contemporary Psychotherapy, 33,* 177–186.

Williams, E. N., Polster, D., Grizzard, M. B., Rockenbaugh, J., and Judge, A. B. (2003) 'What happens when therapists feel bored or anxious? A qualitative study of distracting self-awareness and therapists' management strategies.' *Journal of Contemporary Psychotherapy, 33,* 5–28.

Williams, B. E., Pomerantz, A. M., Segrist, D. J., and Pettibone, J. C. (2010) 'How impaired is too impaired? Ratings of psychologist impairment by psychologists in independent practice.' *Ethics & Behavior, 20,* 2, 149–160. doi: 10.1080/10508421003595968.

Williams, M. B. and Sommner, J. F. (1999) 'Self-Care and the Vulnerable Therapist.' In B. H. Stamm (ed.) *Secondary Traumatic Stress: Self Care Issues for Clinicians, Researchers, and Educators.* Lutherville, MD: Sidran Press.

Wills, E. (2009) 'Spirituality and subjective well-being: Evidences for a new domain in the personal well-being index.' *Journal of Happiness Studies, 10,* 49–69. doi: 10.1007/s10902-007-9061-6.

Wilson, D. (2012) 'The editor's perspective. Spirituality and culture are intertwined.' *International Journal of Childbirth Education, 27,* 1, 4–5.

Winnicott, D. W. (1960) 'Ego Distortion in Terms of True and False Self.' In *The Maturational Process and the Facilitating Environment: Studies in the Theory of Emotional Development.* New York: International UP Inc.

Wise, E. H., Hersh, M. A., and Gibson, C. M. (2012) 'Ethics, self-care and well-being for psychologists: Reenvisioning the stress-distress continuum.' *Professional Psychology: Research and Practice, 43,* 5, 487–494. doi: 10.1037/a0029446.

Wogan, M. (1970) 'Effect of therapist-patient personality variables on therapeutic outcome.' *Journal of Consulting and Clinical Psychology, 35,* 3, 356–361. doi: 10.1037/h0030110.

Wolstein, B. (1996) 'The analysis of transference as an interpersonal process.' *American Journal of Psychotherapy, 50,* 4, 499–509.

Worthington, E. L. Jr. (1989) 'Religious faith across the life span: Implications for counseling and research.' *The Counseling Psychologist, 17,* 555–612.

Worthington, E. L. Jr. (1998) 'An empathy-humility-commitment model of forgiveness applied within family dyads.' *Journal of Family Therapy, 20,* 1, 59–76.

Worthington, D., Barry, J. and Parrott, L. (2001) 'Unforgiveness, Forgiveness, Religion, and Health.' In T. Plante and A. Sherman (eds) *Faith and Health: Psychological Perspectives.* New York: Guilford.

Wrzus, C., Wagner, J., and Neyer, F. J. (2011) 'The interdependence of horizontal family relationships and friendships relates to higher well-being.' *Personal Relationships, 19,* 465–482.

Wurst, F. M., Kunz, I., Skipper, G., Wolfersdorf, M., Beine, K. H., and Thon, N. (2011) 'The therapist's reaction to a patient's suicide.' *Crisis, 32,* 2, 99–105. doi: 10.1027/0227-5910/a000062.

Wylie, K. R. and Oakley, K. (2005) 'Sexual boundaries in the relationship between clients and clinicians practising sexology in the UK.' *Sexual and Relationship Therapy, 20,* 4, 453–456.

Yager, G. G. and Tovar-Blank, Z. G. (2007) 'Wellness and counselor education.' *Journal of Humanistic Counseling, Education and Development, 46,* 142–153.

Yassen, J. (1995) 'Preventing Secondary Traumatic Stress Disorder.' In C. R. Figley (ed.) *Compassion Fatigue: Coping with Secondary Traumatic Stress Disorder in Those Who Treat the Traumatized.* New York: Brurmer/Mazel.

Younggren, J. N. and Harris, E. A. (2008) 'Can you keep a secret? Confidentiality in psychotherapy.' *Journal of Clinical Psychology, 64,* 589–600. doi: 10.1002/jclp.20480.

Zaborowski, Z. and Slaski, S. (2004) 'Contents and forms theory of self-awareness.' *Imagination, Cognition and Personality, 23,* 99–119.

Zeidan, F., Johnson, S, K., Gordon, N. S., and Goolkasian, P. (2010) 'Effects of brief and Sham mindfulness meditation on mood and cardiovascular variables.' *The Journal of Alternate and Complementary Medicine, 16,* 867–873. doi: 10.1089/acm.2009.0321.

Zeidan, F., Martucci, K. T., Kraft, R. A., McHaffie, J. G., and Coghill, R. C. (2013) 'Neural correlates of mindfulness meditation-related anxiety relief.' *Social, Cognitive, and Affective Neuroscience.* Accessed on November 26, 2013 at http://scan.oxfordjournals.org/content/early/2013/06/03/scan.nst041.abstract doi: 10.1093/scan/nst041.

Zondag, H. J. and Van Uden, M. H. (2011) '"Still knockin' on heaven's door." Narcissism and prayer.' *Journal of Empirical Theology, 24,* 19–35.

Zuckerman, E. L. (2008) *The Paper Office: Forms, Guidelines, and Resources to Make Your Practice Work Ethically, Legally, and Profitably.* New York: The Guilford Press.

Zur, O. (2008) *Taking Care of the Caretaker: How To Avoid Psychotherapists' Burnout.* Online Publication by Zur Institute. Accessed on May 25, 2011 at www.zurinstitute.com/burnout.html.

Zuroff, D. C., Kelly, A. C., Leybman, M. J., Blatt, S. J., and Wampold, B. E. (2010) 'Between-therapist and within-therapist differences in the quality of the therapeutic relationship: Effects on maladjustment and self-critical perfectionism.' *Journal of Clinical Psychology, 66,* 7, 681–697.

Subject Index

Author Index